Return of the "L" Word

★ ★ ★ ☆ ★ ★ ★

DOUGLAS S. MASSEY

Return of the "L" Word

A Liberal Vision for the New Century

PRINCETON UNIVERSITY PRESS
PRINCETON AND OXFORD

Library of Congress Cataloging-in-Publication Data
Massey, Douglas S.
Return of the "L" word : a liberal vision for the new century / Douglas S. Massey.
p. cm.
Includes bibliographical references and index.
ISBN 0-691-12303-9 (alk. paper)
1. Liberalism—United States—History—20th century.   2. Liberalism—United
States—History—21st century.   3. United States—Politics and government—2001- I. Title.
JC574.2.U6M27 2005
320.51'3'0973—dc22   2004057502

British Library Cataloging-in-Publication Data is available
This book has been composed in Minion
Printed on acid-free paper. ∞
pup.princeton.edu
Printed in the United States of America
1   3   5   7   9   10   8   6   4   2

Dedicated to Susan Tufts Fiske

Contents

Preface

I decided to write *Return of the "L" Word* after witnessing congressional Democrats lose the elections of 2002. I had been dismayed in 2000 when the party stood idly by and allowed thousands of voters to be disenfranchised without significant protest, but I had hoped that Democrats would return to a serious politics of opposition during the midterm elections. I was disappointed. Indeed, Democratic candidates didn't seem to stand for anything, at least anything they could communicate coherently to voters. As George H. W. Bush might have put it, they lacked "the vision thing." Without a clear message, candidates fell back on the dubious strategy of feinting rightward and portraying themselves as kinder, gentler, and more governmentally competent versions of Republicans. Running in terror from the word "liberal," they allowed conservatives to appropriate a proud label once embraced by America's greatest leaders—Theodore Roosevelt, Woodrow Wilson, Franklin Roosevelt—and turn it into a shameful epithet with the moral valance of a crack whore.

I was mad. Liberal Democrats had ceased to lead. They had become followers, weakly appropriating the slogans of Republicans and serving up focus-group bromides in a desperate but insincere attempt to attract voters. Faced with a choice between Republican candidates who argued from principle and Democrats who lacked clear convictions, voters rationally chose principle over pandering. Although they often disagreed personally with elements of the Republican political program, voters nonetheless preferred Republicans. At least the Republicans articulated a principled, logical, and convincing political program. How much faith can one place in the moral character of candidates who are unable to state clearly their own convictions?

I wanted to address the political fecklessness of the Democrats. At every level and at every juncture in the 2002 campaign, pro-

gressive candidates were out-maneuvered by more effective organizations and conservative strategies. It was as if liberal Democrats had been run over by a speeding locomotive. Rising stunned
and bleeding from the tracks, they stood gaping as the Republican
campaign engine raced away with yet another election. No loss
was more poignant than that of Max Cleland, a popular Democratic senator who left three of four limbs in Vietnam but who
nonetheless fell victim to a conservative smear campaign impugn-
ing his patriotism.

I was also driven to write by my lingering irritation with liberals who continued to support Ralph Nader, friends and colleagues
who argued that there was "no difference" between the major
party candidates and that a vote for Nader was a vote for liberalism, as if voting for the highest office in the most powerful country on earth was simply another expression of lifestyle preference.
Insisting on the right to vote for Nader was like rearranging deck
chairs on the Titanic. "Vote for change," my Nader-supporting
friends told me. Well, Nader's voters gave us change in abundance
after 2000, and here he came again as the nation geared up for the
2004 campaigns.

I thus resolved to lay out a political agenda to serve as a basis for
a liberal revival. My first goal was to review the prior tactical mis-
judgments and political mistakes that Democrats had made to
transform themselves into the minority party. Liberals had to realize it was not all the Republicans' fault and not just a bad dream.
Without a vigorous and effective counter-campaign, the American electorate was not magically going to come to its senses and
return to the Democratic fold. Democrats had definitively lost all
three branches of government and they would not return to power
until they recognized their mistakes and learned from them. Attempting to appropriate conservative ideas to deflect attacks from
the right was a strategy doomed to failure—moving farther and
farther rightward only skewed the center. Democrats would achieve
success only by identifying their political base, articulating a coherent ideology to appeal to it, and then working assiduously to
expand it.

In order for this sort of transformation to occur, the word "liberal"must become a source of pride rather than an emblem of shame. Such a change requires formulating a reasonable political program that can be communicated to voters in plain language to help them understand how liberal policies serve their own best interests. Pointing out the shortcomings and inconsistencies of the conservatives is not enough. Bad ideas are rarely jettisoned because their flaws are known. They are only replaced when better ideas are put forward to take their place. I thus sought to rethink the foundations of American liberalism, moving away from its obsession with identity politics and political correctness and toward a pragmatic materialism that could explain to ordinary people how, by embracing liberal values, they could improve their own welfare. If the Democrats are ever going to win again, they must move beyond a politics of guilt and blame to one of hope and inspiration.

I also wanted to make Democrats in general and liberals in particular understand what they were up against in the conservative movement, to lay out in detail the remarkable structure and organization of what Hillary Clinton termed "the vast right-wing conspiracy." I felt that until liberals understood the unity of purpose, coordination, and resources of the conservative machine, they would continue to fight ineffectually among themselves and stumble blindly into conservative sucker-punches time after time. Liberals had to realize they were facing an implacable, determined, and well-prepared enemy, not an uncoordinated mob of ignorant, redneck hicks. Underestimating the enemy is the first and deadliest sin of political warfare.

Finally, I sought to sketch out a concrete framework for liberal realignment. In addition to laying out a coherent ideology that makes sense to ordinary people, inculcating an appreciation for past mistakes, and engendering a new respect for the capacities of the conservative movement, I wanted to show how a winning political coalition could be built from specific segments of the electorate and to signal the roadblocks that liberals were likely to encounter on the road to power.

My great frustration in early 2003 was that I could not work fast enough. During the spring and summer I read widely in preparation for putting pen to paper, and during the fall of 2003 I wrote intensively, finishing the manuscript in late December. As I shipped it off for review in January 2004, the future was anything but clear. Though a single vote had yet to be cast, Howard Dean had been anointed as the official "front runner" by pundits and the media; John Kerry was on the ropes and widely assumed to be washed-up politically; John Edwards was a distant figure on the horizon; and dark horse candidates like Wesley Clark were still taken seriously.

As 2004 unfolded, it quickly became clear that I was not the only one dreaming of a political realignment. A host of other authors offered up their own proposals for liberal revival. The columnist E. J. Dionne, Jr., issued his call to arms in *Stand Up Fight Back: Republican Toughs, Democratic Wimps, and the Politics of Revenge.* Former Clinton cabinet secretary Robert B. Reich issued his manifesto, *Reason: Why Liberals Will Win the Battle for America.* The journalist and editor Thomas Frank explored the reasons for conservative success in *What's the Matter with Kansas?: How Conservatives Won the Heart of America.* And the entrepreneur John Sperling assembled a team of statistical analysts who described the political fault lines in *The Great Divide: Retro vs. Metro America.*

Despite all the free advice, John Kerry and the Democrats—famously—still lost in 2004, and for essentially the same reason as in 2002: they failed to paint a coherent picture of what America would look like under liberal leadership. Instead, they continued to run from the label "liberal" and did not offer a clear political program that was comprehensible to voters. Rather than making a principled argument for social change, they turned to consultants and "spinmeisters" who helped them guess what voters wanted to hear. Instead of articulating a competing vision for America, they drew upon polls and focus groups to assemble a smorgasbord of disconnected clichés and slogans. Rather than anticipating readying themselves for the scurrilous attacks on Kerry's patriotism that were sure to come, they counted on his Silver Star, Bronze Star, and Purple Hearts to protect him. On all fronts, John Kerry and the Democrats failed to mount an effective politics of opposition.

By campaigning in the absence of principles and lamely repeating what they thought voters wanted to hear, Democrats played directly into the hands of Karl Rove and his minions. Throughout the campaign, the Kerry campaign danced to their tune. Without a clear ideology to connect the candidate's positions to underlying principles he fell victim to charges of "flip-flopping." Without a compelling moral vision to offer voters, he walked into the "moral values" trap set by Republicans. Without an appreciation for the cunning of and determination of the right-wing conspiracy, he was caught off guard by the disinformation launched by the Swift Vote Veterans for Truth.

I will only consider this book a success if liberals in the future take pride in their liberalism. When tagged with the label "liberal" I want people not to shrink and dissemble but to answer back firmly: "Damned right I'm a liberal and this is what I stand for. I believe that government should invest in people by seeing to their health and education, for people are the ultimate resource in society. I believe that markets are not states of nature, but human inventions with imperfections and fallibilities, and that government must work to ensure they function for the good of the many rather than the benefit of the few. I believe it is the obligation of government to make sure that needed markets exist, that competition within them is fair, that transactions are transparent, and that competition is accessible to everyone. I believe that because markets are fallible, and that they can and do break down from time to time, government must create public institutions to protect people from periodic market failures. Finally, I believe that government must ensure equal civil, legal, and political rights for all citizens regardless of background." Only when liberalism is expressed positively and forcefully will voters understand that in a liberal America the largest number of people will enjoy true access to life, liberty, and the pursuit of happiness, finally fulfilling the dream articulated by the Founding Fathers in Philadelphia more than two centuries ago.

Douglas S. Massey
Princeton, New Jersey
December 12, 2004

Return of the "L" Word

CHAPTER 1

Return of the "L" Word

Somehow, during the last quarter of the twentieth century in the United States, conservatives stole the high ground of public debate and were able to depict liberalism as tantamount to a sin, a diabolical philosophy whose unchecked expression during the 1960s led the country to the verge of ruin. If something was wrong anywhere in the world, conservative politicians and pundits were successful in portraying it as the fault of devious liberals and their malevolent policies. Daunting social problems such as joblessness, poverty, crime, delinquency, addiction, family dissolution, and terrorism were laid at the feet of liberals. People who subscribed to a "liberal agenda" were depicted as wasteful, weak, unpatriotic, and self-indulgent—hand-wringing whiners who "blamed America first" and despised working people, viewing them only as little more than a source of tax revenue to support their privileged class position as advocates for the undeserving poor.[1]

That conservatives sought to paint the political opposition in this unfavorable light is hardly surprising. What is truly amazing is their spectacular success at doing so during a period of apparent liberal triumph. As a result of liberal reforms enacted over the course of the twentieth century, Americans in 1970 were freer, healthier, richer, and more equal than ever before in U.S. history. Yet at the moment of liberalism's seeming zenith, conservatives were successful in turning voters away from policies that had brought social and economic well-being to an unprecedented number of Americans. Over the next three decades, an increasingly radical conservative movement took control of the Republican party and sent liberals into full ideological retreat.

With the exception of the anomalous interregnum of Jimmy Carter (notably, a *Southern* Democrat), the Republican party captured and held the presidency during the 1970s and 1980s; and despite losing it during the 1990s to Bill Clinton (again, a *Southern* Democrat), conservative Republicans captured the House and Senate in 1994, and by the end of the decade they had achieved de facto control over the Supreme Court and the federal judiciary as well. Even more remarkably, despite the remarkable peace and prosperity of the Clinton years, in 2000 Republicans once again took the White House. With the restoration of the House of Bush, conservative Republicans controlled all three branches of government, a political realignment that appeared to be ratified decisively by voters in the 2002 elections. As President Bush headed into the second half of his first term, liberalism's demise seemed all but complete.

This dark night of the liberal soul, however, sets the stage for an unexpected rekindling of progressive politics, for the setbacks of 2002 finally demonstrated, once and for all, the futility of conservative accommodation. The movement of the Democratic party away from real opposition and its adoption of a strategy of appeasement alienated the party's core constituencies while doing little to appeal to reluctant voters in the political center. In the ideological vacuum that followed the 2002 electoral meltdown, Howard Dean shocked the Democratic establishment by mounting an unexpectedly successful insurgency based on a forceful and unapologetic politics of opposition, vigorously challenging the Republicans and their Democratic imitators at every political turn—social, economic, and diplomatic.

Although he ultimately did not secure the Democratic nomination, Dean's campaign re-energized the party faithful, mobilized new voters, and made a vigorous politics of opposition not only possible, but respectable, thereby opening a new path for Democrats to follow. As a result, from the ashes of the 2002 elections the phoenix of a liberal alignment is poised to arise. Like so many radical political movements, American conservatism has overextended

itself. Its takeover of the Republican party has moved federal policies far to the right of the electorate. Conservatives now seek to
impose a narrow, fundamentalist morality that is quite out of step
with the relatively open and tolerant social position of most Americans. Conservatives also support a retrograde retrenchment on
civil rights and social entitlements that is wildly out of touch with
the social, economic, and demographic realities of the twenty-first
century.

Not only do the radical conservatives who run the country in
2004 diverge socially from the values and sentiments of mainstream Americans, they also have little to offer the country in practical terms. In the United States, the last quarter of the twentieth
century was one of unparalleled economic polarization. The un-
deniable fact is that since 1975, four-fifths of American households have seen their social and economic well-being stagnate or
even decline. While those in the top 20 percent of the income distribution have gotten richer and more affluent, the rest of the
country is working harder for less money and fewer benefits while
critical services, such as public health and education, continue to
deteriorate.

Although the economic boom engineered by President Clinton
was able to moderate these inequalities somewhat during the late
1990s, forward progress was rapidly and abruptly reversed with
the restoration of the House of Bush. Within a few months of his
inauguration, the boom ended, joblessness returned, deficits increased, inequalities widened, and the tax burden shifted decisively away from the wealthy and onto the middle and working
classes. In material terms, as well as in terms of their social philosophy, the radical conservatives of the Republican party have done
and are doing little for the vast majority of Americans.

Although these facts suggest a historic opportunity for a political realignment, a liberal resurgence is by no means assured or
even likely. The confluence of opportunities won't last long, and a
reconfiguration won't happen without dedication, engagement,
and serious soul-searching by liberals themselves, who face many
serious obstacles on the road to political power. First, liberals
must come to terms with the fact that the mass of voters *did* turn

against them and their policies after 1970. They need to understand how this reversal happened and why so many people voted
against their own material interests in favor of a party openly dedicated to dismantling the system of government that had brought
so many benefits to so many people during the postwar period.
Liberals need to look inward to recognize and acknowledge their
own part in alienating America's middle and working classes and
accept their responsibility for bringing about the resurgence of
plutocracy.

To date, liberals have sought to externalize the blame for their
political demise during the last quarter of the twentieth century.
This all-too-human but ultimately destructive reaction to bad
news serves only to exacerbate the alienation of liberals from the
voters they need to attract in order to return to power—for exter-
nalizing the blame inevitably casts it on the people themselves, ac-
cusing them of racism, sexism, homophobia, social conservatism,
and, perhaps worse, stupidity in not recognizing their own material interests. But voters are neither stupid nor inveterately conservative. While people may resist change in policies and attitudes
toward minorities, women, and gays, liberals must recognize that
deeply rooted values change slowly and that persuasion, patient
argument, and sympathetic understanding are more effective
than strident sermonizing in bringing about political realign-
ments. The public shaming and humiliation of people for holding
"politically incorrect" views only foments reactionary anger and
deepens resistance to progressive change, allowing people's emotional reactions to override their rational economic calculations.

The first step toward recovery, then, is an acceptance of past
mistakes, and this is the subject of chapter 2, which examines
U.S. history to discern the reasons for liberalism's triumph during the first six decades of the twentieth century and its collapse
thereafter. To put it bluntly, in the years after 1965 liberals badly
mishandled conflicts surrounding race, class, war, peace, and
ideology. As long as civil rights meant ending the legal foundations of segregation in the South, liberalism surged ahead; but
once the movement's agenda focused on subtler processes of
racial discrimination that were well-entrenched in the North as

well as the South, progress was no longer easy and the movement faltered.

In the end, liberal elites failed to appreciate the sacrifices being asked of middle- and working-class Americans to remedy the nation's sorry legacy of racial inequality; and rather than reaching a political accommodation to offset the real costs with concrete benefits, they sought to use executive and judicial power to force change upon an apprehensive and fearful public while decrying all opponents as narrow-minded bigots. As a result, the segregation of schools and neighborhoods has continued despite successive civil rights acts, and conservatives were able to use the issue of race to break apart the New Deal coalition.

The liberals who sought to use executive and judicial power to extend civil rights were generally affluent, well-educated, and effectively insulated from the consequences of social change by their privileged class position. In contrast, the people affected by their policies had less education and income, thus opening a class divide into which Republicans quickly plunged a dagger. Rather than recognizing the tenuousness of working-class achievements, liberals more often looked with contempt upon middlebrow Americans who were threatened by change and resisted the liberal policies of the 1960s and 1970s.

This latent class antagonism was exacerbated by the systematic failure of liberals to deal with the real economic burdens imposed by bracket creep and spiraling housing prices during the 1970s. As inflation rose after 1973, middle-class Americans were pushed into tax brackets originally meant for people with much higher incomes, and homeowners of modest means faced real estate taxes well beyond their ability to pay. Rather than dealing with these issues politically, liberals ignored them and gratuitously used the ever-rising tax revenue to expand programs that had by then become quite unpopular, leading to the famous middle-class tax revolt symbolized by California's Proposition 13. Animosity toward affluent liberals was further heightened by the Vietnam War, which was devised in secret by the very same liberal architects of the Great Society, whose own sons and daughters were rarely called upon to sacrifice their lives and bodies.

After steadily losing ground in elections after 1980, liberals compounded their political problems ideologically by retreating to academia to launch a rearguard cultural insurgency under the banner of postmodernism, which came to be known publicly as the doctrine of "political correctness." The arcane language of the movement and its politics of guilt and victimization further divided liberals from the masses and handed conservative writers a propaganda bonanza that they eagerly exploited.[2] Rather than recruit new troops to liberal side, the intolerance, moralism, and self-righteousness of campus radicals more often turned otherwise open-minded and well-meaning, if somewhat innocent, students into rabid, vengeful conservatives.[3]

Although liberals must recognize their own complicity in the conservative resurgence of the late twentieth century and learn from their past mistakes, mea culpas will not win elections or convince voters to return liberal politicians to power. A second reason for the demise of liberalism over the past thirty years was the lack of a coherent program to offer voters. Until liberals can unite around a sensible political philosophy that can be explained to voters in straightforward terms, they cannot expect to win elections. In addition to *opposing* the radical conservative policies of today's Republicans, liberals must themselves *stand for* something—a set of consistent principles that can be communicated widely and translated into concrete public policies.

In chapter 3, I draw upon insights from the new field of economic sociology to derive a principled vision for a liberal society, and in chapters 4 and 5, I apply this liberal vision to outline a practical approach to policies for the domestic and international spheres. Economic sociology studies how interpersonal exchanges are embedded within larger social institutions and how such social embeddedness influences and constrains economic relations.[4] The key insight of economic sociology is that markets are not "free" states of nature, but human-created social systems that citizens of a democratic republic have a duty to supervise and manage in the public interest. Through their democratic decisions, citizens constitute necessary markets and ensure that they are well functioning. To assure the effective operation of markets, citizens build a supporting infrastructure, establish a medium of exchange, enforce equal access and fair competition, and insure citizens from potential market failures.

The recognition that markets are constructed by human beings and that their operation is determined not by nature but by deliberate political decisions leads naturally to a set of domestic policies designed to cultivate the capabilities of citizens and ensure their autonomy as political and economic actors. The cultivation of capabilities boils down to promoting, through whatever combination of public and private means proves to be most effective, the health, education, and independence of citizens. Funds spent on the health and education of citizens are properly viewed as essential investments in human capital formation rather than optional expenditures that detract from economic growth. In a postindustrial global economy where the creation of wealth is based on the application of knowledge and the manipulation of information, the cultivation of the capabilities of citizens is one of the most important things a government can do to ensure its future power, influence, and prosperity. People are truly "the ultimate resource" and failure to make full productive use of their capacities constitutes a serious drag on progress. For this reason, liberal governments must assure that society's markets are open and accessible to all regardless of background, and that they offer citizens equal returns to equal inputs.

Although it has become popular in some liberal political circles to view globalization as the great Satan of our era, a truly liberal viewpoint recognizes that the expansion of markets through international trade and global finance are essential to world peace and prosperity. The negative results of globalization to date have come less from the expansion of trade and markets per se than from the rules and conditions under which this expansion has occurred. Rather than being structured for the benefit of the world's citizens generally, the rules of global competition have been coopted, rewritten and reinterpreted by a small number of corporate and financial actors to serve their narrow economic interests. The solution is not to abandon multilateral institutions and treaties that undergird the global economy, but to embrace them and open up the process by which the rules of global competition are created and enforced to wider democratic participation and greater transparency.

The present era is by no means the first period of economic globalization. An earlier age of global trade and market development evolved from 1800 to 1914. Ultimately, however, the reach of globalism outstripped the ability of extant multilateral institutions to support it, and the world devolved into a World War that was followed by protectionist withdrawal, economic collapse, worldwide depression, and eventually an even larger and more deadly round of global armed conflict. In the ashes of World War II, enlightened liberals managed to create a stronger and more effective set of multilateral institutions to solve the problems inherent to the first era of globalization, leading ultimately to the triumph of market economics in the last decade of the twentieth century and a full return to the globalism of the past.

We now stand at a unique historical crossroads where we can choose either to move the global market economy forward under more democratic and transparent auspices, or retreat from the promise of global capitalism into self-defeating cycles of nationalism, protectionism, and poverty. A retreat from global trade will inevitably have the same disastrous consequences as it did before, only this time the death toll will be higher and the scale of destruction more immense. It is to avoid this frightening scenario that chapter 5 offers a principled defense of globalism and outlines a liberal agenda for reform of the global market economy and the multinational organizations that sustain it.

In addition to admitting past mistakes, setting forth a defensible political philosophy, and translating this philosophy into a practical agenda for domestic and international politics, liberals must accurately appraise the formidable array of conservative forces lined up against them. Based on this knowledge, they must work to develop effective political strategies to counter conservative influence. To date, liberals have been outclassed by the ideological ingenuity and organization capabilities of the conservative right. Chapter 6 analyzes the nature of the radical conservative response to liberalism and surveys the strategy and tactics by which conservatives have come to exercise unprecedented influence on all three branches of the U.S. government. As always, before one enters a campaign it is essential to know the enemy. The time has come for liberals to stop dismissing conservative opponents as benighted ignoramuses on the verge of consignment to the dustbin of history and to appreciate them for the principled, driven, and effective organizational actors that they are. Underestimating one's opponents can lead only to defeat.

Having laid bare the motivations, tactics, and organizational strategies employed by the opponents of liberalism, in the final chapter, I call for a return to a true politics of principled, liberal opposition. Rather than running from the label "liberal," as politicians have done for the past three decades, Democrats and even some Republicans must embrace it and proudly assert, "Yes we are liberals; these are principles we stand for; and this is our program." In advancing their own political program, liberals also need to expose the radical conservative position for what it is: an attempt to dismantle the social achievements of the New Deal and Great Society, roll back the tide of civil rights, erase the wall between fundamentalist Christianity and the state, and ultimately to impose on Americans a restrictive morality that controls their sexual behavior and family formation by institutionalizing gross invasions of privacy and new constraints on civil liberties.

The fight will not be easy, but it must be principled. Attempts by Democrats to win elections by presenting themselves as "Republicans Lite" (as advocated by the Democratic Leadership Committee) or as more competent bureaucratic administrators than their Republican challengers (the appeal made by Democrats from Michael Dukakis to Al Gore) have proven to be ineffective in the past and are doomed to fail in the future. Americans don't like phonies and they disdain bureaucrats. If liberals are to win, they must cease internecine bickering over identity politics and stop looking down on working-class Americans, embrace a liberal vision and present it forcefully and unashamedly to the American public—while working hard to anticipate and neutralize the tactics sure to be employed by organizations and individuals on the conservative right.

In moving toward a liberal alignment, two notable practical problems must be addressed: a self-serving media that is itself out of touch with the public and increasingly unanswerable either to government or the people, and a system of campaign finance that borders on legalized bribery. Not only does current campaign funding perpetuate the status quo and skew the operation of the American political economy away from the interests of the people and toward those with money, but it ultimately undermines the effective operation of markets and pushes the nation toward ever higher levels of economic inequality.

Overcoming these barriers requires developing and implementing a concrete plan to assemble a winning electoral coalition. Opinion poll and survey research data suggest that a working electoral majority can indeed be assembled by appealing to four distinct groups: professionals, women, minorities, and workers. The way to create this new coalition is to return to a materialist politics that builds on the fact that 80 percent of Americans have not benefited from the political and economic policies of the past three decades, and that they are working harder for lower wages and more limited public services. The real political puzzle is not why radical Republicans have been able to restructure the American political economy to benefit the few rather than the many, but why liberals have allowed them to get away with it. It is time for liberals to acknowledge their past mistakes, take destiny into their own hands, and move forward with a positive political philosophy and a practical program of action that will ensure peace and prosperity not only for Americans but for the world. Rather than running from the "L word," liberals must recapture the high ideological ground, define the terms of the debate, embrace the banner of liberalism proudly, and ultimately turn the tables on conservatives to make them run from the "C word." This book offers a blueprint for accomplishing these goals.

CHAPTER 2

Where Liberalism Went Wrong

The first step on the path to a liberal revival is to understand how liberalism failed in the past. The term "liberal" may refer either to a political philosophy or a specific location along an ideological continuum from left to right. In this book, I concern myself more with the latter than the former. Liberalism, in this sense, stems from a basic human impulse to use the powers of government to promote the common good, to ensure that everyone has the same social, economic, and political opportunities. Liberals believe first and foremost that government should be democratic, composed of freely elected representatives who serve the interests of the many rather than the few. In serving the interests of the many, however, liberals also hold that government must respect the rights of individuals, along with those of racial, ethnic, religious, and political minorities, by guaranteeing them the freedom not only to vote but also to speak, assemble, petition, worship, have a speedy trial, and enjoy due process and equal standing before the law.

Liberal sentiments resound in the words of the founding fathers and the charter documents of the United States. The signers of the Declaration of Independence stated, "We hold these truths to be self-evident, that all men are created equal, that they are endowed by their Creator with certain unalienable Rights, that among these are Life, Liberty and the pursuit of Happiness. That to secure these rights, Governments are instituted among Men, deriving their just powers from the consent of the governed. . . ." The U.S. Constitution likewise begins by affirming that "the people of the

United States, in order to form a more perfect union, establish justice, insure domestic tranquility, provide for the common defense, promote the general welfare, and secure the blessings of liberty to ourselves and our posterity, do ordain and establish this Constitution. . . ."

What distinguishes liberals from others is the belief that the rights and privileges outlined in the Declaration of Independence and enumerated in the U.S. Constitution are guaranteed to all people regardless of their characteristics, inborn or acquired. Thus, equality of opportunity should be offered to all persons resident in the United States, whether male or female, black or white, gay or straight, rich or poor, owner or worker; and liberals believe that equality of opportunity should exist not only in theory but in reality.

For those holding these beliefs, the creation of a liberal society represents an ongoing challenge, a life calling. The cultivation and extension of liberty within the United States is very much a work in progress. U.S. history is fraught with many paradoxes, but perhaps the greatest is that at its inception, the nation that came into existence to affirm the freedom of the individual and the right to self-government denied those privileges to most of people who then lived within its boundaries. According to the Constitution, adopted in 1789, full rights of citizenship were not offered to women, most blacks, and, in some states, those without property.[1] At the time of the Constitution's ratification, therefore, only around 43 percent of all U.S. inhabitants—basically free white male citizens over the age of twenty-one—enjoyed full rights under the U.S. Constitution, and in southern states the figure was only 33 percent.[2]

The Triumphs of Liberalism

Liberalism is thus a living enterprise rather than a static ideology; and as such it has had its triumphs and tragedies in the course of U.S. history. Liberal moments, during which rights expanded and liberty was extended, have alternated with periods of retrenchment during which conservatives have sought to stymie the expansion of rights and roll back prior extensions of liberty. The first liberal moment, of course, came with the founding of the United States, which created a constitutional structure for the cultivation of democracy, the assurance of rights, and the expansion of freedom. Since the adoption of the U.S. Constitution in 1789, the primary goal of liberals has been to realize this theoretical structure more fully and extend its benefits to a widening circle of Americans.

The second liberal moment began with the outbreak of the Civil War in 1861 and ended in 1876 with the withdrawal of federal troops from states of the former Confederacy. During these fifteen years, the Union was preserved at great human cost and amendments to the U.S. Constitution were passed to abolish slavery (the thirteenth), guarantee the rights of due process and equal legal standing to African Americans (the fourteenth), and ensure the right to vote for men of all races (the fifteenth). For a brief time federal troops stationed in the South enforced these constitutional rights and saw to it that they were honored, though often more in the breech than in reality. Under the Republican presidencies of Abraham Lincoln, Andrew Johnson, and Ulysses S. Grant, the franchise was extended and civil liberties enforced. By the end of the Reconstruction Era, 46 percent of adult Americans enjoyed full constitutional rights.[3]

In the disputed 1876 Tilden-Hayes election, however, the Party of Lincoln abandoned its historic commitment to enforcing black civil rights in the southern states. In exchange for another term in the White House, Republicans agreed to withdraw federal troops from the South and turn a blind eye as former Confederate states imposed a new system of racial subordination. This caste system, which came to be known as Jim Crow, disenfranchised African Americans politically while subjecting them to separate and decidedly inferior treatment, an arrangement that was shamefully ratified by a conservative Supreme Court in the infamous Plessey decision of 1896.[4] The suffering of millions of black citizens and the systematic abrogation of their constitutional rights was swept under the rug and hidden from sight for generations.

With its racial sins out of sight and out of mind, the nation turned to the business of making money, and lots of it. The end of the nineteenth century was a time of unprecedented wealth creation in the United States. Americans of European origin moved steadily westward to colonize the frontier, clear the land of its aboriginal inhabitants, and turn its natural bounty to fortune. Meanwhile, spurred by massive immigration from Europe, the nation urbanized and industrialized, and new manufacturing centers such as Chicago, Cleveland, and Philadelphia generated huge riches for the owners of factories and the businesses that served them and the new industrial work force.

Just after the Civil War, in 1868, the largest personal fortune in the United States—that of the railroad magnate Cornelius Vanderbilt—stood at $40 million. By 1890 the fortune inherited by his son, William, stood at $200 and by 1912 the nation's richest man, John D. Rockefeller, held $1 billion in assets. Over this period, the ratio of the largest to the median fortune in the United States grew from 80,000:1 to 1,2500,000:1, a sixteen-fold increase in just over forty years.[5] Although the U.S. Constitution, in theory, guaranteed rights and equality of opportunity to all males over the age of twenty-one, in practice the new divisions of wealth translated directly into huge disparities in power and political enfranchisement on the basis of class (not to mention skin color).

The rise of corporate trusts concentrated immense wealth within a small group of interbred families who together owned and managed most of the productive capacity of the United States. In the absence of federal efforts to control corporate power, the task was left to the states, which were forced to compete against one another to attract and retain industries, yielding a race to the bottom with respect to corporate governance and industrial safety and wages. State legislators were notoriously corrupt and were routinely suborned by wealthy interests to secure legislation favorable to themselves but inimical to the general welfare.

The power of families such as the Rockefellers, Vanderbilts, Carnegies, Fricks, Harrimans, Astors, Morgans, and Mellons was immense and amplified by the fact that U.S. senators were not elected by the public, but chosen by state legislatures. With a few modest payments to well-placed political bosses, a cooperative legislature could be purchased to secure the "election" of trusted members of the wealthy elite as U.S. senators. In 1902, one-third of U.S. senators were themselves millionaires, enough to guarantee that any piece of legislation threatening the class interests of the wealthy could be blocked through filibuster.[6] During the "gilded age" of the late nineteenth century, some men were clearly more equal than others.

The third liberal moment came with the Progressive Era, which I date roughly from Theodore Roosevelt's ascension to the presidency in 1901 to Woodrow Wilson's retirement from office in 1921. In the course of these twenty years, the legitimate right of the federal government to control and regulate private business was established and the unbridled power of what Roosevelt called the "great malefactors of wealth" was constrained. Roosevelt, a liberal Republican of patrician origins, used the powers of government to arbitrate the bitter struggle between labor and capital, and to assure economic fairness he became serious in applying the 1890 Sherman Anti-Trust Act, working forcefully to break up corporate monopolies with a zeal and dedication that shocked his wealthy peers.

The Progressive Era reached a crescendo during the presidency of Woodrow Wilson, a Democrat. During his first year in office (1913), the idealistic former Princeton professor presided over the creation of the Federal Reserve banking system, thus establishing federal control over the nation's money supply. To represent the interests of workers he created the U.S. Department of Labor, and to fund the expanded role of government he imposed a graduated federal income tax. Finally, he limited the power of the wealthy by instituting the direct election of U.S. senators, which was shortly followed by a sharp drop in the number of millionaire members.

Later in his administration, Wilson sought to project his liberal ideals into the global arena, calling for the extension of democracy worldwide through national self-determination and leading the charge to create a League of Nations that would preserve international order and avoid the perils of global warfare. Though the latter campaign ultimately failed, during his last year in office

progressive forces finally achieved women's suffrage with the ratification of the Nineteenth Amendment to the U.S. Constitution.
At last women could freely vote in all federal, state, and local elections, and the share of the U.S. adult population enjoying full
constitutional rights finally exceeded half, reaching 90 percent in
that year.[7]

During the ensuing decade, the nation turned inward and once
again focused on the business of making money, closing its doors
to immigration, raising barriers to international trade, and relax-
ing Progressive Era reforms. The 1920s were the heyday of social
Darwinism and laissez-faire economics. New fortunes were made
in automobiles, entertainment, and electronics, and older treas-
ures grew. By 1929, John D. Rockefeller's wealth had mushroomed
from $1 billion to $6.3 billion, and seven other people joined him
in the ranks of the nation's billionaires.[8] On the eve of the stock
market crash in late October, the richest 1 percent of the U.S. population earned 15 percent of the income, a share not reached again
for nearly seventy years.

The collapse of the great speculative stock bubble of the 1920s
ushered in the Great Depression of the 1930s, which set the stage
for the fourth liberal moment, the New Deal, which began with
Franklin D. Roosevelt's election to the presidency in 1932 and
ended with Dwight D. Eisenhower's electoral triumph in 1952.
Franklin Roosevelt picked up where his distant cousin Theodore
had left off, again seeking to use the powers of the federal government to arbitrate the conflict between labor and capital and
manage economic affairs in the public interest.

During his first administration he submitted a veritable bliz-
zard of legislation to Congress in an effort to reform the excesses
of the 1920s and restore the U. S. economy to health. Contrary to
what his conservative critics asserted, he did not seek to impose
socialism in the United States but to create more effective, efficient, fair, and transparent markets. The 1933 Banking Act tight-
ened federal control over the banking industry and established the
Federal Deposit Insurance Corporation to underwrite the deposits
of individual citizens and restore solvency to the nation's financial
system. Additional legislation in 1933 established the Tennessee

Valley Authority as a publicly chartered corporation to promote the construction of dams and the generation of cheap electricity that would promote industry and rural electrification. The 1934 Federal Securities Act established the Securities and Exchange Commission to police the nation's financial and equities markets and curb insider trading and other forms of crony capitalism. To ensure the commission's effective operation, Roosevelt named as its first chairman a well-known financier, a crony capitalist familiar with all the tricks of the trade—Joseph P. Kennedy.

Also in 1934, Roosevelt pushed through Congress the National Housing Act, which created the Federal Housing Administration and established the first federal underwriting program to create a national mortgage market that brought home ownership—and for many citizens the first real chance at significant wealth—to a majority of American families. In 1935 the Social Security Act established the first comprehensive federal retirement system, along with a survivor and disability insurance program and a national program of public relief. At the same time, the Public Works Administration was set up to generate employment through an "alphabet soup" of subsidiary agencies such as the Civilian Conservation Corps (CCC), the National Youth Administration (NYA), the Works Progress Administration (WPA), the Federal Arts Project (FAP), the Federal Theater Project (FTP), and the Federal Writers Project (FWP). Finally, the 1936 National Labor Relations Act affirmed the right of workers to join unions and to bargain collectively through freely elected representatives.

Although opponents alleged that Roosevelt sought to destroy capitalism, in reality he saved it from its own excesses and laid the foundations for unprecedented growth and prosperity during the postwar period, creating what the economist John Kenneth Galbraith in 1958 called the "Affluent Society," one characterized by reliable economic growth and steadily rising material well-being.[9] When he became president upon Roosevelt's death in 1945, Harry Truman worked to maintain the political coalition underlying the New Deal, calling his program the "Fair Deal"; but his greatest success came in fulfilling Woodrow Wilson's dream of creating a liberal world order.

Under Truman's leadership, the United States joined with its wartime allies to establish the fundamental institutions that undergird today's global economy—the United Nations, the North Atlantic Treaty Organization, the World Bank, the International Monetary Fund, and the General Agreement on Tariffs and Trade. Working with his Secretary of State, General George C. Marshall, he channeled U.S. capital through the World Bank to rebuild war-devastated Europe and Japan and contain the militant expansion of the Soviet Union. Then once these goals were achieved, the World Bank's sights turned to promoting economic growth and development in a decolonizing Third World.

Billed as a fight against fascism, World War II brought the issue of black civil rights out from under the rug. How could the United States claim to fight for freedom abroad while denying it to so many at home? In 1942 the Roosevelt administration secured passage of the Fair Employment Act, which required private firms working on government contracts not to "discriminate against persons of any race, color, creed, or nationality in matters of employment." In time of war, Southern Democrats felt unable to filibuster legislation that authorized so much spending on behalf of what Studs Terkel later called "the good war."[10]

In 1948, President Truman attempted to push the civil rights agenda further by desegregating the U.S. Armed Forces and agreeing to a civil rights plank in the party platform at the Democratic National Convention (passed only after an impassioned speech by Hubert H. Humphrey). In response, Senator Strom Thurmond of South Carolina led angry Southern Democrats out of the party to run separately for the presidency as "Dixiecrats" in a failed attempt to deny Truman—and his civil rights platform—victory by stealing the electoral votes of the South. Truman won anyway, but the New Deal coalition was clearly beginning to come undone over the issue of race, liberalism's major piece of unfinished business.

The 1950s were a time of peace and prosperity presided over by the revered patriarch and hero of World War II, Dwight D. Eisenhower, who steered a moderate political course that left intact most of what the New Deal had accomplished. He was not an ideological man and given his immense popularity was courted by both parties as a presidential candidate. Although not a period of retrenchment in rights and liberties, it was not a time of great forward progress either. The most important advancement in civil rights came not from the executive or legislative branch of government, but from the judiciary in the form of the Supreme Court's 1954 *Brown v. Topeka* decision, which declared racial segregation in public schools to be unconstitutional.[11] Only two years into the Eisenhower presidency, of course, most supreme court justices were liberals who had been appointed during the twenty years of the Roosevelt and Truman administrations.

The last liberal moment of the twentieth century came during the 1960s under presidents John F. Kennedy and Lyndon B. Johnson. They faced the daunting task of honoring liberalism's moral commitment to civil rights while attending to the practical problem of keeping populist Southern Democrats within the New Deal coalition. Bowing to political exigencies, support for the civil rights struggle during the Kennedy administration emphasized the moral over the practical. Although Attorney General Robert F. Kennedy enforced the *Brown* decision in Southern colleges and JFK himself publicly sympathized with Martin Luther King and his Southern Christian Leadership Council, meaningful civil rights legislation languished in Congress, presumably awaiting Kennedy's reelection in 1964.

Instead, it was a Southern Democrat, Lyndon B. Johnson, who proved to be the century's great legislator of civil rights. Capitalizing on the moral authority of a martyred president, he used his formidable parliamentary abilities (honed earlier as Senate Majority Leader) to secure passage of the1964 Civil Rights Act, which forbade segregation in schools, accommodations, restaurants, stores, transportation, and public services nationwide. It also prohibited racial discrimination in hiring, promotion, and remuneration; and it created separate commissions on Civil Rights and Equal Employment Opportunity to monitor progress in the achievement of racial equality. In one fell swoop, Lyndon Johnson's signature wiped out the legal basis for Jim Crow in the South and created a framework to combat informal but no less potent discrimination in the North.

With a landslide reelection under his belt in November of 1964, the president gave recalcitrant Southern legislators the "Johnson treatment" (a forceful mixture of reward, punishment, threat, and physical intimidation)[12] to secure passage of the 1965 Voting Rights Act. Often heralded as the Second Reconstruction, this legislation empowered the federal government to enter Southern states to supervise and control local elections to ensure that they adhered to the principle of "one person, one vote" regardless of race. In the same year, amendments to the Immigration and Nationality Act eliminated discriminatory ethnic and racial quotas in the nation's immigration system. Finally, in the wake of Martin Luther King's assassination in 1968 and the subsequent wave of urban riots, Republican Senator Everett Dirksen brokered a compromise that broke a Southern filibuster to secure passage of a long-delayed Johnson project, the Fair Housing Act, which banned discrimination in the rental and sale of housing.[13]

The "Johnson treatment" was not only reserved for legislators who opposed civil rights legislation, however. The former senate majority leader also aspired to be the greatest social legislator in U.S. history and, more particularly, to create a "Great Society" in which poverty no longer existed. By the late 1960s, Galbraith's affluent society had reached its fullest expression. Poverty had declined steadily since 1945, income inequality had dropped, average income had risen, and the fruits of this abundance had been distributed widely as never before. The only thing that remained was to undertake a frontal assault on "pockets of poverty" that persisted in America's inner cities and rural areas.

To accomplish this goal, in his first State of the Union address Johnson called for an "unconditional war on poverty" and submitted to Congress what became the Economic Opportunity Act of 1964, which emulated Roosevelt's New Deal in the "alphabet soup" of agencies that it created to generate employment and foment opportunity, including Head Start, the Job Corps, the Neighborhood Youth Corps, Volunteers in Service to America, and the controversial Community Action Program, which sought to ensure the "maximum feasible participation" of the poor themselves as soldiers in the new War on Poverty.[14]

The flurry of social legislation also included bills to create Medicare (the federal health insurance system for the aged), Medicaid (the program of subsidized medical assistance for the impoverished), the U.S. Department of Housing and Urban Development (to promote desegregation and coordinate to war on urban poverty), the U.S. Department of Transportation (to channel funds into public mass transit), the National Endowment for the Humanities, the National Endowment for the Arts, the Public Broadcasting System (to promote wider access to cultural products), and the Model Cities Program (to clear slums and rehabilitate low-income urban neighborhoods). He also secured passage of the Elementary and Secondary Education Act and the Higher Education Act, which made billions of dollars available for public education, as well as the Air Quality Act and the Water Quality Act to combat pollution of the environment.[15]

Johnson's civil rights agenda sought to guarantee full rights for all citizens not only theoretically but also practically, and new laws forbade discrimination not only on the basis of race but also of sex, religion, and national origin, a list that was later expanded to include age and disability. With the passage of the Twenty-Sixth Amendment to the Constitution, which lowered the voting age to eighteen, the liberal dream of universal suffrage and full equality before the law reached its zenith. In 1972, 98 percent of the U.S. adult population was eligible to vote.[16] At the same time, the War on Poverty was having its effect. From 1963 to 1970, the poverty rate dropped from 22.2 to 12.6 percent, a 43 percent drop in just seven years.[17]

The Retreat of Liberalism

The Johnson administration proved to be the high water mark of liberalism in the twentieth century. By the early 1970s, more Americans had been enfranchised, both economically and politically, than ever before in U.S. history. Average household income was at its height, income inequality had reached a nadir, and the proportion of families in poverty would never again be so low.

Liberalism appeared triumphant. But its moment of triumph was also that of its downfall, as 1968 witnessed the beginnings of a tectonic political realignment that ultimately created a new governing coalition, bringing to power a new cadre of conservatives who were hostile to government and deeply suspicious of the uses to which it had been put under successive Democratic presidents. What brought liberalism's downfall after decades of stunning political successes that had succeeded in benefiting so many people in so many ways?

The Achilles' Heel

There are many reasons for liberalism's demise in the last quarter of the twentieth century, but first and foremost among them is race. Race proved to be the quintessential wedge issue that Republican tacticians could cynically but effectively use to pry apart the New Deal coalition that had steadfastly supported populist, redistributive policies—but only as long as they did not directly benefit blacks and other minorities. From FHA and VA mortgages to Supplemental Security Income, and from Social Security benefits to Aid for Families with Dependent Children, the liberal programs of Roosevelt's New Deal and Truman's Fair Deal had been structured either to exclude minorities from participation or to delegate authority to the states to do so.[18] Once liberals insisted on cutting blacks and Latinos into the populist action, Southern Democrats bolted and Republicans pounced to hack away at the Achilles' heel of the New Deal coalition.

Following a blueprint first adumbrated by Kevin Phillips, Richard Nixon put together a "Southern strategy" that appealed in coded, symbolic ways to antiblack sentiment prevalent in the South as well as to socially conservative working-class values in the North.[19] This strategy became the bedrock of a new political coalition in which Southerners joined the Republican party and allied themselves with nonmetropolitan, fundamentalist Christians, urban blue-collar workers, and wealthy corporate interests to capture first the White House and ultimately Congress. One by one,

Southern Democratic legislators crossed the isle to switch parties, including former Democratic stalwarts such as Strom Thurmond (South Carolina), John Stennis (Mississippi), Jesse Helms (North Carolina), and James Eastland (Alabama). Those Southern senators who remained in the Democratic fold (J. William Fulbright, Albert Gore, Sr.) were targeted for electoral defeat and slowly picked off.

In the course of two decades, the party of the Great Emancipator became the party of a revived neo-confederacy. Republican leadership shifted away from moderate figures such as Nelson Rockefeller (New York), Everett Dirksen (Illinois), Gerald Ford (Michigan), Abraham Ribicoff (Connecticut), and Edward Brooke (Massachusetts) and into the hands of radical Southern conservatives such as Newt Gingrich (Georgia), Trent Lott (Mississippi), Tom DeLay (Texas), John Ashcroft (Missouri), and, of course, George W. Bush (Texas). The Californians Richard Nixon and Ronald Reagan proved to be but way stations on the road to the southernization of the Republican party.[20]

Though shocking to many, Senate Majority Leader Trent Lott's unguarded remark in late 2002 should not have been surprising. At the 100th birthday celebration for the original Dixiecrat, Strom Thurmond, Lott crowed that "we voted for him. We're proud of it. And if the rest of the country had followed our lead, we wouldn't have had all these problems over all these years."[21] Indeed, as early as 1984 he boasted that "the spirit of Jefferson Davis lives in the 1984 Republican platform" and he expressed sympathy for the Jefferson Davis Society, a nonprofit organization founded in 1994 to honor the late president of the Confederate States of America.[22]

The political strategy of Republicans from Richard Nixon onward has been quite simple, a variation on Julius Caesar's classic admonition to "divide and conquer." Focus groups, political polls, and other research conducted during the 1960s, 1970s, and 1980s repeatedly showed the persistence of considerable animus toward blacks on the part of three crucial New Deal constituencies— ethnic blue-collar workers in the North, lower-class whites in the South, and nonmetropolitan whites in the Great Plains and Rocky Mountains.[23] By appealing to antiblack sentiments in these constituencies, Republicans sought to convince lower-income whites to vote against their own economic interests in return for sticking it to "uppity" blacks and their elitist white allies ("limousine liberals"). From Ronald Reagan's deployment of the "welfare queen" imagery, to George H. W. Bush's infamous Willie Horton ad campaign, Republicans have successfully appealed to Americans' baser prejudices and racist sentiments, deliberately dividing white from black to widen a ragged racial schism for short-term political profit.[24]

From the 1970s onward, conservatives have used race to mount a successful campaign to stop and then turn back the rising tide of civil rights, blocking ratification of the Equal Rights Amendment, launching court challenges and referenda to limit the use of affirmative action, watering down civil rights enforcement, and filling the judiciary with people hostile to the advancement of minorities in American society. In return for this symbolic stand against "undeserving minorities," middle- and working-class whites acquiesced to a massive and unprecedented upward redistribution of wealth in American society, supporting the limitation of taxes at the state and local levels, the reduction of inheritance and dividends taxes at the federal level, and cuts in corporate and personal income taxes at all levels.[25]

Between 1970 to 1990, total tax payments became increasingly regressive and inequality surged: the effective tax rate experienced by the top 1 percent of the income distribution dropped from 69 to 26 percent, and from 1970 to 1997 their share of total U.S. income rose from 6 to 16 percent.[26] Whereas the incomes earned by the poorest 60 percent of families actually declined from the mid-1970s to the mid-1990s, the top 5 percent saw theirs increase by a third and the top 1 percent saw theirs go up by 70 percent.[27] Over the same period, U.S. household income inequality rose by a remarkable 13 percent,[28] and inequality of wealth rose even faster as the share of wealth owned by the top 1 percent of households doubled from 20 to 40 percent.[29]

This rise in inequality would have been even greater if it had not been for the increase in hours worked by men and the unprecedented entry of women into the work force, which bolstered household incomes that were sagging in the face of declining real hourly wages. Disposable real earnings declined from an average of around $10.50 per hour in 1972 to under $9.50 in the mid-1990s. As hourly wages stagnated, households and families supplied more hours of labor simply to maintain their standard of living—Americans were running harder to stay in place. At the same time, the middle class was financing a larger share of total government expenses. From 1970 to 2000, the share of the federal tax burden borne by individual payroll taxes climbed from 18 to 31 percent.[30]

The Republican realignment also brought a dramatic decline in the regulation of markets and industries, handing the rich new opportunities to get much, much richer. The mean net worth of the Forbes 400 largest fortunes went from $396 million in 1983 to $1.6 billion in 1997 and over the same period the share of assets controlled by the wealthiest 1 percent of households jumped from 30 to 40 percent.[31] Whereas the ratio between the income earned by chief executives and production workers stood at around 25 in 1968, by 1999 it reached 419. From 1990 to 1998, the average compensation package earned by executives in the largest corporations increased by 481 percent even though corporate profits rose by only 108 percent.[32]

If regressive tax policies were not enough to check the expansion of social welfare in the United States, they were accompanied, during the administrations of Ronald Reagan and George W. Bush, by massive increases in federal defense spending, which boosted the profits of government contractors but put severe fiscal pressures on federal discretionary and entitlement funding. The manufactured budget crisis provided the political leverage needed to enact massive cuts in social spending. Whereas indices of U.S. social health had risen lockstep with increasing GDP through 1970, afterward trends in the social and economic health of the nation departed from one another at an increasing rate.[33] By pandering to the racial animus of white America and using antiblack sentiment as a wedge to force blue-collar Democrats away from their natural party, the southern takeover of the GOP succeeded by 2003 in dismantling much of the New Deal.

Other Reasons for Liberal Decline

As important as race is to understanding the collapse of liberalism in the late twentieth century, it is only part of the story. Whereas liberals might blame conservatives for pandering to American's baser instincts or complain about the lamentable persistence of racial prejudice among whites, other reasons for liberalism's decline are internal to the movement itself. Aside from the scar of race, the remaining wounds to the liberal agenda were largely self-inflicted and, taken together, they heartily abetted the Republican strategy of using race to divide and conquer the New Deal coalition.

Opposition to the programs of the Great Society was based only partly on race. As paradoxical as it may seem, resistance was also based on class, for by the 1970s the ruling elites of the Democratic party had grown increasingly arrogant, self-righteous, and callous toward the sensibilities of their working-class base. In addition to a racially coded symbolic politics, therefore, conservatives also appealed to simmering class resentments within the Democratic coalition, coining terms such as "pointy-headed intellectuals," "nattering nabobs of negativism," "poverty pimps," "limousine liberals," and "brie and Chardonnay activists" to conjure up images of affluent liberals who lived and worked in safe enclaves, where they dreamed up new programs to impose on working people, who bore the costs and experienced the consequences of liberals' decisions.[34]

As the civil rights movement shifted out of the South and the war on poverty confronted concentrated disadvantage in the urban North, liberal Democrats naturally encountered resistance from entrenched social and political interests that were threatened by the changes.[35] Rather than acknowledging the sacrifices that were being asked of working-class whites and their political bosses, and attempting to reach a *political* accommodation that offered benefits to counterbalance them, liberal elites treated lower-class opponents as racist obstructionists to be squelched using the powers of government. Rather than outlining a political argument to explain why desegregation was in their interests and providing money to ease the pain of transition, liberals increasingly turned to the courts and executive branch to *force* working-class whites and local political bosses to accept whatever changes they mandated from above.

During the 1960s and 1970s, well-educated, affluent liberal planners created urban renewal programs that blithely deemed working-class neighborhoods to be "slums," systematically stripped workers of cherished homes, and, after razing the dwellings, converted the land to "higher" (i.e., middle-class) uses from which the original inhabitants received little or no benefit.[36] Without prior consultation or compensation, public housing for poor families was plunked down within stable, working-class neighborhoods to undermine property values and impair safety, something that residents bitterly noted never happened to the neighborhoods where the liberals themselves lived.[37] High-priced lawyers, well-educated bureaucrats, and upper-middle-class activists worked assiduously to end the passing of jobs, union memberships, and apprenticeships through family and friendship networks, which perforce excluded minorities.[38] These liberals themselves, however, benefited from an institutionalized system of "legacy admissions" that guaranteed places for their children at the nation's best colleges and universities, thus ensuring the reproduction of their own privileged class position.

The well-schooled children of the baby boom came of age during a period of unprecedented affluence in which material security was taken for granted.[39] They believed education and jobs were permanent birthrights rather than fragile gains achieved through hard-won economic and political struggles.[40] In the 1972 presidential election, youthful activists took control of the Democratic party and managed to communicate quite clearly the contempt they felt for the patriotism, faith, and social conservatism of the white working class, whom they derided as "hard hats," "red necks," and "racists." Faced with such overt contempt and welcomed as a "silent majority" by Richard Nixon, Northern ethnic voters and Southern whites deserted the Democratic party in droves to produce a landslide for the Republicans. The self-destruction of Richard Nixon in Watergate was followed by the anomalous

victory of Jimmy Carter in 1976 and sent the wrong signal to liberal Democrats, who preferred to see Nixon's Southern strategy
as a bad dream. They continued to neglect the warning signs of
1972, leading to a predictable return to Republican landslides in
the 1980s.

The arrogance and self-righteousness of liberal elites mani-
fested themselves in yet another way that had disastrous effects.
The supreme irony of the Great Society is that the same liberal architects who promoted civil rights and social welfare also prosecuted a costly foreign war on the basis of lies, deception, and
subterfuges that once again callously abused the faith and trust of
the working class. As subsequent tapes and archives have clearly
shown, liberals in the Johnson administration—including the president himself—manufactured a supposed attack on U.S. warships
in the Gulf of Tonkin to secure a congressional authorization for
military intervention in Vietnam. Then they systematically lied to
voters about the costs and consequences of that engagement and
its ultimate prospects for success.[41]

Aside from the betrayal of public trust, the Vietnam War also
contributed to the demise of liberalism through fiscal means after
1968. Economically, Johnson's attempt to support guns and butter
without raising taxes laid the foundation for inflationary spirals
and stagflation in the 1970s. The 1973 oil boycott would have dealt
a serious blow to the U.S. economy under any circumstances, but
the fiscal excess of the Great Society, combined with the Vietnam
War, turned what in Europe and Japan were severe but manage-
able recessions into a disastrous brew of inflation, unemployment,
and long-term recession in the United States.

A particular challenge to liberals stemmed from the fact that
high rates of inflation in the 1970s produced rising nominal wages
but declining spending power in real terms, causing a serious
problem of "bracket creep" in the federal tax system. In the course
of the 1970s, more and more Americans were pushed by inflation
into income tax brackets that were originally intended to apply
only to the very affluent. Middle-income Americans were working
harder for less money in real terms, but were being taxed at higher
and higher rates.[42]

High inflation also brought about an escalation in the value of real assets, particularly housing. Families with modest incomes suddenly found themselves owning homes—and paying real estate taxes—far above what they could really afford.[43] Rather than sympathizing with the plight of middle-class families struggling to pay taxes in an era of stagflation, however, liberals viewed rising tax revenues as a source of easy money. Bracket creep and asset inflation offered legislators a seemingly costless way to raise taxes steadily without ever voting to do so.

But there were indeed costs. The unwillingness of Democratic legislators to adjust tax brackets or accommodate the inflation of housing prices set the stage for a middle-class tax revolt. As is often the case, the revolution began in California. By a large majority, voters in that state passed Proposition 13 in 1979 to cap property taxes permanently at unrealistically low levels, which led directly to a sustained decline in the quality and quantity of California's public services, notably education.[44]

Riding the wave of middle-class anger and resentment, Ronald Reagan promised "morning again in America" and won a landslide victory over the hapless Jimmy Carter in 1980. One of his first acts was to cut tax rates sharply and to reduce their progressivity, which, when combined with a massive increase in defense spending, shut off the flow of money that had financed the expansion of liberalism. Following a path that led from intervention in Vietnam to hyperinflation to bracket creep, liberal Democrats—through a remarkable combination of arrogance and self-righteousness—dug their own graves in the 1970s and created the political conditions whereby conservatives could achieve their cherished goal of "de-funding" the New Deal.

The Vietnam War had one more effect on the American electorate that was less tangible but no less powerful: it forcefully underscored that liberal elites made the decisions while working-class whites paid the price, thus reinforcing a politics of class resentment manipulated so effectively by conservative Republicans. The soldiers who fought and died in Vietnam were disproportionately drawn from the America's working and lower classes.[45] The sons and daughters of upper-middle-class professionals—the people who held power, influence, and prestige in the Great Society—by and large did not serve in Vietnam. On the contrary, they evaded the draft through a combination of student deferments, personal connections, and a skillful use of medical disabilities. To add insult to injury, as they sat out hostilities on campus, they very vocally and visibly protested the war in southeast Asia and branded U.S. soldiers as "war criminals" and "baby killers." Tellingly, once the system of student deferments was abandoned and the children of the upper-middle class faced the real risk of being drafted through random assignment, direct U.S. participation in the war quickly ended.

To blue-collar workers in the North and poor whites in the South (the latter always being over-represented in the U.S. military) it seemed as though liberal lawmakers favored the war as long as someone else's children were serving and dying as soldiers, but as soon as their precious offspring were put at risk, they quickly ignored the sacrifices of the working classes, forgot about the 60,000 dead, and abandoned hundreds of POWs and MIAs in their haste to leave Vietnam. The ultimate result was the evolution of a working-class mythology of sellout by unpatriotic liberal elites ("America haters"), epitomized cinematically by the movies and roles of Sylvester Stallone, Chuck Norris, and Clint Eastwood, whose tag lines were appropriated to great political effect by Ronald Reagan. Although liberal Hollywood critics turned up their noses at Rambo and his ilk, the movies were immensely successful at the box office and clearly tapped into a rich vein of popular resentment against liberal elites, which liberals once again ignored at their peril.

During the 1980s and 1990s, as liberal Democrats began to be driven from the public sphere by the politics of race, combined with their own self-righteous blindness and arrogance, they responded in two equally unproductive ways. One response sought to remake Democrats as Republicans under the aegis of the Democratic Leadership Committee, positioning candidates in the political market as "Republicans lite."[46] This group achieved power and prominence under the charismatic leadership of Bill Clinton; but absent his charisma and lacking a clearly defined ideology to oppose the Republican right, they had the rug pulled out from under them in 2000 and went on to humiliating defeat in 2002. After all, faced with a choice between real and ersatz Republicans, why not pick the real thing? Americans never like phonies.

As the mainstream of the Democratic party turned rightward in a failed bid to emulate Republicans, other liberals retreated to the safe confines of academia, where under the banner of postmodernism, deconstructionism, critical theory, or, more popularly, "political correctness," they prosecuted what became known as the "culture wars."[47] In the course of this new campaign, liberalism on campus became an Orwellian parody of itself, suppressing free expression to ensure liberal orthodoxy and seeking to instill through indoctrination what it could not achieve politically at the polls.[48] To the delight of conservatives everywhere, liberals often ended up attacking each other—seeking to unmask a white male as a closet racist, and ferreting out the last vestiges of racism, sexism, classism, and ageism wherever they might remain, even in the nation's most liberal quarters. Authors such as Dinesh D'Souza, Alan Bloom, Roger Kimball, and Robert Bork had a field day lampooning the tortured logic, breathless rhetoric, and impenetrable jargon offered up by the priesthood of postmodernism, further alienating liberals from their base among the poor and working classes.[49]

The essence of postmodern ideology is that there is no such thing as objective truth. There is only a subjective reality constructed by the powerful through a "hegemonic discourse" that serves the narrow interests of the privileged.[50] The goal of postmodern scholarship is to "deconstruct" the hegemonic discourse to reveal how it serves the interests of power and privilege and then to substitute a counter-narrative that advances the interests of persons formerly marginalized in terms of class, race, ethnicity, gender, and sexual preference, and that celebrates their characteristics.

There is nothing illiberal about defending the interests of the marginalized and advocating the rights of the oppressed, of course. But whereas the instinct to stand up for the little guy may be liberal, the conceptual apparatus of postmodernism is not. Ultimately it is a neo-fascist ideology that seeks little more than to replace one tyranny for another. Rather than seeking to advance an open society in which the rights and opinions of all citizens are protected, it seeks to create a new social world in which an alternative hegemonic discourse favorable to the oppressed is imposed by an intellectual vanguard acting in the "interests of the people."

The vocabulary of postmodernism, however, is so arcane, the prose so dense, and the propositions so convoluted that they can be mastered only with a great investment of time and energy by a leisured class of intellectuals, either independently wealthy or working on someone else's nickel. Anyone who has ever tried to digest a postmodern tract quickly realizes that contempt for the uninformed and un-elect is built into the corpus of critical social theory. Is it any wonder that right-wing critics like Dinesh D'Souza find a ready mass audience when they rise to oppose the avatars of academic liberalism?

Liberalism at the Crossroads

Liberals accomplished great things during the first three-quarters of the twentieth century. They extended full constitutional rights to women, racial minorities, and young adults, finally giving the right to vote to a true majority of the U.S. population.[51] They achieved the direct popular election of U.S. senators and established control over corporate trusts to reign in the power of the wealthy. They established the right of the federal government to manage the U.S. economy in the public interest and secured a place for workers at the economic bargaining table. They created a limited but serviceable system of social welfare that protected citizens from the worst ravages of market failures and provided basic access to health care. They created programs to underwrite markets for credit, capital, and insurance that dramatically increased household wealth and protected family incomes. Finally, they enacted programs to ensure that the civil rights of all Americans were honored and that the natural environment—air, water, land, forests—was protected.

As a result of these achievements, in 1975 Americans were healthier, wealthier, and more affluent than ever before, and collectively they had a greater say in their own governance than at any time in U.S. history. Since that time, however, liberals stumbled badly and let down key elements of their constituency—and the nation as a whole—in a variety of fundamental ways. When they encountered resistance to black civil rights among poor and working-class whites—some of it racially motivated, some of it not—rather than dealing with the resistance politically, liberal elites sought to impose solutions from above by taking advantage of their privileged access to judicial and executive power. Then, rather than telling Americans honestly about the likely costs and consequences of a military intervention in southeast Asia and trusting them to make the correct decision, they used lies and deception to trick voters into supporting an unwinnable war that was fought mostly by the poor and working classes; and when the war came too close to home, they quickly forgot about the lower-class combatants and the sacrifices that they had made. Then, after liberals' attempt to support guns and butter set off hyperinflation to erode the real value of wages, they callously thought up new ways to spend the windfall of tax revenue rather than adjust tax brackets to relieve the unsustainable burden on the middle class. Finally, when faced with political revolt because of these misguided policies, they either sold out and attempted to appropriate conservative positions for the sake of election or they retreated into arcane ideologies to wage a rearguard cultural insurgency from the safety of the ivory tower.

From several perspectives, then, the last quarter of the century was a disaster for the cause of liberalism and a travesty for those constituencies it ostensibly represented. Rather moving forward to extend and enforce civil rights, liberal strategies since 1975 sparked a counter-revolution that steadily chipped away to reduce earlier gains. Liberal arrogance drove poor and middle-class whites into the waiting hands of conservatives, who used their support to engineer a massive upward redistribution of wealth and income. As a result, since 1975 the rich have become richer, middle-class families have worked harder to stay in place, and the poor have steadily grown poorer. As the needs of the poor and middle class grew in response to the rising inequalities, social services were cut and the safety net trimmed.

As a result, on virtually every indicator of social and economic well-being, the vast majority of Americans are no better, or are even worse off, than they were in 1975. At the dawn of the twenty-first century, the United States has evolved a political economy that clearly and consistently benefits only the top fifth of the income distribution. These people enjoy unprecedented wealth, magnificent health, and they increasingly live and work in safe, secure, and luxurious enclaves that are removed socially and spatially from the rest of American society. To preserve the status quo that has lavished upon them this beneficence, they vote in large numbers, participate heavily in politics, and donate substantial sums to candidates and political organizations that reflect their interests. Just as earlier in the century, the U.S. senate has increasingly become a club for millionaires (there are at least forty at last count) instead of a deliberative body that is representative of the American people.[52]

The obvious question is why and how a political economy that fails to deliver social and economic welfare to four-fifths of the population is allowed to persist in a democratic society. Part of the answer lies in the low rates of political participation and voting among those not in the top fifth of the class distribution. The explanation also lies in the disproportionate resources at the disposal of the favored classes and of the growing importance of money in politics. But a more fundamental problem is the lack of a coherent political alternative, the absence of a clear and convincing program of opposition that the unfortunate 80 percent can believe in, contribute to, and ultimately vote for.

The limitations of current social and economic arrangements are clear in national statistics that chart trends and differentials with respect to income, health, wealth, and work. People are aware of the situation and are eager for change, but liberals have not been able to articulate a salable political vision. Neither the watered-down Republicanism of the Democratic Leadership Committee nor the inward-looking identity politics of the campus offer an appealing model for political progress. In politics a failed paradigm is rarely discarded because it is seen to have problems. As in science, a paradigm is rejected only when a better model is available to serve as an alternative. During the past quarter-century, liberals have failed miserably at offering such an alternative.

The first national elections of the millennium were embarrassments. In 2000, Al Gore sought to replicate Clinton's success without his political skills or personal magnetism; but whereas Clinton's chameleon personality could read the political winds, shift course, and still offer a convincing message to voters, Al Gore's wooden attempts to do the same thing simply made him look phony, insincere, and ultimately untrustworthy. With no coherent ideology and a candidate lacking in charm and grace, voters had little reason to support the Democratic platform, creating circumstances in which the election could be stolen against the wishes of most voters. Liberal ineptitude let George W. Bush became minority president through political chicanery at the state level and suborned justice at the national level.

Given the closeness of the 2000 elections, many looked to the midterm elections of 2002 for a corrective. But it didn't happen. Despite a weak economy, the steady movement of the nation toward war in Iraq, and little tangible progress in the war on terror, the Republicans retook control of the Senate and increased their margin in the House of Representatives. The problem, once again, was the lack of a coherent, believable platform of opposition. If one needed convincing evidence that the strategy of "Republican lite" was a loser, the elections of 2002 supplied it.

The purpose of this book is to offer a coherent liberal alternative to the reigning conservative ideology. The Republican coalition is weak and vulnerable, out of touch with the mainstream and disconnected from the values, beliefs, and aspirations of most Americans. What is missing to convert this vulnerability to political victory is a convincing platform that tells voters why it is in their interests—and in the interests of the nation—to support liberal causes and candidates. Electoral victory cannot be accomplished by running away from the liberal label, by donning the garb of Republicans. If Americans are good at one thing, it is spotting phonies, and they will never support people who try to be something they are not. The time has come to end the charade and for candidates to step forward and say "I am a liberal and this is what I believe." This book offers them something to say and a program of action to undertake.

Chapter 3

Liberalism and the Market

During the twentieth century liberals often displayed considerable ambivalence toward the market. They remained skeptical about markets and their desirability as mechanisms for producing and distributing goods and services in human societies. Many people of liberal sentiment disliked the inequalities and concentrations of private wealth that accompanied markets and believed that rational planning would do a better job of ensuring the general social and economic welfare. In their view, enlightened, technically trained specialists would use hard data and scientific methods to improve material conditions through rational planning. Rather than leaving important decisions to the vagaries of a market motivated by selfish interests, public officials empowered by the people would sift through the facts, weigh the evidence, and then apply their theoretical knowledge to evaluate the conflicting claims and counterclaims to reach a decision that was in the best interests of society as a whole, ensuring the greatest benefit for the greatest number of people.

Underlying this faith in the ability of government agents to solve human problems was a near-religious belief in the inevitability of "progress" and the perfectability of human societies through enlightened rational action. During the first half of the twentieth century, liberals differed from one another mostly with respect to the nature of the government that they hoped would make the necessary decisions. Progressives saw government as a means by which the people, through their elected representatives, could moderate the excesses of capitalism, restrain the power of the wealthy, and manage markets in the public interest. Socialists generally sought to have democratic government assume ownership of key sectors of the economy, which could then be operated strategically in the public interest rather than to make a profit. Communists, of course, sought to create a full-blown command economy in which the state assumed responsibility for most economic decisions and central planners were empowered to make decisions on behalf of the people.

Thus, political liberalism was originally a big tent that encompassed a wide range of beliefs about the market. People who wished to regulate, partially take over, and eliminate markets could agree to support the initial steps necessary to build a better society while disagreeing on the ultimate relationship between the state and the economy. When Franklin D. Roosevelt first came to power in 1933, his supporters included progressives, who mostly got what they wanted in the ensuing years; aspiring socialists, who saw the New Deal as an interim milepost on the road to state socialism; and frustrated communists, who grudgingly settled for Roosevelt while they waited for the revolution to break out.

Mass markets came into existence and globalized during the nineteenth century, and much of the ensuing century was taken up with societal experiments that tried out different alternatives to capitalism. At one point, about a third of the way through the twentieth century, many of the proposed alternatives seemed not only viable but also preferable to the market model. By the 1930s, global capitalism had seemingly collapsed and fascism emerged as an alluring alternative. By the end of the decade, fascism seemed to restore social order and economic growth to countries that only a short time earlier were wallowing in disorder and decline, such as Germany, Japan, and Italy. In the Soviet Union, meanwhile, the Bolsheviks ended civil conflict, imposed order, and through command mechanisms proceeded to jumpstart industrialization in a way that repositioned Russia on the world stage as a significant international power.

In contrast, during the 1930s liberal democratic nations such as England, France, and the United States were mired in deflation, unemployment, and bitter class conflict, leading many intelligent people to conclude that markets and democratic government were on the verge of extinction. To many hopeful observers, it seemed possible that centralized planning might trump the market as the organizing principle for modern human societies.

Subsequent events proved them wrong. The utopian vision of fascist order died in the ovens of Auschwitz and the communist hope for a worker's paradise was strangled in the Gulag Archipelago. The unprecedented scale of death and destruction that could be visited upon human beings by centralized planners with too much power, too much arrogance, and too little conscience was evident in Stalin's collectivizations, Hitler's exterminations, Mao's Great Leap Forward, and Pol Pot's killing fields. If it did nothing else, the bloody history of the twentieth century should have convinced people of liberal sentiment—those seeking to use government to promote the common good—that the market is the only economic system that is consistent with democratic values and that it offers the best possible means of ensuring social and economic welfare for large human populations.

Indeed, China's decisive shift away from communism in the 1980s and the collapse of the Soviet Union in 1991 leaves no credible alternative to the market as a model for organizing economic production and distribution in developed human societies. Neither the anarchist utopias envisioned by anti-globalization activists nor the stern theocracies envisioned by fundamentalists offer much hope for improving human welfare. If liberalism is to have any hope of success, therefore, it must accept the inevitability of markets in human affairs.

Rather than seeking alternatives to markets, liberals must work to manage them in ways that promote a more even distribution of social and economic benefits within the United States and throughout the world. To accomplish this goal, liberals must unabashedly adopt the language of market economics and, in doing so, take the high moral ground away from conservatives. Governing a postindustrial market society that is increasingly integrated on a global scale is far too important a task to be left to conservative ideologues and corporate cheer leaders. The place to begin is by exposing the conservative bromide of the "free market" for the myth that it is.

The Myth of the Free Market

The concept of the "free market" is one of the most misleading tropes ever devised. The pairing of the words "free" and "market" suggests that capitalism somehow exists autonomously, as a state of nature, and that in the absence of human "interference" markets will spring into existence to operate smoothly and effectively, as natural processes do. The metaphor of the free market implies that human actions undertaken to influence market outcomes represent unwarranted "interventions" that artificially "constrain" the operation of naturally functioning systems, in the same way that building a dam constitutes an intervention to create an artificial lake from what used to be a river. Whereas the construction of dams, highways, and bridges are usually viewed positively, however, actions undertaken to influence markets are portrayed as detrimental—undermining, however good one's intentions, the market's efficient operation so that it cannot produce the greatest good for the greatest number.

In fact, markets, like dams and highways, are very much human creations.[1] Indeed, in the panorama of human existence markets are a very recent invention. For the vast majority of the time that humans have inhabited the earth, they exchanged resources almost exclusively through nonmarket mechanisms.[2] It was not until the fifteenth century that markets began unambiguously to grow, and for a long time they covered a relatively small share of human transactions.[3] It has only been within the past two hundred years that markets have expanded geographically and socially to subsume large swaths of human behavior.

Functioning markets ultimately rest on certain institutional foundations that generally do not exist in small-scale societies. Until around 10,000 years ago, virtually all human beings lived in mobile groups no larger than 150–200 persons, and these were spread fairly uniformly at low densities through the environment. The economy was one of subsistence through hunting and gathering, and there was little differentiation between people or social classes.[4]

The nineteenth-century sociologist Max Weber identified four crucial preconditions for the emergence of markets: private property, buyers and sellers, money, and information.[5] Among hunter-gatherer societies, there is little private property, and interpersonal behavior is dominated by relationships based on communal sharing, turn taking, and, in larger groups, authority ranking; but little, if any, human behavior is influenced by the mechanisms of market pricing.[6] Before the agricultural revolution, population densities were so low that potential buyers and sellers rarely came into contact with one another; and although objects were often endowed with symbolic value, money per se did not exist.[7] Information among early hunter-gatherers was generally limited to whatever knowledge could be accumulated and passed down through oral tradition.[8] Under these circumstances markets could not realistically emerge.

Significant market relations became feasible only with the urbanization of human society, which itself was made possible by the domestication of plants and animals. Although the first cities came into existence around 6,000 years ago, it has only been within the past two centuries that more than 5 percent of human beings have been able to live in them; and it is only within the current decade that more than half of the world's population has urbanized.[9] Paralleling the urbanization of the human population, markets emerged slowly, beginning with a revival of long-distance trade between Europe and the rest of the world during the fifteenth century and continuing steadily through the mercantilist and early capitalist eras of the 1600s and 1700s.[10]

Markets began to expand dramatically during the nineteenth century because they proved to be remarkably effective at organizing the production, distribution, and consumption of goods and services under an industrial system. Industrialism offered a new approach to manufacturing things that substituted inanimate for animate sources of power. Unfortunately, however, early capitalism was associated with regular market failures, instability, and a high degree of inequality, leading many social theorists and political actors to consider alternatives to market pricing as a means of organizing human affairs. Despite these drawbacks, a vigorous transatlantic economy emerged during what Eric Hobsbawm has called "the long nineteenth century" (which lasted from 1800 through

August of 1914), one characterized by the relatively free movement of materials, goods, capital, and people among continents.[11]

The first global market economy blew itself up during World War I, and in the ashes of that cataclysm several nations undertook experiments with command economies.[12] Some political theorists believed that centralized planning and the rational allocation of resources would avoid the inequalities, instabilities, and injustices of the market, and spare future generations the horrors of another global war. Whether justified by an ideology of the right (fascism) or the left (communism) or the center (socialism), experiments in state control of the economy distinctively marked the seventy years between 1919 and 1989.

Whatever their form, however, command economies have to have two fatal flaws. First, with everything owned by the state, workers labor on behalf of the commons rather than themselves, yielding insufficient motivation to run a modern economy effectively. Second, and more serious, to function effectively command economies require a concentration of economic and political power within a single bureaucratic structure. Decisions about the production, distribution, and consumption of goods and services are made by a central planning authority rather than by private consumers and producers interacting in a market.[13] The resources of land, capital, and labor are mobilized by administrative fiat rather than by market signals. For allocation decisions to be effective, planners must have sufficient power and authority to make them stick, and the consequent monopolization of economic and political power within a single bureaucratic structure means that whoever controls the state wields near-absolute power in society.

Once people enjoyed such power, of course, there was nothing to stop them from wielding it in their own interests rather than for the benefit of the masses that they ostensibly represent. Rather than being aberrations, brutal tyrannies proved to be the rule wherever command economies were established, and the resulting dictatorships of Stalin, Hitler, Mao, and Pol Pot proved to be far more destructive and deadly than anything ever produced by the likes of Rockefeller, Ford, or Vanderbilt, yielding tens of millions of deaths over the course of the twentieth century.[14] One by one, the world's command economies either self-destructed or were overthrown by their citizens in favor of a return to market mechanisms, though not always straight into a fully formed market economy.

Not all the social experiments of the twentieth century entailed repression, of course. Some European nations peacefully attempted to create socialist economies that combined private enterprise and state ownership within the framework of a parliamentary democracy.[15] In these countries, however, the demand for state-provided services proved to be inexhaustible, leading to a growth of public bureaucracy at the expense of the private enterprise, the ultimate engine of economic expansion and wealth creation. As the bureaucracies of welfare states expanded, special interests grew up around particular programs and prevailed upon legislators to support them for reasons of narrow self-interest rather than the general good.[16] Ultimately, planning bureaucracies turned out to be too slow, too inflexible, and too ponderous to manage a rapidly changing information economy,[17] and in country after country they (and the taxes required to support them) became so onerous that voters rebelled to elect center-right politicians committed to shrinking the size of the state.

By the end of the twentieth century, therefore, markets had come to prevail throughout the globe, embracing ever-more remote geographic zones and entering increasingly recondite areas of social and economic life.[18] Although markets now rule, their evident triumph does not, however, signal a victory of the natural over the human. Despite paeans to the inevitability of markets delivered by star-struck apostles of globalism such as Thomas Friedman,[19] they are still human creations. In a very real way, citizens throughout the world, by their conscious actions, have *chosen* markets as the least tyrannical and the most effective human-designed system for generating societal wealth while preserving individual freedom and ensuring widespread material well-being.[20]

It is thus incumbent upon liberals to counter the myth of the "free market" promoted by conservatives, not by proposing alternatives to the market, but by embracing it as the societal instrument of choice. Citizens do not stand *apart* from markets, but by their public actions they *constitute* them. The issue is not *whether* to regulate markets. Markets are necessarily regulated by the decisions made (implicitly or explicitly) in creating them. The real issue for liberals is whether the markets created by past decisions are presently yielding outcomes desired by a majority of citizens, and whether there are actions that might be taken by elected representatives to bring the performance of markets into closer conformity with the democratically expressed preferences of the people.

Government and the Market

Ultimately, markets are nothing more than competitions among people that occur within particular arenas according to specific rules using some medium of exchange. By building the arenas, defining the rules of play, and defining a medium of exchange, societies necessarily regulate competition and constrain outcomes. The true liberal project is not to end markets or substitute bureaucracy for pricing mechanisms. Rather, the proper role of government in the postindustrial world is to ensure, on behalf of citizens, that needed markets exist; that appropriate arenas are constructed to enable necessary transactions; that there is a recognized medium for the exchange of goods and services; that all members of society have equal access to markets; that competition within markets is open and fair; that people are well prepared to participate in the market; and that citizens are protected against the deleterious consequences of market failures. Rather than a "free market," what liberals should aspire to is a "democratic market" that reflects the preferences of all citizens.

Creating Markets

If markets are constituted by the societies in which they are embedded, then there is no inherently correct number, distribution, or nature of markets. Markets may take a variety of forms. The nature and number of markets may be expected to change as societies change socially, demographically, and culturally; as new technologies emerge; and as new knowledge is created. As a result, in any society actions must be undertaken regularly and periodically to develop new markets, modify old ones, and eliminate those that have become obsolete. After local markets for goods and services, the first long-distance markets to emerge were those associated with finance and trade, followed by insurance markets. Fully functioning labor markets developed only in the nineteenth century, in concert with the urbanization and industrialization of society. Later still to emerge were markets for futures, options, financial derivatives, and consumer credit.[21]

Over the past two decades, the range and efficiency of markets has expanded dramatically both within and among nations, in response to improvements in social organization, transportation, communication, and information processing.[22] Markets are most thoroughly developed in wealthy industrialized nations, of course. Although developing nations are presently being incorporated into global trade and financial networks, their internal markets are often weak and ineffective. Many countries in the Third World continue to be hampered either by missing or by poorly functioning markets in a variety of crucial areas.[23]

A good example is the market for home mortgages—financial instruments that allow people of modest means to purchase a dwelling that is valued at many times their annual income. Even in the United States, mortgage markets are of very recent origin.[24] Prior to World War II, they were inaccessible to all but a privileged few. Although home-purchase loans existed before Roosevelt's New Deal, lending markets were incomplete and poorly functioning. Banks typically required half the cost of a home as a down payment and demanded very short payback periods. To purchase a home, buyers had to post a large amount of cash up front and make high monthly payments. As a result, home loans were available only to those with considerable wealth and income. In essence, only those who really didn't need a loan to buy a home could afford to get one.

In the course of the New Deal, however, the U.S. government deliberately acted to create a mass home-lending market by setting up mortgage guarantee programs through the Federal Housing Administration and later, the Veteran's Administration. The federal government agreed to underwrite private mortgages for up to 90 percent of assessed home value and extended amortization periods for up to thirty years. Under these circumstances, as long as a buyer put down 10 percent of the cost of the home, banks experienced no risk in making a loan. If the home-buyer defaulted, the bank retained the equity and collected the outstanding balance from the federal government as insurance. As a result, banks were eager to make loans, and the minimal outlay and low monthly payments meant that most Americans could afford to purchase rather than rent. Through its loan guarantee programs, and later through the establishment of institutions such as Fannie Mae and Freddie Mac (which created a secondary mortgage market to expand the pool of mortgage capital) the U.S. government created a mass market for home lending where none had existed before.[25] In doing so, home ownership and the possibility of building wealth through home equity became accessible to a majority of Americans. At present, more than two-thirds (67.4%) of all American households own their homes, compared with just 43.6 percent in 1940.[26]

Most developing nations, in contrast, lack well-functioning mortgage markets and the desire to overcome this particular market failure constitutes a leading motivation for international migration today.[27] Contrary to popular belief, most contemporary immigrants from the developing world do not move to developed nations intending to settle permanently. Rather, they seek to work abroad *temporarily* to amass savings that will enable them to construct or purchase a home in their country of origin. In the absence of well-functioning mortgage markets, households are *compelled* to migrate internationally to self-finance the acquisition of housing and thus overcome a key market failure. Other markets where failures and omissions are rife include those for investment capital, consumer credit, and various forms of insurance, the absence of which also serves to motivate much of the world's international migration.

Creating Infrastructure

For transactions to occur, buyers and sellers must come together within a mutually accepted arena. Sometimes the arena is delimited physically (such as the trading pit in the New York Stock Exchange), and at other times it is geographically diffuse (as with NASDAQ, where securities are traded electronically in cyberspace); but always the competitive arena is defined *socially* by mutually agreed-upon rules, both formal and informal, that govern transactions. As markets have evolved, the rules have increasingly shifted from the informal to the formal realm.[28]

Formal rules are laws and regulations that are written down by authorities to recognize private property, define the rights of buyers and sellers, establish a basis for the execution and enforcement of contracts, and define acceptable behaviors within a competitive arena. Informal rules are unwritten codes of conduct and practice that are implicitly understood by market participants and reinforced through mechanisms of enforceable trust such as ridicule, gossip, shaming, exclusion, and ostracism. Whereas some markets are predominantly formal (e.g., U.S. mortgage markets) others remain highly informal (e.g., the global diamond trade), but most remain mixtures of formal and informal mechanisms (jobs and hiring).[29]

In addition to being supported by a social infrastructure of laws, regulations, expectations, and conventions, many competitive arenas also require a physical infrastructure. The necessary structure may be erected by public or private efforts, but as with social infrastructure, the construction of arenas generally involves a mixture of the two. Whereas private interests may finance the construction of factories to produce consumer goods, for example, the public builds highways and ports, and subsidizes air and rail travel that enables producers to bring the goods to market. A core responsibility of the state is to make sure, by some combination of public and private means, that the physical and social infrastructure necessary for markets is created and maintained.

U.S. economic history is full of examples where public investments were made to create a competitive arena for markets that ultimately led to the formation of significant private wealth. Despite the self-image of entrepreneurial independence so dear to inhabitants of the western United States, for example, the West was actually "won" more by publicly subsidized collective action than by individual enterprise. Without public sponsorship and governmental subsidies for homesteads, railroads, highways, dams, canals, pipelines, ports, and harbors, many of the West's great fortunes would never have been accumulated, and most certainly Los Angeles and many other western cities would not and could not exist.[30]

Establishing a Medium of Exchange

Markets may exist, of course, without a well-defined medium of exchange. Indeed, when economists speak of a "marriage market" they generally do not refer to a system where brides and grooms are traded on the basis of price.[31] In the absence of a common currency, the system that people use to exchange goods, services, or commodities is known as bartering. Suppose, for example, I have three blankets that you, the reader, desire to keep warm with and you have two chickens that I want to eat. Through bartering we arrange a trade. I give you three blankets and you hand over the two chickens. By trading in this fashion we both enhance our well-being and satisfaction. We are both happy with the exchange.

The earliest economic exchanges between human beings were of this form, and within small-scale societies where most interpersonal behavior involves relations of sharing, turn-taking, and authority ranking, bartering offers an effective and relatively efficient mode of exchange.[32] As societies grew in size and scale, however, and as the volume of goods, services, and commodities that needed to be exchanged rose accordingly, bartering proved to have serious drawbacks as a framework for economic exchange.

First, bartering is time-consuming. Each transaction must be negotiated, usually face-to-face, which requires that humans spend time traveling to a site where they can meet and then argue over suitable terms. Moreover, each exchange must be independently negotiated. In effect, each transaction requires setting a new price. In addition, the terms of the exchange are not particularly transparent and are difficult to observe and compare with others. If another person gets two chickens in exchange for three bear hides, who gets the better deal? Me, who received two chickens for three blankets, or my neighbor, who got two chickens for three bear hides? In bartering, there is no common metric with which to express value. Bartering also entails extra costs of shipping and transportation. Not only do I personally have to show up at an agreed-upon location to bargain, I have to bring with me all the blankets, bear hides, and other goods or commodities that I wish to trade.

In essence, the lack of a medium of exchange exacerbates transaction costs, which are trivial in small hunter-gatherer groups but grow very large as the size and scale of society increases.[33] As settlements grew over the course of human history, and sedentary towns expanded into dense cities characterized by a significant accumulations of material wealth, money gradually emerged as a medium of exchange to facilitate market transactions, finally making possible widespread human interactions based on market pricing.

Some 4,200 years ago the first tangible money was invented by Cappadocian Greek kings, who smelted silver ingots and guaranteed their weight and purity to ensure their acceptance as a standardized form of payment. The first coins were minted by a people in Asia Minor known as the Lydians between 700 and 600 B.C., and the idea of coinage spread to Greece in the following century. Eventually coins were adopted throughout the Hellenistic world and later embraced by the Romans. By the time of Caesar Augustus, the imperial treasury was minting a variety of gold and silver coins, and the existence of a common currency within a network of cities linked together via well-developed networks of transportation and communication under a single legal authority prompted a surge of trade and market expansion.[34] The end of the Pax Romana, of course, ended this era of market creation.

For most of the past two thousand years, precious metals have been used to define media of exchange, first in the form of actual coins and later in the form of paper instruments that were backed, publicly or privately, by specified amounts of gold or silver that were stored in some central location and could be presented, at least theoretically, upon demand. With the advent of money, the value of any good, service, or commodity could be expressed in a common metric. Price did not have to be negotiated independently for each exchange and two sets of goods or commodities did not have to be shipped: one party could simply send money in payment for the later shipping and delivery of materials by the other party. As a result, transaction costs were dramatically reduced, greatly enhancing the efficiency of markets.[35]

Although the use of precious metals to create common currencies and consensual standards of exchange offered a great advance over barter economies, a major problem was that the money supply remained tied to the supply of a particular metal rather than to the needs of the market or its participants. Economic expansion could be stunted if supplies of precious metals did not keep pace with the demand for coinage or reserves, and inflation tended to follow the discovery and exploitation of new ore deposits irrespective of the needs of the economy and its ongoing levels of production or consumption.

By the late nineteenth and early twentieth centuries, many economic observers realized that something was amiss with a money supply that was tied to arbitrary and capriciously distributed quantities of scarce metals. Rather than focusing on the essence of the problem, however, the public debate was sidetracked to focus on *which* precious metal, gold or silver, was best to adopt as a reserve standard. Only with the collapse of the global economy in the 1930s did governments begin to shift away from precious metals as a means of valuing currencies. Britain and Japan abandoned the gold standard in 1931, followed by France in 1936.[36]

During World War II, however, the United States emerged as the world's largest creditor nation and in 1944 took the lead in establishing a new system of convertible currencies and fixed exchange rates based on gold-backed dollar reserves. This system was known as the Breton Woods regime in honor of the New Hampshire town where it was negotiated. Although the 1956 publication of Milton Friedman's classic treatise, *A Restatement of the Quantity Theory of Money*, caused economists to question the wisdom of a precious metal standard, the Breton Woods agreement continued to function into the 1960s.[37]

In 1968, however, the United States ran its first trade deficit since 1893, putting new pressure on the Breton Woods regime and causing a large drop in U.S. gold reserves. Following a rapid increase in foreign claims on the dollar, the U.S. government was forced to suspend convertibility to gold in 1971; and in 1973 it finally abandoned the gold standard altogether. After this date, most national governments adopted monetarist policies that peg the supply of money to the level of economic output and, in so doing, prevent the inflation or deflation of currencies, thus solving a problem that had long bedeviled market economies.[38]

A crucial task of government is thus to establish a secure medium of exchange, but the history of money suggests that the best way to accomplish this task was by no means obvious before the fact. The invention of something called "money" was not inherent in the logic of the market itself. Rather, the idea of money was invented independently and then imposed through a series of trials and errors that revealed only gradually the best course of action. If human beings had done nothing and simply "let the market decide," the instrument of money would not have come into existence in the form that we know it, and the institutions that make it a reality would not have been created.

Ensuring Equal Access

Democratic governments are not only responsible for bringing necessary markets into existence, creating the infrastructure required for their operation, and maintaining a stable and reliable currency; a well-functioning liberal government must also ensure that citizens who wish to participate in markets have the opportunity to do so. If a society uses markets to allocate production, distribute goods and services, generate wealth, and produce income, then it is incumbent upon government to ensure that all citizens have the right to compete freely in all markets. In a market society, lack of access to markets translates directly into a lack of equal access to material well-being and ultimately into socioeconomic inequality.

The minimum of access that a government must provide its citizens is the right to participate in markets regardless of ascribed characteristics such as race, ethnicity, religion, gender, sexuality, and disability. U.S. history is replete with examples where market access was denied to people on the basis of inborn characteristics. Examples range from housing covenants that prohibited the rental or sale of property to members of specific racial or ethnic groups (in force until 1948)[39] to laws specifying separate (and inferior) services for minorities in stores, hotels, and restaurants (allowed under federal law until 1964).[40] They also include the refusal to hire or pay the same wages to qualified applicants of different races, ethnicities, or religions (legal until 1964),[41] and prohibitions on lending to people with certain ascribed characteristics (permissible until 1974).[42]

In addition to securing a place for racial and ethnic minorities in the political arena, therefore, the history of the civil rights movement in the United States has also been one of assuring equal access to markets for goods and services.[43] Indeed, the Civil Rights Act of 1964, which sought to guarantee minority access to markets for goods, services, and employment *preceded* the Voting Rights Act (passed in 1965), which sought to guarantee the political rights of minorities. A society in which all social groups do not have access to all markets cannot be considered just.

Guaranteeing Fair Competition

Of course, simple access to markets, in the sense of being admitted as a participant, does not guarantee equality of opportunity; for in addition to being allowed merely to compete, the contest must be "fair" in both perception and in reality. If markets are set up and the rules written in such a way that certain social groups consistently and disproportionately "win" the competition, then over time the legitimacy of the market itself will be called into question, leading to revolts by excluded groups. If they succeed in achieving real power, those formerly excluded from markets may seek to impose an authoritarian, nonmarket system, so much will be their hatred for the system that had exploited them (witness the construction of the Soviet Union under Lenin and Stalin). If political power remains out of reach, the excluded may simply withdraw wholly or partly from market competition to establish alternative social fields—subcultures—within which they can earn respect and esteem despite the unfairness of a rigged market (witness the proliferation of oppositional subcultures in poor urban neighborhoods throughout the world). Neither long-term outcome bodes well for human welfare.

Unlike access, however, whereby a person is either admitted or not, "fairness" has no ready definition and has been the subject of lengthy debates in the social and political literature.[44] When it comes to markets, especially, the concept of fairness can be quite subjective. What seems fair to one market participant may seem to be quite unfair to another, depending on his or her relative position and power in the marketplace. To circumvent this conceptual problem, the philosopher John Rawls defined as "just" any set of institutional arrangements that would be approved by people without knowing their position in the resulting social order.[45]

In practical terms, a doctrine of fairness requires that people who enter a market with equal inputs should achieve, on average and in the long run, equal outcomes. Whites and blacks with equal qualifications should not be paid different wages for the same work; Latinos and Anglos with the same buying power should not be charged different prices for the same goods; the quality of services provided to customers should not vary by gender; the interest rate charged on home loans should not be greater for Asians than whites; and so on. According to public opinion polls, Americans evince remarkable consensus on the principle of equal treatment for equal qualifications,[46] though as recently as the 1960s this was not so.[47]

More controversial have been efforts to take the doctrine of "fairness" a step further and grant a special status in markets to those who, through no fault of their own, cannot muster equal inputs. As

President Lyndon Johnson argued in his famous speech at Howard University in 1965, "You do not take a person who, for years, has been hobbled by chains and liberate him, bring him up to the starting line of a race and then say, 'you are free to compete with all the others,' and still justly believe that you have been completely fair."[48] The view that fairness demands "affirmative" steps to redress past inequities has been especially controversial.[49]

Since the notion of market fairness will always be subject to debate, perhaps the most important function of a democratic government is to provide accurate and unbiased information about how markets are performing. Reliable public data on prices, wages, salaries, wealth, income, education, and health are essential inputs for policy debate in a liberal democratic society. When such data are broken down by gender, age, race, and ethnicity, they provide a good indication of who the winners and losers are in any market. If one group is consistently observed to win while others regularly lose, it provides prima facie evidence that something is amiss in the way that markets are performing, and that tough questions about fairness need to be asked and publicly debated.

Investment in Human Capacities

A crucial responsibility of government in a liberal market society is to ensure that comparable investments are made in the capacities of all citizens, so that all social groups enter competitive markets with a similar, or at least basic, array of personal resources. All people, regardless of their characteristics or circumstances, should be guaranteed some socially defined minimum level of human investment, one sufficient to enable reasonable participation in society's markets and political processes. If markets are used to distribute resources in society, then groups lacking the capabilities required for effective participation in those markets—health, skills, education—cannot have equal access to the goods, services, income, and wealth they distribute.[50]

In all societies, human capabilities are cultivated through a mixture of public and private actions. The private institution most fundamentally and universally involved in producing capable human beings is the family.[51] Within families children are born, fed, housed, clothed, and taught. Within the confines of the family people learn to walk, speak, behave, and think. As a result of conscious instruction and unconscious emulation, children learn to value and follow certain patterns of thought and action and to devalue and shun others. The configuration of family members responsible for child rearing varies across time and space, yielding a variety of cultural forms; but throughout all of human history, the family has been the social institution primarily responsible for inculcating and nurturing human capabilities.[52]

As the size and complexity of human populations have increased over the past two centuries, however, other social institutions have assumed a relatively greater role in the creation of human capabilities, and in the last quarter of the twentieth century the importance of nonfamily institutions in the inculcation of ability has increased dramatically. This growth in the relative importance of nonfamily institutions reflects both changes in the family and in society itself.

Within the family, the most important change has been the rise in female labor-force participation and the corresponding increase in the social and economic autonomy of women.[53] As a result, compared to the past, women in today's wealthy postindustrial societies are much less likely to marry; are older when they do marry; are less likely to choose childbirth; are likely to have many fewer children when they do decide to reproduce; and are more likely to experience marital disruption whether or not children are present. The net effect of these changes is to reduce quite substantially the number of person-hours available within the family for the labor-intensive tasks of child raising. As a result, far more of the work of raising young children is now being done by nonfamily members and institutions, such as day-care centers, nursery schools, hired nannies, live-in au pairs, and salaried babysitters.[54]

Within society, changes in the ability of families to engage in capacity-building have been accompanied by an equally important expansion in the number and complexity of the capacities necessary for effective participation within markets. Over the past two hundred years, the economic basis of society has shifted from the growth and cultivation of food, to the industrial manufacturing of goods, to the provision and extension of services, and finally to the creation of knowledge and the manipulation of information. In the course of this evolution, the set of skills and capacities required for effective citizenship and market participation has grown exponentially and continues to expand at a remarkable rate.[55]

The resulting gap between the declining ability of families to engage in capacity-building and the rising demand for human capabilities has been filled by social institutions, notably those delivering education. In peasant societies dedicated to labor-intensive agriculture, little education is required, and little was historically provided by the state. Schooling was mostly arranged privately and confined to a ruling urban elite. Industrialization created new needs for literate workers and led governments to require and provide primary and secondary schooling to citizens on a mass basis. The shift toward services in the twentieth century was accompanied by rising public investments in higher education, and the recent shift to a knowledge-based, information economy has even further accelerated the rate of investment in post-graduate education, research, and lifetime training.

In the advanced-market societies of the postindustrial world, a critical responsibility of government is to ensure that citizens receive a level of education and training sufficient not only to permit effective participation in a growing array of complex markets, but also to assure sustained personal income growth and the continued creation of societal wealth in a competitive knowledge-based global market economy. Reflecting this societal transformation, the share of Americans aged twenty-five or more with some college education went from 25 percent in 1940 to around 50 percent by the year 2000.[56]

In addition to inculcating knowledge, the other major investment of governments in human capacity comes in the form of health care.[57] The desire for a long and healthy life is universal among human beings, and societal actions undertaken to promote this goal may be justified on purely moral grounds. But government actions taken to ensure public health and elevate life expectancies also carry a compelling economic rationale. The provision of education and training appropriate to the needs of a knowledge-based economy is necessarily labor-intensive and in a high-wage economy quite expensive. The cost of raising and educating a child from birth through high school is now estimated to be $231,000 for the typical middle-class family, plus an additional $34,000 for a four-year college education at a public college or university, or $81,000 at a private institution.[58]

The total investment in producing a capable middle-class work force for the postindustrial knowledge-based economy is thus on the order of $265,000–$312,000. Death or any impairment sufficient to prevent labor-force participation before a person reaches adulthood represents a deadweight loss of that investment, and morbidity and premature death after adulthood prevents a full return on earlier investments in human capacity. As educational levels have risen, therefore, postindustrial societies have invested higher shares of their wealth and income in prolonging the life and improving the health of their citizens.

Protection from Market Failures

Markets can never achieve all the goals that citizens would like to see accomplished, nor are they foolproof mechanisms for the seamless production, distribution, and consumption of resources. The history of capitalism is replete with examples of failed and missing markets.[59] As we have seen, mortgage markets were effectively absent in the United States before the 1940s and do not exist in most developing nations today. Likewise, from 1929 to 1939 markets failed on a variety of fronts around the world, yielding insufficient employment for workers, goods for consumers, profit for producers, and income for farmers.[60] The widespread market failures of the 1930s were instrumental in creating a new consensus in the United States that it was the responsibility of government to protect citizens from capitalism's downside.[61]

Although improvements in management and technology have reduced the depth and frequency of market failures, the hazard can never be eliminated entirely from a capitalist economy. Citizens of developed countries by substantial majorities agree that law-abiding citizens should somehow be protected from vicissitudes of the market that lie outside their control.[62] Bowing to this sentiment, democratic governments have erected a variety of social "safety nets" to prevent citizens from falling too far down the economic ladder, creating aid programs such as unemployment insurance, welfare payments, medical insurance, old age benefits, and food subsidies.[63]

The principal problem with any safety net is the "moral hazard" it creates, for in protecting people from market failures it also shields them from the consequences of their own bad choices and reckless behavior.[64] As a result, safety nets end up encouraging irresponsible decision-making and antisocial actions. For this reason, democratic societies have long debated where, exactly, to place the social safety net: high enough to keep people from misery, yet low enough to discourage reckless judgment and indolence. In the United States, this debate has been expressed over time in cycles of social experimentation, as the welfare system has shifted from one of selective entitlement (widows and veterans) to universal entitlement (all those below a certain income threshold), and most recently to contingent entitlement (those below an income threshold who demonstrate a willingness to work).[65]

Public attention to the moral hazard has focused mostly on the poor; but the rich also face their own moral hazard arising from government protection. Perhaps the best example is the federal bailout of the savings and loan industry during the late 1980s. In this case, the existence of federal deposit insurance programs encouraged bankers to make speculative, high-risk loans. Banks profited immensely from origination fees and interest payments, but when the loans went bad they did not suffer the full consequences of their actions, as their institutions were bailed out by the federal government.[66] Despite the independent, swashbuckling self-image of American entrepreneurs, they are as fond as any

worker of relying on government to privatize the gains while socializing the risks of market participation.

Liberals, Conservatives, and the Market

In an ideal liberal world, markets would be constituted by citizens
and managed effectively through the actions of democratically
elected officials, who would work on behalf of the public to identify
and create the markets that are needed; erect the infrastructure necessary for their operation; provide a reliable and balanced supply of
money; protect citizens from potential market failures; and ensure
fair competition, open access, and basic human capacities. These responsibilities require the state to produce reliable and timely public
data about the performance of markets in different areas of social
and economic life. Engaged citizens then use this information to
monitor outcomes and, through their elected officials, make sure
that market performance matches democratic preferences.

The foregoing is the ideal, of course, and in the real world the
supervision of markets for the public good is threatened by the in-
trusive realities of class: the unequal distribution of resources generated by the market itself and the use of those resources to create
infrastructures and write rules of competition that benefit the few
rather than the many. Although the self-interested abuse of markets by the wealthy is not inevitable, it nonetheless constitutes a
serious threat that requires constant vigilance by those of liberal
conscience.

The primary tactic used by conservatives to rig markets in their
favor is a principled defense of "the free market." As markets are
not states of nature but human creations, in reality there is no
principle to defend. Free-market rhetoric usually serves as a smoke-
screen to allow producers of goods and services to arrange the
rules and arenas of competition so that they win as often as possible and are able extract the maximum in resources from other
market participants. In concrete terms, producers—owners, corporations, the wealthy—hire lobbyists and make political contributions to shape the legislation and regulations as they are written

to create markets and determine their operation. They make generous contributions to political candidates who are sympathetic to their interests and who seek to use their influence to place sympathizers on the commissions, boards, and agencies that are charged with managing, monitoring, and regulating markets. To the greatest extent possible, they seek to have the public pay for the construction of competitive arenas and underwrite risks to private investment, while minimizing their own tax payments for these government services.

Most galling of all, from a liberal point of view, is that while conservatives work so assiduously behind the scenes to offload investments, socialize risks, and maximize gains at public expense, they very loudly and publicly deride those who represent the interests of other market participants as Luddites seeking to "interfere" in the operation of the "free market" through "interventions" that inhibit "private enterprise" and prevent economic growth. It is the responsibility of liberals to call the conservative bluff and to make such hypocrisy apparent to the public. By cowering in the shadows for the past twenty-five years and fearing to take a principled stand, liberals have been handmaidens to the systematic reconstruction of the American political economy for the benefit of the wealthy and the affluent.

Not only is it unjust and hypocritical to let producers determine the rules of competition and the organization of markets, it is also bad economics. History has repeatedly shown that when those who profit from a market are left free to determine its operation, they undertake actions and implement policies that over time undermine competition and liquidity, and ultimately bring about the collapse of the market itself, typically leaving the public to pick up the pieces. Such is the sad tale of the savings and loan collapse of the 1980s and the Enron fraud of the 1990s.[67]

Not only do conservatives take every opportunity to rig markets in favor of the wealthy and powerful, they also seek to prevent the public from learning about their actions by, whenever possible, conducting regulatory business in closed-door sessions from which the public and the press are excluded, and by working covertly with legislators to slip beneficial loopholes, favorable regulations, lucrative tax incentives, and targeted subsidies into federal legislation while no one is looking.[68]

The most recent egregious example of the use of secrecy to obfuscate attempts at market manipulation is the Bush administration's Energy Task Force, convened in 2001 to develop a national energy policy. The task force was chaired by Vice President Dick Cheney, former CEO of Halliburton Corporation, which according to the firm's website "is one of the world's largest providers of products and services to the oil and gas industries. The Company adds value through the entire lifecycle of oil and gas reservoirs and provides and integrates products and services, starting with exploration and development, moving through production, operations, maintenance, conversion and refining, to infrastructure and abandonment."[69] Despite, or perhaps because of the apparent conflict of interest built into the task force by Cheney's former position in the energy industry, the Bush administration has sought to keep all proceedings and deliberations of the task force secret and inaccessible to the public.

A lawsuit was filed by the National Resources Defense Council, and in 2002 a federal judge order the Department of Energy to release 3,500 pages of the task force's previously secret proceedings. Although Bush administration officials heavily censored the documents before their release, they reveal that the Cheney task force "sought extensive advice from utility companies and the oil, gas, coal and nuclear energy industries, and incorporated their recommendations, often word for word, into the energy plan."[70] Under a veil of secrecy, the Bush administration gave control of energy markets over to companies with a self-interested stake in their operation, which subsequently allowed them to manufacture electricity shortages that bilked consumers and taxpayers in California of millions of dollars.[71] It also permitted the Enron corporation to continue its questionable accounting and business practices outside the scrutiny of hobbled regulators in Washington, leading to the systematic defrauding of Enron's owners (its stockholders) of billions of dollars.[72]

Transparency and public access to information about the construction, operation, and regulation of markets is thus critical to the success of a market economy, not only to protect the interests of the public but also to protect greedy corporate interests from themselves. Time and time again, when company officials and private entrepreneurs have been given disproportionate control and influence over a market, they ended up destroying it and bringing down the very companies they were appointed by shareholders to protect and serve.

Conservatives have sought not only to shield their attempts to rig markets but also to prevent public documentation of the consequences of their actions through the systematic suppression of data. It is no coincidence that the coming to power of both Ronald Reagan and George W. Bush was accompanied by deliberate attacks on the federal statistical system, seeking to prevent the collection, publication, and dissemination of social, economic, and demographic data about the state of the American people. Attempts to sabotage the U.S. statistical systems were accompanied by attempts to limit and politically control government funding of social scientific research.

Information about how markets are performing is essential in a liberal democracy—not simply data about prices, interest rates, assets, income, and trade, but also indicators of the distribution of social and economic well-being—health, education, and housing— along with demographic characteristics such as race, ethnicity, marital status, and, of course, sex and age. Since markets are constituted by voters in a democratic society for the general good, the public has a right to know whether different markets are indeed working to promote the overall welfare; and the government has an obligation to provide such statistics as are necessary for the public to determine the degree to which current market-regulating policies are working to improve the welfare of the many or preserve the wealth of the few.

The liberal stance with respect to markets is thus clear. Markets are neither to be feared nor worshiped. They are neither evil nor good. They are simply a tool that citizens have chosen democratically as the best means for producing and distributing the goods and services that they desire while respecting their freedoms. Markets do not exist to provide profits to producers. Profits are merely the reward that a liberal society offers to producers to make markets work. Markets are not states of nature but human creations, and it is the duty of citizens in a liberal democracy to monitor their operation and to insist, through elected representatives, that markets operate in accordance with their collective wishes and that over time they function to ensure the general welfare of the population.

There is no such thing as a "free market" and one cannot simply "let the market decide," for that begs the question of who creates the market and for what purpose. Through their failure to adopt a clear and coherent position on the role of markets in a liberal democracy, liberals let conservatives in the late twentieth century hide behind the hollow rhetoric of free market capitalism as they systematically restructured markets to benefit the few rather than the many. The time has come for liberals to tell the public that markets are not "free," but human-created institutions that citizens have a right to supervise and manage for their own benefit. Liberals need to abandon their lingering hostility toward market mechanisms, embrace them, and substitute a new rhetoric of "democratic markets" for the false metaphor of the "free market."

CHAPTER 4

Domestic Policies

In the last chapter, I argued that in a democratic nation citizens have a duty to monitor the operation of markets. Markets must be evaluated regularly to determine whether they are working fairly to distribute goods and services to all citizens, and whether their social and economic outcomes are consistent with democratic preferences. Such vigilance is necessary because conditions invariably change—new technologies emerge, populations grow, tastes and values evolve. Over time old markets wither and disappear while new ones arise and grow. Because the nature and character of markets undergo constant change, it is necessary for elected officials and the public to monitor their operation on an ongoing basis to make sure that they continue to function in the public interest.

Vigilance is also needed because owners and producers—who, unlike consumers, are small in number and thus amenable to collective organization—have strong incentives to enact market policies that benefit themselves rather than serving the interests of the whole. Although producers may sincerely believe that the measures they propose are in the general interest, and they may argue fervently for their implementation as a matter of the highest national priority, citizens must be skeptical of their claims and demand accountability. The risk of self-deception is so great whenever policy proposals carry tangible benefits for those who propose them. One should always be wary of foxes who volunteer to guard the chicken coop.

Since the mid-1970s, citizens in the United States have been hoodwinked into ceding their responsibility for managing the

U.S. political economy to an elite of investors, corporate managers, and upper-class professionals. During the past quarter of the twentieth century, actions taken by government to define the rules of competition, set monetary policies, create competitive arenas, determine market access and fairness, invest in human capabilities, and protect citizens have worked to the benefit of the few rather than the many.

The proof is in the pudding. For heuristic purposes, American society may be divided into three classes of people whose fortunes diverged sharply after the mid-1970s. Those fortunate few in the top fifth of the household income distribution—whose class position is based on access to various forms of capital—saw their wealth and earnings increase substantially in the thirty years between 1973 and 2003; and the higher up in the top fifth one looks, the greater the improvement.[1] Those located at the 15th percentile of the income distribution did better than those at the 20th; while those at the 10th did better than those at the 15th; and those at the 5th did better than those at the 10th. The top 1 percent, of course, did the best of all. On virtually every indicator of social and economic well-being, those at the very top of the income distribution are much better off now than before 1975. Their earnings are higher, their taxes lower, their health better, their wealth greater, and they have access to more resources and personal services than ever before, though these lavish services are increasingly offered under private rather than public auspices.

In contrast, since the mid-1970s people in the middle 60 percent of the household income distribution worked harder just to stay in place. Individual wages in this segment of the income distribution fell in real terms, especially for men, and to prop up sagging family incomes women entered the work force in record numbers. Were it not for the massive entry of women into the paid labor force after 1975, incomes would have *fallen* for many middle-class households. As it was, household incomes in the middle three-fifths of the distribution simply stagnated.[2] By 2003, the typical American family was collectively working more hours to earn about the same amount of money it had received in 1973.

At the same time, public services, on which the middle class critically depends, underwent a slow but steady deterioration. Public education suffered particularly, as households in the top fifth of the income distribution withdrew to private schools, taking their tax dollars and political clout with them. A growing number of middle-class families found themselves cut off from good schooling and decent health care; and those who retained access to these critical resources were paying a larger share of their income for worsening and more limited services.[3]

As grim as trends for the middle of the income distribution were, they were even worse for the poorest 20 percent of American households, who saw their well-being fall on virtually every indicator.[4] During the last quarter of the twentieth century, incomes of the poor dropped in real terms, entry-level wages sagged, welfare payments eroded, the minimum wage stagnated, and, except for a brief surge in the late 1990s, joblessness persisted at high levels. Conditions in the schools and neighborhoods inhabited by the poor deteriorated markedly, their physical safety and security decreased, and access to all but the most rudimentary services evaporated.[5]

At a time when wages and incomes were stagnating for all but the most affluent families, conservatives were scaling back the federal supports and social protections enacted under the New Deal and Great Society. Federal payments for unemployment, welfare, and supplemental security income all fell sharply after the late 1970s.[6] Low-income housing assistance offers a convenient illustration. Targeted federal housing assistance fell from a peak of $76 billion during the Carter administration to $14 billion during the last year of the Reagan administration, and, despite modest increases during the Clinton years, it stood at just $18 billion in the year 2000, 76 percent below its liberal peak.[7] As a result, during the 1970s and 1980s, the poor increasingly came to inhabit isolated zones of concentrated poverty, and the concentration of socioeconomic disadvantage within neighborhoods was particularly acute for African Americans and Latinos.[8]

In sum, data unambiguously indicate that the political economy constructed by conservatives during the late twentieth century worked to benefit a small minority of Americans who comprise no more than a fifth of the U.S. population. The remaining 80 percent of citizens were either working harder for less money and fewer benefits or were actually getting poorer in both relative and absolute terms. That liberals have not been able to make political hay out of this regressive economic structure and use it to achieve consistent electoral victories is a remarkable indictment of our fecklessness. To a large extent, it reflects the lack of a coherent political program that makes sense to ordinary voters.

The Capabilities Approach

Achieving growth within any economic system necessarily involves marshaling the classic factors of production—land, labor, and capital—and deploying them in a coordinated way to produce the goods and services demanded by human beings. Naturally, as one moves from hunting and gathering, to farming, to industrialism, to postindustrialism, the relative importance of the various factors shifts. Land is more important in an agrarian economy and labor relatively more important in an industrial system. Financial capital is always important, but its centrality to growth and development has generally increased across successive economic transitions.

Within any economic system, however, human beings inevitably constitute "the ultimate resource,"[9] for at any point in time it is *they* who must figure out how to use the land, labor, and capital at their disposal for maximum benefit. It is always through the talents, energies, and capabilities of individual human beings that material improvement is achieved. Moreover, as with financial capital, the capital embedded within human beings—*human capital* such as skills, knowledge, and experience—has become increasingly important over time. Indeed, many economists believe that human capital has become *the critical factor* of production in a postindustrial economy, where wealth is created by generating knowledge and manipulating information rather than manufacturing goods; human capital now represents an *essential* input for sustained economic expansion.[10]

This reality has led development economists such as the Nobel Laureate Amartya Sen to emphasize the importance of cultivating human capacities in promoting economic growth, an approach that Martha Nussbaum has extended and labeled "the capabilities approach."[11] She lists ten fundamental human capabilities on which human social welfare and economic growth ultimately rest: the capacity to live out a normal human life span; the capacity to remain in good health during this life span; the capacity to control one's own body; the capacity to use one's senses to imagine, think, and reason; the capacity to form emotional attachments with other things and people; the capacity to form an individual conception of what is good and moral; the capacity to engage in social interactions with other human beings; the capacity to live sustainably within the natural world; the capacity to laugh, play, and enjoy recreation; and the capacity to control one's social environment, politically through particpatory government and materially by enjoying rights to property and full access to markets.

Although Sen and Nussbaum focus primarily on the cultivation of these capabilities in developing nations, they are equally, if not more, important for achieving economic growth in advanced, postindustrial societies. Conservatives typically portray government spending on human capabilities as some kind of "waste," a kind of frivolous consumption, and thus a misappropriation of taxpayers' hard-earned money. The liberal response should be that spending to promote human capabilities is *not* wasteful or frivolous, but *essential* and a fundamental *investment* required for economic growth. To the extent that a government invests in human capabilities, it promotes *human capital formation*, and the creation of human capital has increasingly become *the critical process* ensuring growth in a knowledge-based economy.

To the degree that government is successful in promoting the formation of human capital, money spent will not be lost, but securely invested; it will be repaid with interest in the form of future economic expansion and material development. As economic history and contemporary circumstances clearly reveal, absent capable human beings, even the most abundant endowments of land, labor, and capital by themselves cannot produce wealth or achieved sustained economic growth.[12] If it were that simple, the economy of Argentina would today be on a par with those of the United States or the European Union.

As noted in the last chapter, human capacities are generally developed through a mix of public and private auspices, most notably the state and the family. In a free and democratic society, the cultivation of certain of Nussbaum's capabilities is probably best left to families and other private institutions. A hard lesson learned at great cost through centuries of religious warfare and communal violence in the West is that it is better for all concerned if the state does not attempt to instruct its citizens in what is moral and good or to create capacities to form stable emotional attachments with others. The teaching of right and wrong and of how to get along with others is better left to families and churches rather than government.

However, other human capabilities—such as the capacity to control one's one body, to participate in government, to enjoy property rights, and to participate freely in markets—must be *guaranteed* by the state; and other capabilities—such as the capacity to enjoy a normal human life span; to experience good health; to imagine, think, and reason; to engage in social interactions; to live harmoniously through the natural world; to be able to laugh, play, and enjoy recreation—are best achieved through a *combination* of public and private auspices. As a matter of liberal policy, I consider here only those capabilities in which government clearly has a role in guaranteeing, creating, or otherwise promoting them.

Government-Guaranteed Capabilities

In the United States, the capacity to control one's one body, to participate in government, to enjoy property rights, and to exchange freely have been elaborated on and extended by the Constitution, the Bill of Rights, congressional legislation, and successive generations of state and federal jurisprudence. As noted in the first chapter, the extension of basic human rights to all Americans regardless of their characteristics represents one of liberalism's great historical triumphs. With the abolition of slavery, the increased protection granted to women from rape and physical abuse, and the establishment of female rights to contraception and abortion, more and more Americans have achieved full autonomy over their bodies. Successive constitutional amendments and legislative acts have formally enfranchised all citizens aged eighteen and older, and the civil rights legislation of the 1960s and 1970s has guaranteed everyone the right to exchange goods and services freely within U.S. markets.

Although the de jure rights of U.S. citizens may appear well-established at this point, an important part of a liberal agenda must be to guard against covert rollbacks attempted by those who prefer the subordination of women, blacks, and other minorities. Despite a constant need to look out for and resist backsliding on civil rights and liberties, however, a more important goal for liberals is to move beyond the mere enumeration of de jure rights to secure their de facto achievement in the real world. This goal represents the unfinished business of the civil rights era and an ongoing challenge to people of liberal sentiment.

Despite the legal protections of the thirteenth, fourteenth, and fifteenth amendments, for example, the year 2000 elections were marred by shameful attempts by Republicans to suppress the black vote in Florida and other states, in direct violation of the 1965 Voting Rights Act. The intentional disenfranchisement of black voters was achieved by a variety of means: by systematically allocating older, error-prone voting machines to black precincts; by illegally purging black voters from registration rolls through a variety of ruses; by systematically blocking the access of African Americans to polling places through police activity; and by blanketing black precincts with direct mail and fliers announcing that it was illegal for anyone arrested for a "crime" (as opposed to convicted of a felony) to vote and that "illegal" voting would be prosecuted to the fullest extent of the law (thus frightening many would-be voters).[13] Given the tiny margin of Bush's victory in Florida, it is absolutely clear that systematic violations of electoral law and especially the 1965 Voting Rights Act cost Al Gore the presidency. More shameful than conservative actions taken to steal the election, however, was how few liberal Democrats rose in protest for fear of making the electoral fraud a "racial issue," which of course it was.

An even more important arena for civil rights enforcement lies in securing the de facto access of all Americans to all markets. Despite substantial progress in securing both de jure and de facto political rights for women and minorities, less progress has been made in securing their practical access to American markets and their fair treatment within them. Strong social scientific evidence exists showing that relatively high rates of discrimination persist in markets for housing,[14] lending,[15] and employment[16]—by far the most important markets for achieving socioeconomic mobility in the United States. As a result of ongoing discrimination in these and other important markets, African Americans continue to lag well behind other Americans in terms of earnings and employment, and even further behind with respect to wealth, after controlling for human capital and demographic characteristics.[17]

As argued in the opening chapter, liberalism foundered on shoals of race after the civil rights era. But conditions now exist for liberals to develop a new civil rights agenda that has the political support of white America. Rather than using courts and the federal bureaucracy to force unpopular and coercive measures—school busing, public housing, affirmative action—down the throats of the middle and working classes, a new liberal agenda should focus on guaranteeing universal access to all markets regardless of a person's characteristics.

Exclusion and unfair treatment within housing, lending, and job markets has always lain at the root of minority disadvantage in the post–civil rights era, but liberal Democrats were afraid to confront this reality through congressional action for fear of losing the South. In an effort to make civil rights legislation more palatable to Southern senators and representatives, most enforcement mechanisms were stripped away and federal agencies were not authorized to police markets to identify bias or eliminate discrimination. Instead, the enforcement of anti-discrimination law was fobbed off on individual victims, who could sue and obtain relief in federal courts on a one-by-one basis.

The reluctance of Democrats to antagonize the South has out-lived its time. The South is now solidly Republican, and survey data indicate a quiet revolution in white racial attitudes throughout the country, even in states of the former confederacy. Representative polling data show that whites, by large majorities, support the principle that everyone should have equal access to jobs, mort-gages, and housing regardless of race, ethnicity, or gender, even though some respondents may indeed express opposition to spe-cific policies such as school busing and affirmative action.[18] Lib-eral politicians need to build a case for civil rights enforcement on the basis of widely held, principled beliefs and make market access the keystone of a new campaign for equality. Even Republicans will have a hard time arguing publicly that blacks and women shouldn't be guaranteed equal access to markets.

Fortunately, social science has developed a low-cost tool to de-tect and measure market discrimination, and the Supreme Court has upheld the validity of the evidence it produces to be used in courts of law.[19] The tool is known as the audit study. In such a study, investigators randomly or purposively select advertised jobs, housing units, or lending institutions for investigation. Then they have a mixed team of testers—white and black, male and female, Anglo and Latino, or disabled and unencumbered—approach the person or institution marketing the job, housing unit, or loan to inquire about availability, price, and terms.[20] The information, treatment, and product provided to testers by marketing agents is recorded and entered into a database.

Once a series of audits has been completed across multiple tri-als, the data are examined statistically to determine whether mem-bers of different groups achieve the same market access and terms of exchange. If female, African American, Latino, or disabled testers achieve systematically less access or less favorable treatment in the course of a transaction, it provides strong evidence that discrimi-nation is occurring in the market under scrutiny. To date, audit studies have been implemented sporadically for research purposes by the federal government, but not much for purposes of civil rights enforcement. Most auditing for civil rights enforcement has been carried out by local nonprofit organizations that are small, poorly funded, and limited in scope.[21] Nonetheless, once in federal court, their record of achieving convictions, relief, and penalties is quite good.[22]

What is needed is a wider application of audit studies by the federal government, and this should be the focus of a new liberal agenda for civil rights in the United States. Statistical branches of the U.S. Department of Justice and the U.S. Department of Housing and Urban Development should be authorized to conduct statistically reliable audit studies in cities around the country on a regular basis, thus enabling the public and enforcement agencies to identify those markets in which discrimination is greatest. Enforcement agents could then implement a second round of audits targeted specifically to these areas to identify, charge, and prosecute those caught discriminating under relevant civil rights statutes. The prosecutions would then be publicized to build public awareness that discrimination is illegal and that civil rights laws are being enforced, and the resulting publicity would encourage groups that have historically been excluded from key markets to renew their efforts at participating, thus increasing the demand for homes in integrated neighborhoods and raising expectations for better employment, higher wages, and freer access to loans.

This strategy, however, requires an important shift away from strategies favored heretofore by liberals and civil rights leaders— away from attempts to extract guilt payments from white Americans in the form of set-asides, special treatment, and compensation—and toward the vigorous assertion of market rights for all Americans. Too often liberals have indulged in the fantasy, propounded by some black nationalists, of a segregated black America that is somehow, against all odds and evidence, the equal of white America. It didn't work for the tribal homelands and townships in the Union of South Africa, and it won't work for segregated counties and neighborhoods in the United States.

This strategy does not require abandoning a commitment to affirmative action in the short term; but the recent Supreme Court decision in the University of Michigan case clearly indicates that preferential treatment of minorities as a means of overcoming past discrimination, while still acceptable, will not be allowed to remain in place forever. Hence, liberals need to move *now* to embrace a strategy for the long term, one that is politically salable and consistent with American values and upheld by public opinion.

Public-Private Partnerships

The creation of many human capabilities has historically involved a mixture of public and private institutions. The capacity to live a full human life span in good health obviously requires private efforts from families and individuals, who must take care of themselves physically and make ongoing investments in preventive and, when necessary, curative health care. After all, no institution will ever be more concerned with an individual's welfare than the person him- or herself and those to whom he or she is connected socially. Research conclusively shows that people who are connected socially to spouses, family, and friends live longer and healthier lives than those who are not,[23] and that paying close individual attention to diet, exercise, and lifestyle can significantly improve health and longevity.[24]

At the same time, however, the prolongation of life and health always requires the expenditure of public resources. Tax revenues pay for the construction of water and sewage plants to reduce the spread of water-borne infectious diseases such as cholera, dysentery, and typhus; and public health departments and the U.S. Centers for Disease Control use the methods of epidemiology—inoculation, education, and quarantine—to check the spread of airborne, insect-borne, and blood-borne diseases such as smallpox, malaria, and AIDS. Likewise, the U.S. Food and Drug Administration employs inspectors and laboratory tests, and oversees rigorous evaluation procedures and approval mechanisms to safeguard the supply of food and drugs. Since the nineteenth century, publicly subsidized but relatively inexpensive efforts to prevent and check the spread of infectious diseases and improve nutrition have been responsible for most of the remarkable increase in human life expectancy.[25]

Although hospitals and clinics, along with the specialists and equipment located within them, are partially funded through

private auspices, even in the United States they are heavily subsidized by the state. Although private medical schools, hospitals,
and clinics exist, much of the healing, training, and research done
within them is subsidized by taxpayers through health care transfers, public training fellowships, and federal research grants. Although private hospitals and medical schools may not receive
direct budgetary subventions from state or local authorities, they
nonetheless depend on these broader public subsidies to stay afloat.

While conservatives would like to think that they are standing
on their own two feet when they use their own money to purchase
a physician's time or pay for medical care in a private institution,
they ignore the huge public investment that has gone into generating the scientific knowledge and medical technology used in their
treatment, and the taxpayer money that went into training person-
nel how to use these tools effectively. At present, the budget of the
National Institutes of Health, the federal institution most responsible for health research and medical training, stands at $28 billion
per year.[26] Because of this public investment in health science and
medical technology, there has been a remarkable increase in human
life expectancy above age fifty since the 1970s, allowing Americans
to live longer than ever before.[27]

Economists often classify goods as public or private. A private
good is one that is consumed by individuals for their own satisfaction and produces little or no benefit to others. A public good is one
that is consumed by a community as a whole and is not readily di-
visible among individuals.[28] Food products offer a good example of
a private good. If I buy a box of Cheerios at the supermarket and
take it home to enjoy my favorite cereal at breakfast, no one else enjoys the satisfaction of their consumption. Not even my family will
derive much satisfaction from seeing me eat them. At the other extreme, national defense is a public good. The existence of a strong,
well-trained, and well-equipped army, navy, and air force protects
everyone in the United States from attack by hostile interests, and
no one can really purchase national defense privately.

Many conservatives see the world in binary terms and view
nearly all goods except national defense as private; accordingly,
they support the use of public funds only for defense and national

security.[29] In reality, most goods fall somewhere on a continuum between purely private and purely public goods, and health care is a good example. One obviously derives a personal benefit from being healthy and living a long life, so naturally people devote a significant share of their personal resources to health maintenance. In this sense, health is a private good. But each of us also benefits if those around us are healthy, and to this extent health is also a public good. Infectious diseases, in particular, can exist only in populations, and the larger and more dense the aggregate, the greater the potential for the incubation and spread of epidemic diseases. In a large urban society, no matter how much one spends individually on health and medical care, one cannot remain healthy or survive long in a population within which infectious diseases are raging, as even conservatives eventually discovered in the AIDS epidemic.[30]

If everyone were to invest the same amount in health and medical care, then there would be no particular problem—health care could indeed be treated as a private good. But income is unevenly distributed and some people are not able to afford a quality of health care sufficient to keep infectious diseases at bay. Although morality alone would seem to suggest that life and health should not be rationed to human beings strictly on the basis of income, many diehard libertarians are not convinced by moral arguments and for them, the issue must be presented as one overcoming a market failure for self-interested reasons.

Markets for health care fail because at any given distribution of income, some people will not have the funds necessary to purchase privately all the health care they need. Unlike many goods and services, when it comes to health care, consumers are not always in a position to substitute less costly alternatives or forego the service altogether, especially when it treats a life-threatening condition. When one arrives in an emergency room bleeding profusely, one is not in a position to haggle over price. By guaranteeing that everyone has access to some minimum level of health care regardless of wealth or income, the government improves the disease environment for everyone, helping even the selfish libertarian from succumbing to an infectious disease agent.

To the extent that health care, or any other good, is public, a second difficulty arises. If everyone invests in health care to prevent infectious diseases from spreading, then a single individual can get away with making no investments. He or she can act as a "free rider," taking advantage of the fact that everyone else has paid for immunization and hygiene, so that diseases like polio, measles, and plague cannot gain a foothold and spread. He or she can avoid paying the costs of health care and rely on others to do so. Of course, the more such free riders there are, the more likely it is that a disease agent will encounter sufficient numbers of unprotected people to spread; and if there are too many free riders, the public good will simply cease to exist. The only reliable way to overcome the free rider problem is to undertake collective action to force everyone to contribute their fair share to the common good—hence the necessity of government and taxation.[31]

According to Nussbaum, recreation is also essential to human productivity, and public funds accordingly have been used to create and maintain venues within which people can laugh, play, and cheer, such as sports stadiums, parks, playgrounds, and theaters. Government manages access to scarce public resources such as broadcast bands and airwaves. Tax revenues are widely used to subsidize and promote the creation of cultural products and to educate people in their consumption. Such is the purpose of the National Endowment for the Arts and the National Endowment for the Humanities, as well as the Public Broadcasting Corporation, all liberal programs enacted during the presidency of Lyndon Johnson. These institutions are frequent targets of attack by conservative politicians, though the same people rarely train their sights on public subsidies for sports teams owned by wealthy conservatives. Indeed, George W. Bush owes a substantial part of his fortune to the good citizens of Texas for their subsidy of the Texas Rangers baseball team, a sports franchise he co-owned.[32]

Whatever the importance of play and recreation for enhancing human well-being, a more central goal in the twenty-first century is to build human capacities to imagine, think, and reason, for these abilities lie at the core of a rapidly changing information economy. As already noted, economic changes and demographic trends have reduced the ability of families to provide children with the skills and abilities necessary for economic success, while at the same time the amount and sophistication of the knowledge required for success in a postindustrial economy has grown dramatically.

Whereas most human capital formation used to occur within the family, the tasks of child-rearing and education have increasingly been taken over by nonfamily members and institutions, and this situation is unlikely to be reversed. Women are unlikely to withdraw from the labor force in large numbers, men will not work fewer hours, marriage rates will not rise, divorce and separation rates will not return to the levels of the 1950s. The feminist and sexual revolutions will not be undone and the pace of structural and social change in the postindustrial information economy will not slow down.

Under such circumstances, it is in the self-interest of society and its citizens for public institutions to fill the gap between what is needed with respect to human capital development and what can be provided by increasingly hard-pressed families. To date, the pubic response has been woefully inadequate. Public schools are wracked with "savage inequalities" to the extent that many are simply incapable of providing an education sufficient to ensure a reasonable chance of success in contemporary society;[33] and even the most successful schools are straining under the large and growing body of knowledge that must be imparted during the fixed term of childhood.

Although the amount and complexity of human knowledge has grown dramatically in recent decades, schools are still organized according to the needs of a nineteenth-century agrarian economy, with three months of summer annually spent away from classes and learning, and early daily dismissals that leave working parents scrambling to arrange child care. Moreover, the typical curriculum is more suited to preparing workers for a regimented factory than for taking part in a dynamic, flexible, and increasingly networked economy.[34] Finally, in many jurisdictions, pay scales and professional opportunities for teachers are insufficient to attract the best people, despite teaching's growing centrality to national economic success in the information age.[35]

In the past, public schools were staffed by women who could be paid relatively low wages, partly because other, more lucrative avenues were closed to them and partly because of cultural norms—women were expected to perform "caring labor" on behalf of others because it was part of their role in society, not because they expected to get rich.[36] Teachers tended disproportionately to be unmarried or childless women who left teaching upon marriage or childbirth, perhaps returning later in life after children had grown. Women who pursued lifelong careers in education fulfilled the hoary stereotype of the "spinster teacher"; and even though these women didn't need much money to survive individually, they often experienced penurious retirements that depended on the charity of their extended families.

Although the condition of women changed dramatically during the 1960s, the incentives offered to people to become teachers—that is, crucial specialists in the essential task of human capital formation—have not kept up with the times. Because women are now free to pursue lucrative careers in law, medicine, and business, those who in the past would have become teachers now go into these professions instead. Moreover, women can no longer count on the institution of marriage to ensure their social and economic welfare. Given current rates and age patterns of marriage, childbearing, divorce, remarriage, and widowhood, the typical American women coming of age today can expect to expend at least half of her adult life alone, or at least without the direct support of a male partner.[37] Women have become careerists and breadwinners, and they need to be paid as such.

Obviously the days when we, as a nation, could rely on a captive market of capable, caring women to undertake the critical tasks of human capital formation for low prestige and minimal pay are gone. Yet the current social organization of education in the United States continues to pay teachers poorly and hold them in low esteem, with predictable results. If we are to succeed economically in a nation, we must invest more in our future; we must offer salaries, prestige, and professional opportunities sufficient to attract the best and the brightest people—both male and female—into this most crucial of economic tasks; and we must pay more to people who undertake the arduous task of working with those who are hardest to teach.

Giving people the capability to engage in meaningful social interactions was also primarily a function of the family in the past; but it too has increasingly fallen into the public realm. In an immobile agrarian society where most families are sedentary, communities are small, social change is slow, and few people move any great distance from their birthplace, the family is readily able to assume responsibility for socializing children into the values, beliefs, and mores of the community in which they will live. But as society urbanizes and becomes more diverse, the number of subcultures it houses proliferates;[38] and as the economy globalizes, Americans are routinely brought into closer and more intense contact with a wide variety of languages and cultures.[39] The pace of change is now such that the world into which children are socialized is vastly different socially, culturally, and technologically from that of their parents, and light years away from that of their grandparents.[40]

In an urbanized, globalized, and rapidly changing information society, no single family can provide access to all the cultural information that a person might conceivably need to socialize harmoniously with the people whom he or she will meet in a lifetime—hence the growing emphasis on diversity (racial, ethnic, linguistic, national) within institutions of higher education and the proliferation of courses introducing students to a range of racial, ethnic, and national experiences. As societies grow more diverse in terms of race, ethnicity, and national origin, the repertoire of cultural and linguistic skills that a person needs to advance socially and economically correspondingly increases.

Social Organization as a Factor of Production

The foregoing discussion suggests that to the classical categories of land, labor, and financial capital we must add human capital to the list of critical factors of production. But the effective creation of human capital itself, as well as its deployment with other factors to create wealth, requires an important fifth ingredient—social organization. No matter how rich a society's endowments of land, labor, financial capital, and human capital, little economic growth will occur unless an infrastructure of social institutions exists to put these resources to effective use. Markets are always embedded within a matrix of social institutions, some of which (such as the family) precede the market, and others of which (such as the corporation) were invented to facilitate its operation.

Although computers came into existence during the 1950s, for example, and were widely used by the 1960s, the administrative organization required to employ them efficiently and effectively did not fully emerge until the 1990s.[41] As a result, despite dramatic gains in computing power and a corresponding drop in costs, productivity lagged through the 1970s and 1980s.[42] Computers were used mainly to automate the routine tasks of mass markets organized by large bureaucratic structures. They facilitated the movement of paper up and down organizational hierarchies and helped distribute uniform products to a mass market.

In the 1990s, however, the social organization of work was radically reordered to take advantage of new productive possibilities enabled by prior increases in computing power. During this decade, mass markets fragmented into specialized niches and computers were used to design and distribute distinctive products tailored to specific demographic segments. At the same time, in sector after sector the size of business organizations shrank, bureaucratic structures flattened, hierarchical layers condensed, and top-down linear relations of authority were replaced by fractal networks of co-equal responsibility. The reorganization of work brought about a renewed surge of productivity growth, beginning in manufacturing during the 1980s and then moving into services during the 1990s.

Because of their intensive use of skilled, educated workers, bureaucracies and the service sector generally tended historically to be resistant to improvements in productivity. But the advent of inexpensive micro-computing suddenly enabled a single, well-trained worker at a workstation to manage huge inventories, track complicated bureaucratic procedures, and jockey paper trails that used to involved dozens of low-level white-collar workers employed at different levels, and it created new pressures for a complete restructuring of business organizations. After an initial "white-collar recession" during the early 1990s, the economy exploded to produce an unprecedented burst of growth based on cheaper and faster information processing, which came to be known as the dot.com boom because of its association with the growth and spread of the Internet.

A critical bottleneck in most economies historically, and a principal cause for the stagnation and decline of nations, has been a lack of institutional flexibility.[43] Once social, economic, and political institutions come into existence, they tend to become rigid and inflexible. Organizational inertia sets in because people who profit from prevailing institutional arrangements mobilize politically to ensure their perpetuation. Social structures are reproduced not because they maximize current or future well-being, but because the status quo is the path of least resistance to ensure the continued dominance of those who currently benefit from those arrangements. It is always difficult to imagine an alternative set of social arrangements when one is profiting so handsomely from present circumstances.

The system of political alliances and governmental institutions created during the New Deal had, by the late 1970s and early 1980s, fallen into such a state of inertia. Owing to shifting factor prices, the globalization of markets, and the revolution in telecommunications and computing, the social and economic environment had changed in profound ways, but New Deal institutions failed to adapt. Instead, the politicians and special interests tied to them sought to perpetuate past structures and practices, even as they were rapidly being rendered irrelevant by ongoing social and economic changes, with counterproductive effects.

The "Reagan Revolution" demolished the old set of arrangements and set the stage for a restructuring of labor markets, business organizations, and government that provided a foundation for the explosive growth of the 1990s; but now the Reagan Revolution has itself become narrow and sclerotic. Rather than working to promote new organizational forms to perpetuate future economic growth, a narrow cabal of corporate owners, investors, professionals, and conservative ideologues are working to preserve an outmoded political economy and to milk it for all they can while they can, despite obvious negative consequences for the nation—ballooning deficits, rising joblessness, and growing international hostility to the United States—yielding what Paul Krugman has called the "great unraveling,"[44] which sets the stage for a new liberal revolution.

Toward a New Liberal Agenda

The foregoing discussion illuminates the desiderata for a liberal program of government that will work in the best interests of citizens who inhabit postindustrial societies, where wealth is generated through the creation and application of knowledge and the manipulation and control of information within globalizing factor markets. In a liberal political regime, the ultimate goal of government should be to maximize human capabilities, for human beings inevitably constitute the ultimate resource for progress. It is they who develop knowledge, devise new forms of social organization, and creatively combine existing stocks of land, labor, and capital to ensure the expansion of markets that are capable of ensuring steady material improvement and of broadening access to wealth and income.

As a matter of domestic policy, the highest priority should be given to promoting, through a democratically agreed-upon combination of public and private auspices, the health and education of U.S. citizens, functions that are now being accomplished very poorly. We spend billions of dollars annually to preserve the health of citizens whose productive lives are over or drawing to a close while we invest little in the children who are the bedrock of future economic growth and productivity.[45] What is required is not a reversal of resource transfers to the elderly, but a greater balance in health expenditures by generation. Through some combination of public and private means, we desperately need to improve the health and well-being of the American young.

With respect to ensuring the health of its children, the United States lies at the bottom of the developed world. Out of thirty nations in the Organization for Economic Cooperation and Development (OECD), the United States currently has the seventh highest rate of infant mortality, exceeded only by Turkey, Mexico, Poland, Hungary, Slovakia, and South Korea.[46] If the United States could achieve the same average rate as the twenty-three OECD countries below it in the distribution of infant mortality (4.78 infant deaths per 1,000 births) instead of its current level (6.69 deaths per year), some 7,600 innocent lives could be saved each year (assuming 4 million births per year, the current rate); and if we could somehow achieve the infant mortality rate observed in Japan and Scandinavia (3.69), the number of children who would reach their first birthday would rise by 12,000. Before worrying about the lives of the unborn we should make a greater effort to protect the lives of the recently born.

With respect to educating its young, the United States fares little better. According to a report by the U.S. National Center for Educational Statistics, the United States currently spends about 3.8 percent of its GDP on primary and secondary education, including all public and private institutions.[47] While this fraction is slightly above the OECD average of 3.6 percent, it is well behind countries such as Australia, Belgium, Denmark, France, Korea, New Zealand, Norway, Portugal, Sweden, and Switzerland, whose fraction each exceeds 4 percent. Our expenditures are closer to those of nations such as Mexico and Spain, where the percentage is 3.7 percent. Paradoxically, the United States spends far *more* of its GDP than other countries on post-secondary education, devoting 2.3 percent of GDP to this purpose compared with 1.3 percent for the OECD in general. Only Canada and Korea spend higher fractions of their national income on post-secondary education (2.5% and 2.4% respectively).

Given this pattern of educational investment, the United States theoretically should not be able to prosper in a global economy where wealth is generated through the creation and application of knowledge. Indeed, our starving of primary and secondary education while lavishing resources upon higher education *does* produce a large annual shortfall in the number of people who are prepared to attend the best colleges and universities. If the United States had to rely solely on domestic sources for its supplies of human capital, the economy would have ground to a halt long ago.

The only reason we as a nation can get away with this skewed pattern of educational investment is that we have bridged the gap by importing human capital from abroad. First, the United States selects top high school and college graduates from around the world and offers them entrance into the world's finest system of higher education, choosing the best and the brightest to earn doctorates and other advanced degrees. From 1990 to 2000, the number of student visas issued for entry to the United States nearly doubled from 326,000 to 659,000 per year.[48]

Second, the United States waits for college and university graduates to appear in distinguished institutions elsewhere in the world and engages in "cherry picking," inducing them to enter the United States through special provisions built into U.S. immigration law. Between 1990 and 2000, the number of legal immigrants admitted in skilled occupational categories grew from 16,000 to 108,000 per year and the number of temporary workers admitted for skilled labor or training increased from 145,000 to 544,000 per year.[49] As a result, over the past two decades, immigrants have formed an ever-larger share of the nation's scientific, technical, and professional work force.[50] To a significant degree, the United States has been free-riding on the back of the rest of the world's better-funded primary and secondary educational systems.

Thus, a clear goal for liberals in the United States is to bring educational funding at least up to a par with the best-funded systems of primary and secondary education now in existence elsewhere in the world (4.6% in New Zealand). If educational expenditures were increased merely to match "the best of the rest," the cost would be just $266 per person, but that would raise an additional $77 billion to improve the nation's primary and schools (some $10 billion less than President Bush's 2003 request for assistance to Iraq). This money should not be seen as frivolous consumption but as a critical investment in the nation's economic future.

The question is not only the amount of money to devote to basic education, but also to spent it; how and there is no question that the provision of education is badly organized in the United States. What is required is no less than a comprehensive overhaul of institutions responsible for the care and education of children from birth through college, what sociologist Mary Brinton has called the nation's "human capital development system."[51] A nationwide system of daycare centers should be created through a combination of public and private means to provide affordable yet intellectually enriching daycare for infants and children too young for school, building on the experience of the nation's very successful but chronically underfunded Head Start program.

The schools that these children go on to enter must be completely reorganized. New buildings must be constructed, replacing the dilapidated structures prevalent in inner cities and rural areas with state-of-the-art learning centers that are wired for the needs of an information economy. In addition to enhancing the nation's productive infrastructure, this effort would also provide needed jobs in the construction industry. Given this new educational infrastructure, the school year would be extended to twelve months (with seasonal vacations) and the school day expanded to an 8–5 schedule, with options for subsidized, extended-day coverage for working parents. Public institutions of primary and secondary education would be transformed from schools that are vacant most of the time into intensively utilized centers for both the care and education of children.

Teaching also needs to be transformed from a regimented rote transmission of information carried out by poorly paid people with minimal skills and low status into a highly paid profession with significant incentives for training, improvement, and professional recognition. According to data from the College Board, the average combined SAT score for intended education majors was 963 in 1998, compared with an overall average score of 1017.[52] Of the majors listed, only those intending to major in home economics (917), public services (912), and a vocational track (888) scored lower. Salaries must rise, benefits increase, and class sizes decline markedly to attract and retain the best and the brightest people in one of the nation's most important jobs.

In a liberal education system designed for the twenty-first century, moreover, education would cease to be something that was pursued early in life and then ended; instead it would come to be an ongoing task to be accomplished throughout a worker's lifetime. During the evening hours, public schools could serve as centers for continuing adult education, offering subsidized training for workers who wish to retool or augment their knowledge and skills, especially for those of immigrant origin who wish to improve their English and knowledge of U.S. society. In addition to using public schools as centers for adult evening education, community colleges would be expanded to provide daytime education not only to young people but also to workers dislocated by the ongoing structural transformations within a healthy, growing economy.

The government would protect workers against market failures by generous transfers but they, in turn, would be required to retool and refresh their human capital as necessary to stay employed. Displaced workers would be supported by temporally limited unemployment benefits or welfare payments on condition that they either look for work or attend a certified educational institution. Under current federal regulations, education does not substitute for employment in putting off time limits for welfare transfers and for retaining eligibility for public support, forcing many low-income workers into an endless circuit of dead-end jobs with no realistic chance of escape. With children taken care of in a comprehensive, full-time system of care and education, and with their immediate material needs met by transfer payments, adults would have no excuse for not working or investing their energies in additional training when the need arose.

These measures would not be cheap, but they would be cheaper than our current labor force policy: building and staffing a huge criminal justice system. The United States now has the highest rate of incarceration in the world, and if incarcerated men had been included in labor market statistics in the 1990s, they would

have contributed about two percentage points to the U.S. unemployment rate.[53] Whereas Europeans pay marginalized workers a
stipend to stay at home and out of trouble, Americans build hugely
expensive prisons to contain them.[54]

Over the period 1985 to 2000, state-level spending on higher
education increased by 29 percent; but state spending on corrections increased by 175 percent. At the same time, the ratio of
spending on colleges and universities to prisons went from 3.74 to
1.74, and the fraction of total state spending on education fell
from 8 to 6.3 percent while spending on prisons went from 2.9 to
4.3 percent, despite a sustained decrease in violent crime during
the 1990s.[55] If we were to return to the incarceration rates of the
mid-1980s, the effect on the crime rate would be trivial,[56] but it
would free up an additional $20 billion for investment in the
human capital of the United States. There is no greater waste than
spending billions to lock up human beings during their most productive years of labor force participation. It is hard to imagine a
more illiberal policy than funding incarceration to the exclusion
of education.

Thus, the liberal domestic agenda boils down to two overriding
goals: better management of markets so that they operate in the
public interest and greater investment in the capabilities of Americans. Rather than handing over the operation of markets to a narrow cabal of producers and financiers with a self-interest in their
operation, markets are portrayed politically as a *public resource* to
be managed in a transparent way by elected representatives for the
good of society in general; and rather than viewing spending on the
health and education of Americans citizens as a frivolous luxury, it
would be presented to voters as a critical investment *required* for
the continued growth and expansion of the U.S. economy. Offering these two broad goals to the American people as a political
platform is not only good politics; it is also good economics.

CHAPTER 5

Global Policies

Although the term "globalization" came into vogue during the late twentieth century to describe the emergence of markets on a worldwide scale, the 1990s were not the first time the earth's inhabitants had witnessed such a transformation. From 1800 to 1914, the world underwent a similar expansion of international trade and commerce as industrialization spread outward from its point of origin in northwestern Europe to affect distant corners of the globe. As industrialism spread, the costs of transportation and communication fell, unleashing unprecedented transoceanic flows of goods, commodities, capital, and labor, which moved between trading nations with relative ease and in ever-rising volumes.[1]

Capital accumulated through industrialization in Britain and Germany was invested in the emerging markets of southern and eastern Europe, as well as in Asia and, especially, in the Americas. As successive nations were incorporated into global networks of trade, production, and finance, their economies were radically transformed. Machines replaced human labor and inanimate sources of power (steam and electricity) supplanted animate sources (horses and oxen) to increase productivity dramatically. In the countryside, mechanization brought about the consolidation of land and the massive displacement of peasants, who migrated by the millions in search of alternative means of support. Some moved internally to rapidly growing industrial cities, thus bringing about the urbanization of society; but many others traveled internationally to labor-scarce regions overseas that were themselves in the throes of rapid industrial development. In the course of Europe's industrialization, some fifty-four million people emigrated, the largest mass movement in human history. Their arrival in the United States, Canada, Argentina, Australia, and New Zealand transformed these societies and made them rich.[2]

Over the course of the nineteenth and early twentieth centuries, economic growth followed a well-defined cycle. European investment in an emerging market overseas was followed by a surge of emigration to that place. When economic activity there declined, investment and migration were redirected back toward European cities. Bursts of economic development in Europe oscillated with spurts of economic growth in immigrant-receiving cities abroad, yielding successive waves of growth development that gradually ratcheted trading nations up the scale of wealth, leading over time to a global convergence of wages, income, and living standards.[3]

To facilitate this rising volume of trade, political and economic leaders created a series of rudimentary but serviceable multilateral institutions to facilitate the international movement of goods and capital and to ensure international liquidity and the convertibility of currencies.[4] Over the course of the long nineteenth century, trading nations grew wealthy as incomes rose at an astounding rate compared to earlier times.[5] At the same time, the worldwide circulation of people, ideas, information, and investments brought about a new cosmopolitanism. Steady growth in living standards, along with increasing interdependence among nations created new faith in secular "progress." War among nations began to seem "unthinkable" to many, or at least unlikely because the material interests of each country so obviously lay in avoiding conflict and perpetuating trade to accumulate more wealth. People came to believe that whatever problems existed would somehow be solved by advances in science and technology. Even perplexing social issues such as poverty and communal conflict seemed amenable to rational human solution.

Yet at the peak of this spectacular period of wealth creation, there were serious fissures lurking below the surface that would break the system apart. Whereas rapid industrialization brought wealth to some, it yielded hardship to others and created new inequalities of material well-being within nations even as it promoted convergence among them.[6] Urbanization produced a proletariat of poor workers and an expanding middle class, both of whom sought a bigger piece of the social and economic pie. As they organized politically to press their demands in Europe, they encountered rigid, inflexible states in which power and wealth were confined narrowly to a hereditary elite of nobles and monarchs.

The unwillingness of European elites to share power and the unequal distribution of wealth and income was met by a rising tide of demonstrations and strikes and the formulation of counter-ideologies such as anarchism, socialism, and communism. At the same time, rising wealth and the new technologies of mass transportation and communication gave voice to nationalist aspirations among Europe's repressed ethnic minorities. Frustrated ethnic and class ambitions were expressed through violence—bombings, kidnapings, and assassinations—a wave of what we would today label as terrorism.[7]

In the absence of sound national and international political institutions capable of handling these tensions, leaders in the great European powers viewed their populations and each other warily. Despite its rapid rise to industrial might, Germany remained insecure, chary of irredentist Slavs to the east and envious of Britain's naval hegemony to the west. Austria-Hungary feared restless national minorities seeking recognition within its sprawling empire; and France harbored a bitter grudge and its own territorial claims against Germany, stemming from the Franco-Prussian war. Hereditary elites everywhere feared the rising power of the masses.[8]

In August 1914, there was no formalized mechanism for arbitrating these cross-cutting pressures, no forum within which nations could talk, bargain, and compromise rather than fight; and no way that a decision to go to war could be debated publicly before fateful actions were taken. Thus the stage was set for the cataclysm of global war; and, as Germany's Iron Chancellor Otto von Bismark had once acidly predicted, it all began with "some damn fool thing in the Balkans."[9]

After a Serbian terrorist assassinated the Austro-Hungarian heir in the province of Bosnia, the emperor declared a "war on terror" and issued an ultimatum to Serbia demanding that it cease harboring terrorists and dismantle its nationalist networks. Although resistant at first, Serbia ultimately acceded to the demands; but not before Austria-Hungary declared a unilateral right to self-defense through preemptive invasion. Its preemptive attack on the Slavs of Serbia triggered military mobilization by Russia, which caused the mobilization of the German military, which brought about the mobilization of France, which by treaty required the mobilization of Britain, which eventually culminated in the entry of the United States.

Thus the global trading regime, once it degenerated into conflict, led to something entirely new: a global war. From August 1914 through November of 1918, approximately eight million soldiers died on the battlefield; another two million were classified as missing and presumed dead; somewhere around 1.5 million Armenians died in the century's first genocide; and untold millions of civilians died from starvation and disease. Within roughly half a decade, at least fifteen million people perished in the inferno of World War I.[10] When the blood finally stopped flowing, the global system of trade and investment that had produced prosperity and peace for more than a century was gone, and the international political economy lay in ruins.

Despite the heroic efforts of U.S. President Woodrow Wilson, liberalism failed miserably to put the pieces back together in the aftermath of World War I. During the 1920s, nation after nation turned inward economically, socially, and culturally. In the United States, the Senate refused in 1919 to ratify American entry into the League of Nations, thus dooming the first attempt to create a structure for global conflict resolution. In 1920 and 1924, Congress passed restrictive quota laws designed specifically to curtail the flow of immigrants from southern and eastern Europe, thus reducing immigration to a trickle compared with pre-1914 levels. In 1921, Congress imposed tariffs on forty agricultural products and in 1923 added duties to manufactures. Further protections were piled on throughout the decade, culminating in the Smoot-Hawley Tariff Act of 1930, which consolidated and raised duties across a wide spectrum of raw materials, agricultural products, and manufactured goods, including many things the United States did not even produce.[11]

As other nations followed suit, the size of markets progressively shrank, leading to depression at home and abroad. The collapse of liberal capitalism during the 1930s lent new legitimacy to the counter-ideologies developed in the prior century, leading to the foundation of a dictatorship of the proletariat in Russia and a tyranny of the *herrenvolk* in Germany, Japan, and Italy. Whereas communism sought to create a worker's paradise by expropriating the means of production on behalf of "the people," fascism sought to create social order through a deadly mixture of racial myth and national economic autarky. The violence unleashed by fascists against their internal and external enemies produced the Holocaust and World War II, catastrophes that proved to be even bloodier and more destructive than the events of 1914–1918.[12]

To defeat fascism, the capitalist and communist worlds temporarily banded together at the cost of some 23 million military deaths and 17 million civilian casualties worldwide.[13] This time, however, the deaths were not in vain, for leaders in the United States and elsewhere were determined not to repeat the mistakes of the past. Led by liberal Democratic presidents Franklin D. Roosevelt and Harry S. Truman, the United States joined with other nations to build a new set of multilateral institutions to promote international stability, stimulate global trade, and, in so doing, create global prosperity and secure world peace.

In an effort to provide a mechanism for diffusing international conflict, offer a platform for discussing multilateral issues, and create a venue for collective action in the global interest, the world's sovereign states in 1945 joined together to form the United Nations. The centrality of the United States to this venture is indicated by the American venue for the UN charter convention (San Francisco, California); the American location of the UN headquarters (New York City); and by President Harry S. Truman's opening address to the delegates at the United Nations organizational conference in April 1945.[14]

The United Nations is governed by a General Assembly of all nations and a Security Council that includes a rotating subset of

nations from the General Assembly plus the world's major powers
as permanent members. The executive branch, the UN Secretariat,
reports to these bodies and supervises a far-flung bureaucracy of
international agencies. The International Labor Organization
(in Geneva) coordinates labor policies across nations. The World
Health Organization (also in Geneva) works to control the spread
of infectious diseases. The Food and Agricultural Organization
(based in Rome) seeks to raise agricultural productivity and increase global food supplies. The Educational, Scientific, and Cultural Organization (in Paris) promotes the exchange of ideas
and information; and other, less-known agencies monitor and coordinate international policies with respect to civil aviation, mar-
itime practices, postal services, telecommunications, and weather
forecasting.[15]

Two of the most important specialized agencies included under
the United Nations umbrella were conceived at a conference in
Breton Woods, New Hampshire during July and August of 1944.
The International Monetary Fund (IMF) was created to guarantee
international liquidity and assure the ready convertibility of currencies, and the World Bank was established to finance the reconstruction of Europe and Japan (through the International Bank for
Reconstruction and Development). Later the World Bank would
be adapted to promote economic development in the Third World
(through the International Development Association). Three additional agencies were ultimately added to the World Bank's portfolio
of responsibilities: the International Finance Corporation, which
promotes investment in high-risk sectors and countries; the Multilateral Investment Guarantee Agency, which offers risk insurance for investors in developing countries; and the International
Center for Settlement of Investment Disputes, which mediates
disagreements between lending institutions and financiers and
the countries in which they invest. Both the IMF and the World
Bank are headquartered in Washington, D.C., once again indi-
cating the centrality of the United States to the global political
economy.[16]

The final institution created in the wake of World War II was
the General Agreement on Tariffs and Trade (GATT), inaugurated

in 1947 and progressively broadened through successive "rounds" of negotiations: the Kennedy round of 1964–67, the Tokyo round of 1973–77, and the Uruguay round of 1986–94. The latter culminated in the creation of the World Trade Organization, which came into existence on January 1, 1995, to monitor and enforce international trade agreements. Although early rounds of the GATT focused on reducing tariffs, successive rounds expanded the treaty's purview to address nontariff barriers, intellectual property rights, agricultural subsidies, textile policies, as well as environmental and labor standards.[17]

Despite the creation of this new international infrastructure, global markets did not recover quickly, for several reasons. First, in 1950, around a third of the world's people were cut off from markets and isolated within the command economies of China, the Soviet Union, and their various satellites. Second, at the end of World War II the global distribution of economic resources was highly uneven. The United States emerged from the conflict as the world's largest creditor nation and reigning industrial power, accounting for the lion's share of global investment capital and industrial production.

During the 1950s and 1960s, the United States occupied an enviable economic position. It lent Europe and Japan money to rebuild their productive facilities. It then recouped these funds when they were used to purchase capital goods made in the United States. Meanwhile, while factories in Europe and Japan were being rebuilt, consumers around the world bought U.S. products. American banks and industries could not help making money. With Europe and Japan preoccupied with reconstructing their productive bases and domestic markets, U.S. industries experienced little international competition, and for two decades the American economy seemed to grow effortlessly. Median wealth increased, average income rose, inequality fell, and the era of the mass American market reached its zenith.

By 1970, however, Europe and Japan were fully rebuilt and their producers were looking to expand sales in U.S. consumer markets. The Oil Boycott of 1973 exposed structural weaknesses in the U.S. economy and provided an opening through which overseas competitors moved to increase their U.S. market share, notably in automobiles and electronics. In the years between 1945 and 1973, U.S. producers had grown fat and lazy making products for a huge, insulated market. No matter what kind or quality products they produced, American consumers bought them, providing few incentives for investment or innovation. Over time, U.S. plants grew old and inefficient, leaving them in a weak position to compete with the new industrial infrastructures of Germany and Japan. The recession induced by the Oil Boycott of 1973 simply aggravated an already-bad competitive situation.[18]

During the 1970s and early 1980s, U.S. industries competed mainly with other developed nations; but as the 1980s gave way to the 1990s, industrial competition grew with developing nations in the Third World. It was not until the end of the Cold War, however, that the world was truly in a position to resume the trajectory of international trade it had so abruptly abandoned in 1914. With the fall of the Berlin Wall, the parting of the Iron Curtain, the collapse of the Soviet Union, and the shift of China from command to market mechanisms, the international trading regime for the first time became truly global in scope. As a result, in 1990 international trade as a share of U.S. GDP finally reached 15 percent, a level it had last attained on the eve of World War I.[19]

During the last half of the twentieth century, as trade resumed and the global economy steadily expanded, the multilateral institutions created in the aftermath of World War II generally performed well. Despite periodic confrontations between the Soviet Union and the United States, global warfare was averted for four decades during the tense standoff known as the Cold War. At the same time, prosperous, democratic societies were established in former fascist countries throughout Europe and Asia, and served as models for the extension of industrial development elsewhere.

International trade and the security enabled by multilateral institutions such as the UN, GATT, and WTO allowed development to spread faster and more widely than at any point in human history; and despite widespread beliefs to the contrary, over the last quarter of the twentieth century global trade generally worked to *close* the gap between rich and poor nations.[20] National economic growth during the postwar period was enabled by access to large markets and by the formation and deployment of human capital. Countries that made basic investments in health and education while integrating within global markets generally advanced socially and economically; those that failed to take these steps did not.[21] National development in many countries would have been impossible in the absence of trade, because their internal markets were simply too small and too weak to support the economies of scale necessary for industrial production.[22] To destroy the system of global trade, therefore, is to condemn a large share of the world's population to permanent poverty.

The preservation and extension of global trade is essential to assuring global peace and prosperity, now and in the future. Despite its successes, however, globalization and the institutions on which it depends have recently come under serious attack. Just as in 1914, the system is under strain because of foolhardy policies implemented by unaccountable political leaders acting out of a combination of narrow self-interest and ideology; and just as before, counter-ideologies have arisen to argue against the creation and extension of markets in human society. The community of nations, in general, and the United States, in particular, once again stand at a crossroads. One path requires hard work and sacrifice but leads to a future of peace, progress, and prosperity. The other requires less effort and fewer investments in the short run, but will lead ultimately to collapse, poverty, and violence on a scale that will be difficult to imagine. Let us hope we choose better than our predecessors did in 1914.

The Washington Consensus

In the world, as in the United States, the management and supervision of markets has increasingly been given over to free market ideologues and a set of narrow corporate and financial interests. According to Susan Aaronson, a leading scholar of global trade, "[T]rade policy was developed by a small circle of elites in government, with advice from leaders from business, labor, academia, and agriculture. Environmentalists, consumer activists, and human rights activists were not part of that inner circle."[23] This takeover was accomplished under an ideological umbrella known as the "Washington Consensus." The term was coined in 1990 by the economist John Williamson of the Institute for International Economics, and it refers to a package of "policy advice being addressed by the Washington-based institutions to Latin American countries as of 1989."[24] Also known as "neoliberalism," this advice stressed the importance of balanced budgets, tax reduction, decontrolled interest rates, free exchange rates, trade liberalization, foreign direct investment, deregulation, and privatization.

During the 1990s, these policies were increasingly forced upon nations in the developing and postcommunist worlds with religious zeal by officials of the IMF.[25] Nations in desperate need of loans from the World Bank and other international institutions were compelled to accept the "structural adjustment" policies demanded by IMF officials, for without the blessing of the mandarins of the IMF, the spigot of international investment funds from the World Bank would be twisted shut. Paradoxically, although the IMF was originally chartered to protect nations against *failures in international markets*, during the 1980s its officials came to view *markets as the solution* to virtually all national ills. Through a steady process of "mission creep" the IMF became a central player in imposing the Washington Consensus upon a dubious but compliant world.[26]

According to the Nobel Laureate Joseph Stiglitz, who served as Chief Economist for the World Bank during 1997–99, "[T]he IMF took a rather imperialistic view of the matter . . . [and] viewed almost everything as falling within its domain. The IMF had all the answers (basically, the same ones for every country), didn't see the need for all this discussion, and while the World Bank debated what should be done, saw itself as stepping into the vacuum to provide the answers."[27] So much faith had the high priests of the Washington Consensus that Stiglitz has labeled them "market fundamentalists," people who knew "*by assumption* [that] markets work perfectly and demand must equal supply for labor as for every other good or factor [so] there cannot be unemployment, the problem cannot lie with markets. It must lie elsewhere—with greedy unions and politicians interfering with the workings of free markets" (emphasis in original).[28]

Policies adopted under the Washington Consensus proved to be even more destructive when applied to developing nations than when implemented in the United States, for at least the latter had well-developed institutions to protect citizens against market failures and to mitigate the structural consequences of reckless policies. It is one thing to promote privatization and deregulation in a rich country with well-established property laws, enforceable contracts, functioning democratic institutions, a secure financial system, widespread insurance, and agencies capable of market oversight and regulation. It is quite another to propose these policies in a country where these institutional foundations do not exist.

The poster child for the Washington Consensus was the Latin American nation of Chile. But this initial test case succeeded more because of its strong institutional foundations than because of the gospel according to Washington, causing the high priests of the Potomac to draw all the wrong conclusions. Prior to the CIA-sponsored coup of 1973, Chile had been a relatively stable, middle-class nation with a long democratic tradition characterized by respect for private property and the rule of law. The communist government of Salvador Allende was an *elected* one, and it came to power only in 1970. It had thus taken relatively few steps toward socializing the Chilean economy when it was toppled with U.S. assistance in 1973.[29]

After leading the successful coup d'état, General Augusto Pinochet invited down a group of Ph.D. economists who became known throughout Latin America as "los Chicago Boys." Their charge was to revamp the Chilean economy along the lines recommended by their spiritual master, Professor Milton Friedman of the University of Chicago. In pushing forward an agenda of privatization, fiscal austerity, and deregulation, however, the boys unwittingly benefited from Chile's well-established infrastructure of reliable social, economic, and political institutions. Moreover, despite the emphasis of the Washington Consensus on privatization, the Pinochet government curiously never saw fit to return

Chile's leading industrial enterprise—copper production—to the private sector, preferring to use it instead as a source of exchange earnings.[30] Even given the advantages of well-established property rights, the rule of law, strong societal institutions, and a secure source of foreign income, however, Chilean poverty rates soared initially and inequality rose quite markedly before the economy stabilized and more balanced growth resumed.[31]

In his critique of the Washington Consensus, *Globalization and its Discontents*, Joseph Stiglitz points out that when it comes to constructing a well-functioning market system, timing and sequencing are everything.[32] Governments necessarily play an important role in building the infrastructure (legal, institutional, and cultural) that enables the effective functioning of markets, as well as in creating the human capital (through investments in health and education) upon which economic growth ultimately rests. Unless the necessary infrastructure and human capital have been created *first*, one cannot expect to achieve prosperity and stability by suddenly opening an economy to unencumbered private exchanges.

In the case of Chile, the preconditions for success fortuitously existed, and from this the high priests of the IMF in Washington drew the mistaken conclusion that all a government had to do to achieve development was get out of the way and "let the market decide." As a result, the Washington Consensus was imposed by rote in country after country by technocrats with a limited comprehension of economics and virtually no understanding of the history, culture, or language of the societies they were entering. Because every nation has a different history and comes to the process of market creation with a different matrix of social institutions and practices, *there can be no single path to the market.*[33]

The starting point for economic development must always be an appreciation for a nation's existing social structures, economic institutions, and cultural systems. Only then can one know what features of social organization need be created for the operation of markets and, more importantly, how existing social structures might be adapted for the purpose. According to development theorist Hernando de Soto, the most fundamental problem plaguing market creation throughout the world is a lack of legal structures to protect private property and to define the terms for its exchange.[34] For a functioning market economy to exist, a nation must abandon informal, extralegal property systems and replace them with a codified system that is formal, legal, and unified. This requires developing a body of law that specifies how individuals gain title to the land and material artifacts they control, and that defines when, where, and how they may dispose of titled property. Without clear title to property and rights for its disposition, the capital it contains remains "dead" economically—it cannot reliably be sold, rented, or mortgaged to realize value, creating a huge drag on development. Most of the world's people live in societies where property rights remain informal and ill-defined and therefore inaccessible for purposes of development.

A particular article of faith in the sacred scriptures of market fundamentalism is that capital markets must be deregulated, thereby giving free reign to what Thomas Friedman calls the "golden horde"—a galloping herd of international currency speculators, financiers, and investors who stampede into a country to place "hot money" bets on different activities hoping to maximize their returns as quickly as possible.[35] In the absence of controls on the movement of such investments, capital markets are notoriously volatile, leaving newly developing nations at risk of serious economic damage from rapid and uncontrolled capital flight, even though other macroeconomic fundamentals may be sound. Stiglitz argues that "premature capital market deregulation"— allowing for the free mobility of capital before an adequate institutional foundation is in place—is one of the most important single failings of the Washington Consensus and a central cause of the wave of financial meltdowns that swept global markets during the 1990s.[36]

Not only has the market fundamentalism of the Washington Consensus proved destructive within countries of the developing and postcommunist worlds, it has also proved deleterious for globalism generally. Under the guise of promoting "free trade" (a hollow trope much like that of the "free market"), decisions about the rules and infrastructures for global competition were turned

over to a narrow set of economic interests who structured the operation of international markets to benefit themselves rather than
the world's people generally. As a result, the process of economic
globalization has functioned disproportionately to advance the
material well-being of investors, financiers, and multinational
corporations with little attention to the interests of workers, consumers, or the world's citizens in general, thus doing much damage to the natural environment and social fabric of many nations.
Indeed, those countries that followed the prescriptions of the
Washington Consensus most faithfully often suffered the most.[37]

The negative consequences of globalization observed during the
1990s, however, are not inevitable by-products of global capitalism, but artifacts of specific choices made by the people and interests who hijacked the process of market creation and management
to write the rules of global competition in their favor. At the end of
the twentieth century, the problems of globalization as managed
by market fundamentalists and their corporate allies have become
increasingly obvious. But rather than calling for reform—rewriting
the rules of competition and restructuring multilateral institutions
to improve the terms of international trade and represent the interests of a broader cross-section of the world's population—many
observers have come to reject markets and their global extension
entirely. Counter-ideologies of both the right and the left have
emerged, and their realization threatens peace and prosperity
throughout the world.

Globalization Backlash

Unfortunately people are more likely to see what globalization has
not accomplished during the last quarter of the twentieth century
than what it actually delivered. The failings are indeed spectacular
and have been widely publicized. The financial implosions and
subsequent bailouts in nations that followed the advice of the Washington Consensus—Mexico, Korea, Malaysia, and Argentina—
have been widely reported.[38] The economic stagnation, internecine
violence, spreading disease, and social disintegration that has

befallen sub-Saharan Africa are likewise well documented;[39] and people have been rightly appalled by the human pain and social turmoil inflicted on people throughout the postcommunist world through the blind pursuit of fiscal austerity, deregulation, and privatization for their own sake.[40]

But these failings should not obscure the very real successes achieved during the latter half of the twentieth century. Global warfare and nuclear conflict were averted. Former fascist nations were rebuilt and transformed into prosperous democracies. The Iron Curtain parted so that a political and economic union of twenty-five free, democratic states could evolve to bring prosperity and peace to the whole of Europe. In Asia, "tigers" such as Taiwan, South Korea, Hong Kong, Singapore, and Malaysia entered the global trading system and, by pursuing a strategy of export industrialization, joined the ranks of developed nations. Command economies in Eastern Europe, China, and South Asia gave way to decentralized and increasingly open market societies, leading to rapid improvements in the material living standards of millions of people.[41]

The formula for rapid growth and development has been much the same everywhere: expand the size of markets by joining the global trading regime; form new human capital by investing in health and education; create the social organization necessary for the effective operation of markets; and steadily liberalize society to offer people a wider range of freedoms and choices. Much of the pain and suffering in the world today stems from the failure of states to achieve one or more of these essential milestones on the pathway to development, either through their own mistakes or through the failure of international organizations to promote their realization in an appropriate sequence.

Rather than seeking to rectify the deficiencies of globalization as it has been practiced over the past two decades, many critics of global trade and multilateral institutions call for its curtailment. Unfortunately, ending global trade will not solve the world's problems. Indeed, it will make them worse. If human progress is to continue in the twenty-first century, globalization must be reformed, not ended. It is thus crucial to combat forcefully the growing backlash against globalization on both the right and the left, especially in the United States, whose voters—for better or worse—hold so much of the world's fate in their hands.

Unilateralism from the Right

If American conservatives are mistrustful of the federal government, they are even more wary of anything that smacks of "world government." After all, they have traditionally championed "states' rights," defending state autonomy to the point where they staunchly upheld the right of states to permit chattel slavery and systematically subordinate African Americans through legal segregation. Such people are unlikely to have much sympathy with global institutions and governance. Indeed, the principal criticism of globalization from the right is that it undermines national sovereignty and that it opens the country up to a multitude of suspect "foreign" influences.[42]

The entry of the United States into a multilateral agreement, of course, *does* impinge on its freedom of action as a nation.[43] Joining the United Nations, the General Agreement on Tariffs and Trade, or the World Trade Organization commits the United States to eschew certain actions and behaviors while embracing others. The point is that the United States enters into multilateral agreements *voluntarily*, expecting to reap benefits in exchange for relinquishing some measure of its autonomy. Officials trade off some portion of their right to unilateral action (e.g., the right of Americans to build as many nuclear missiles as they see fit) to achieve an even more desirable outcome (a world in which nuclear annihilation is less likely).

The benefits achieved through multilateralism are obvious. By cooperating with other nations through multilateral institutions, the United States won the Cold War, averted a nuclear exchange with the Soviet Union, and positioned itself at the core of a prosperous global economy during the 1990s. Despite these achievements, conservative leaders of the radical right have worked assiduously over the past decade to undermine multilateralism and the institutions and treaties that promote it. For many years, the Republican-controlled Congress systematically withheld payment of UN dues owed by the United States (only to relent quietly in the wake of September 11); and since coming to power the Bush administration has accelerated the pace of subversion, renouncing the Kyoto Accords on global emissions, rejecting the authority of the International Criminal Court, and abrogating the Anti-ballistic Missile Treaty first negotiated by President Richard M. Nixon, someone who could hardly be considered as "soft" on international security issues.

Then, as part of his self-declared "war on terrorism," President George W. Bush announced a new first-strike doctrine, asserting the unilateral right of the United States to launch a preemptive attack on any nation it deems a threat. Against the wishes of a majority of the world's nations, and in violation of basic principles of international law, the Bush administration then exercised this putative right by mounting a full-scale military invasion of Iraq at a cost to date of around $100 billion, 15,000 Iraqi deaths, and 450 U.S. combat deaths and 2500 American wounded, despite heated opposition by several of America's closest allies.[44]

Although the invasion was originally justified as necessary to counter the threat to the United States emanating from Saddam Hussein's possession of weapons of mass destruction, when evidence of these weapons failed to materialize in the aftermath of the invasion, the rationale was subtly shifted to promoting democracy in Iraq (even though the United States was untroubled by Hussein's authoritarianism a few years earlier, when he was at war with Iran). In a few short years, the radical right has succeeded in abrogating the fundamental principles that have guided every congress and administration—Democratic or Republican—since 1945.

In doing so, U.S. authorities have undermined rather than enhanced American national security. In much the same way that the Soviet invasion of Afghanistan made Russia a legitimate target for Islamic terror in the 1980s, the unprovoked invasion of Iraq by American forces has mobilized Muslims throughout the world to enjoin a new holy war to expel the infidels from the *umma*, the lands of Islam, and creating Iraqi links to international terror organizations where none had existed before.

The assertion of an American right to unilateral action in foreign affairs has been accompanied by a new militarization of the domestic sphere. Increasingly repressive measures have been implemented in the name of defending Americans from a host of invasive foreign threats—drugs, terrorists, and immigrants (with much elision between the last two categories). Even before September 11, the nation had grown quite hostile to immigrants, systematically stripping foreigners—even those legally here—of rights and privileges, and massively increasing the application of repressive force along the border with Mexico, a peaceful nation that is a close ally and top trading partner.[45]

After the destruction of the World Trade Center and the anthrax attacks in the fall of 2001, the Bush administration capitalized on the upsurge of national fear and media hysteria to push the USA Patriot Act through Congress with virtually no debate.[46] In addition to expanding the power of the executive authority over noncitizens, it granted the president sweeping powers to define a "terrorist" or "terrorist organization" and take to whatever steps he deemed necessary to combat the resultant threat, including permission to trace and intercept private communications among American citizens without judicial authorization. Under this expanded authority, the Bush administration has declared numerous people—citizens and noncitizens—to be "enemy combatants" and has held them in indefinite detention without presenting evidence against them or filing formal charges, all while denying those detained the right to legal counsel, a court hearing, or judicial review.

The world that the radical right seeks to create is thus eminently clear from the behavior of conservative authorities since taking over Congress in the mid-1990s and the White House in 2000. Internally, the United States will militarize its borders and restrict the civil liberties of its citizens. Internationally, it will seek to preserve itself as an unrivaled military superpower that retains the right to attack any nation wherever and whenever it wishes for whatever reason. Multilateral treaties and institutions are to be undermined and the exchanges of people, ideas, goods, and capital will be curtailed and regulated. In the world of the radical right, the United States will not cooperate with other nations to construct a stable world order. It will act unilaterally strictly on the basis of its perceived national interest, irrespective of the wishes of other nations. This stance closely resembles that of the United States during the 1920s, which set the stage for global economic collapse and world war.

Anarchy from the Left

At the opposite end of the political spectrum, the counter-ideology proposed by the left is equally troubling, though perhaps not quite as frightening because it is less coherent and so far away from political realization. In response to the failings and inequities of global trade as practiced during the 1980s and 1990s, the radical left has coalesced around a disparate "anti-globalization movement."[47] The radical left's critique of the globalization is that it is undemocratic and that it is destroying local cultures and replacing them with a homogenized consumer society designed and controlled by Western corporate interests for their own profit.[48] They seek to prevent expansion of the GATT, the WTO, and regional trade pacts such as the Free Trade Agreement of the Americas. Many seek the actual demise of these and other multilateral institutions, such as the World Bank and the IMF.[49]

What is not clear is what radical leftists envision as a replacement for the system of global trade and multilateral relations. Some clearly advocate reforms along the lines of what I am suggesting here.[50] Many others, however, seem to be motivated by a visceral hatred of global capitalism and seek only to destroy it, whatever the consequences. On the far left, an anarchist ideology has revived and spread for the first time since it was eclipsed by communism and socialism in the 1930s.[51] Committed anarchists believe that all national and transnational structures inevitably are controlled by wealthy corporations and financial interests, and that the global market economy and the institutions that sustain it—the World Bank, IMF, WTO—must be smashed through direct action. They envision a return to some idyllic preindustrial past of small, self-sufficient communities living in harmony with the earth and with each other.[52]

Leaving aside the fact that the preindustrial, communal past was not so idyllic in the first place,[53] we have little choice but to continue along the organizational and technological path we have followed since 1800 and try to improve it. There is no conceivable way that preindustrial technologies can sustain today's population of six billion people. We are locked into a technology trap whereby our survival depends on the social, economic, and material inventions of the past two centuries, even though the misapplication and misappropriation of these same inventions carry serious risks for our future.[54] The alternative systems of government that were attempted during the past century—fascism, socialism, and communism—failed miserably, leaving liberal capitalism guided by representative democracy as the only viable and humane option.

Many on the left argue that a particular sin of economic globalization is that it is destroying the world's traditional cultures and supplanting them with standardized ideas and mass-produced products that cater to tastes inculcated by global media, thus bringing about the transformation of the rich tapestry of human culture into a bland corporate-inspired McWorld.[55] It is true, of course, that the totems of American popular culture—Big Macs, Coca Cola, MTV, Hollywood action movies—have spread worldwide and have insinuated themselves into disparate cultural settings the world over.[56] It is also true that aboriginal peoples throughout the world are under intense cultural pressure and that in the next century many human languages will disappear and their associated cultures will be radically transformed.[57]

One trend does not necessarily cause the other, however, and the transformation of languages and cultures is inherent to the human condition. Although the products of American popular culture are indeed ubiquitous, to a great extent they have spread because people throughout the world *enjoy* consuming them. They like drinking Cokes, eating Whoppers, and watching Schwarzenegger, movies, at least when they are not at home watching an episode of *Baywatch* on television. Although consumption may be influenced by Western advertising that glorifies the products of global capitalism, thus giving Third World consumers a feeling of being "modern" when they purchase them, their demand is by no means solely a function of commercial propaganda, and the introduction of global products does not necessarily involve a one-to-one trade-off with local goods and services.[58]

Indeed, globalization expands the range of choices available to the world's citizens. Through global trade and international exchange, citizens of developing countries get access to hot dogs, hamburgers (and increasingly tacos and salsa), while inhabitants of the United States get to know the cuisines of China, Japan, India, Thailand, and Greece, not to mention those of France and Italy. Africa, Asia, and Latin America receive exports of American rap and rock music, but Americans increasingly consume the fruits of regionally produced "world music." And the intermingling of music, cuisines, and other cultural artifacts through globalization juxtaposes cultural elements that would never have come into contact before, creating synergistic possibilities and entirely new cultural products. Rap may have entered the popular culture of Africa and Latin America, but there it was transformed and sent back to influence musical styles in its American birthplace.[59]

The marginalization of aboriginal cultures has been occurring since the invention of agriculture some 8,000 years ago.[60] What we are observing now is the final stage of a long process of global cultural change, social assimilation, and biological amalgamation. A properly structured liberal globalization, however, offers as many possibilities for the preservation of traditional cultural forms as it takes away. It gives aboriginal peoples and regional societies access to much larger markets to support the production of their artifacts for global consumption, preserving artistic skills and cultural knowledge that might otherwise have disappeared.[61] Global culture also offers tools not simply to preserve cultural products (text, tape, film, video) but introduces new elements (paints, tools, colors, fabrics) that offer new possibilities for elaboration and extension.

In the end, culture is not a museum piece to be preserved. Rather, human culture is a dynamic and constantly changing repertoire of words, concepts, behaviors, and artifacts that real people use to adapt to the natural, social, and material environments they encounter in their daily lives.[62] "Traditional" cultures are not now nor have they ever been constant and unchanging—though that is often the myth passed along about oral cultures. The objects, beliefs, and practices have always changed in the course of being transmitted across time and between people.[63] Attempts to seal off a particular people to preserve their culture ultimately denies them their full humanity. Rather than attempting to preserve aboriginal, local, and regional cultures as they happen to be at a moment in time, liberals should make sure that institutions exist to give them the time and space they need to adapt to globalism on their own terms, in ways that make sense given their own aspirations for material improvement and attachments to particular cultural products.

A fundamental problem with the left-wing vision is that an imagined idyllic past never existed, and that a rejection of industrial and postindustrial technologies would condemn billions of people to starvation and death. Ultimately, it is only through the application of scientific knowledge, the development of new technologies, and the extension of markets that the world has been able to clothe, feed, and house a population that grew from 2.5 to 6 billion during the last half of the twentieth century. The destruction of the first global market economy early in the twentieth century ushered in the bloodiest period in human history. Two world wars, dozens of regional conflicts, mass starvation through failed social planning, and a succession of genocides left tens of millions of corpses. A similar collapse of the global market economy in the early twenty-first century would lead to calamity on an even greater scale, with deaths in the hundreds of millions or perhaps billions.

Progressive Globalism

If human beings are to survive and prosper with freedom and dignity, therefore, they must circumvent the ideological fantasies of the right and the left and adopt a liberal approach that focuses on restructuring the global market economy and reforming its institutions. The problem is not so much globalization as it is the terms under which globalization has occurred for the past two decades; and these, in turn, have come about through concrete decisions made by real human beings, not a global deus ex machina. Globalization is neither an unstoppable juggernaut that must be accommodated nor a malicious conspiracy that must be confronted and destroyed. It is, rather, an ongoing social and economic program of action and institutions designed and implemented by human beings, one with great potential to increase the well-being of humanity, but also with significant potential to inflict damage and misery throughout the world. The choice of pathways is ours.

Constructing a global trading system that is both fair and efficient is difficult because of the constant possibility of cheating by national free riders. Absent sanctions to force compliance, it is always in the immediate self-interest of a nation to cheat, assuming that other nations follow the accepted rules of international competition. If one nation attempts to ride free on the compliant behavior of other countries that play by the rules, then the cheater will prosper. Obviously a country can maximize its earnings by selling its products freely to other nations while blocking the entry of foreign goods and services into its markets through tariffs, regulations, quotas, and other trade barriers. But if other nations do the same thing, the whole system breaks down and everyone loses.

Attempts to cheat in trading are likely because international commerce invariably affects special interests who then beseech national authorities to restrict the entry of competing products. American steel producers, for example, implore the U.S. government to apply a tariff on imported steel to make it more expensive than the steel they produce, forcing American consumers to buy their product. Elected representatives, of course, do not justify their actions by admitting that they are acting to protect the profits of inefficient companies whose officers made generous contributions to their reelection campaigns. On the contrary, they usually glorify protective policies by insisting that they were taken "to preserve American jobs." Of course the tariff probably cost jobs in some other industrial sector, where firms were forced to pay more for steel, thus requiring them to shed workers to maintain profitability. It also ignores the interests of consumers who end up paying higher prices for the goods they purchase.

To minimize cheating and preserve the integrity of the trading regime, the WTO was created to adjudicate trade disputes, decide whether a policy constitutes an unlawful barrier to trade, and to apply sanctions if the policy is not changed. Suppose, for example, that the U.S. government levies a tariff on foreign steel imports. Under WTO rules, governments of countries that contain competing steel firms may lodge a complaint, alleging that the United States is in violation of the agreed-upon rules of trade. Efforts are first made by WTO officials to mediate the disagreement, but if these fail, then the complaint is referred to a dispute panel made up of experts in trade and international law. This panel hears arguments on both sides and then issues a decision, which goes to member countries for ratification.[64] Although by international agreement, ratification must be unanimous, approval of the settlement is usually pro forma.

In this example, once the ruling has been confirmed, the United States would still retain the ultimate decision-making authority, however.[65] U.S. officials could decide to alter tariff policies to come into conformity with the WTO ruling, pay a fine to the WTO, offer compensation to the foreign producers, accept equivalent foreign retaliation against U.S. products, or, in the final analysis, it could withdraw from the General Agreement on Tariffs and Trade and leave the WTO entirely. To preserve the trading system and to ensure continued access to global markets in the future, however, most countries accede to the WTO, though sometimes they elect to pay fines, compensation, or tolerate counter-tariffs.

Because politicians in trading states always come under pressure to protect special interests, WTO dispute panels are specifically designed to be insulated from political pressure.[66] Their proceedings are secret, and adjudication is undertaken by unelected international civil servants, in the same way that courts are insulated from political pressures by having juries deliberate in secret in trials that are supervised by judges who are appointed for life. By insulating dispute resolution from political lobbying, and by giving politicians a villain to blame for a negative decision, the WTO is intended to prevent free riding and preserve the integrity of the trading system as a whole.

Thus, if one wishes to reform the global system to make it "fairer" and to redistribute economic outcomes, the place to focus attention is the body of rules that defines the rights, obligations, and terms of international exchanges—the set of rules and regulations by which dispute panel judges adjudicate trade disputes. Opening up the process of dispute resolution to greater scrutiny or making members of dispute panels accountable to national governments—as critics of free trade such as Ralph Nader advocate—will not solve the problem.[67] These actions will only compromise the global system of trade. To the extent that dispute panels decide whether nations have violated the rules of international change, it is the rules that must be changed to effect a different outcome.

Although the adjudication of tariff disputes may be contentious, they are much less controversial and easier to resolve than disputes over nontariff barriers—regulations that govern how products are produced rather how much they cost or what they contain—*process regulations* as opposed to product regulations.[68] The adjudication of nontariff barriers is problematic because this is where international trade intersects with a nation's social compact—the agreement between a government and its citizens to uphold environmental and labor standards and to protect public health.[69]

A nation's social compact, for example, may ban tuna caught by certain environmentally hazardous methods, prohibit drugs manufactured using certain procedures deemed risky to public health, or forbid the manufacture of products using convict labor. To date, in conflicts between domestic social standards and free trade, WTO and GATT dispute panels have tended to favor the interests of trade over others; but this need not be the case, and the balance has shifted in recent years in response to pressure from environmental, labor, and human rights advocates and the anti-globalization movement. To a greater extent than many critics realize, the real task facing reformers is one of making multilateral institutions such as the WTO comply more fully with their own charters rather than adding new strictures to their missions.[70]

Article XX of the General Agreement on Tariffs and Trade, for example, very clearly allows nations to restrict the importation of goods and services for environmental, moral, or health reasons. It states that "nothing in this Agreement shall be construed to prevent the adoption or enforcement by any contracting party of measures: (a) necessary to protect public morals; (b) necessary to protect human, animal or plant life or health . . . (d) relating to the conservation of exhaustible natural resources."[71] A clarifying declaration issued by WTO ministers in Doha, Qatar, in November of 2001 reaffirmed this principle: "[W]e recognize that under WTO rules no country should be prevented from taking measures for the protection of human, animal, or plant life or health or of the environment."[72]

The key to a regulation's acceptability before the WTO is that it apply *equally* to foreign and domestic producers. The United States may ban imports of tuna caught using certain methods as long it also prohibits domestic producers from using the same methods. This requirement is known as the principle of *equivalency*.[73] As explained by the WTO itself, "[Y]ou cannot be lenient with your own producers and at the same time be strict with foreign goods and services."[74] If such discrimination were allowed, countries would be free to erect a variety of nontariff barriers to international trade—restricting the importation of foreign goods by imposing burdensome requirements that are not applied to domestic products—and so unravel the delicate system of international exchange.

Despite this seemingly forthright declaration of principle by the WTO charter and the organization's official propaganda, dispute panels, being dominated by trade specialists and lawyers rather than environmentalists or labor representatives, have tended to decide cases against environmental and labor regulations and in favor of free trade. However, in the wake of the demonstrations in Seattle and subsequent political pressures, dispute panels have increasingly relented and allowed social regulations to stand, declaring them *not*, in fact, to constitute violations of international free trade rules.[75]

Thus, the WTO *can* be induced to change and reflect a wider array of interests in regulating the world economy. For liberals, the political program with respect to reforming global trade is clear. First, political pressure must be applied to ensure that dispute panels honor the WTO charter with respect to environmental regulations.[76] Second, efforts must be made to build fair labor regulations into the structure of the WTO by bringing it into closer cooperation with the International Labor Organization and by adopting the latter's recommended international standards, which include freedom of association and the right to collective bargaining; the elimination of forced or compulsory labor; the abolition of child labor; and the elimination of discrimination in employment and remuneration.[77] Third, the WTO as a whole must be held accountable to elected representatives and should be supervised through regular meetings by heads of government rather than unelected secretaries of trade or commerce.[78] Finally, an important step toward democratization is the elimination of the requirement of unanimous consent among member nations for the adoption of trade policies, which amounts not to a democracy but a veto system, and replace it instead with approval by a super-majority of two-thirds of all members.[79]

These reforms will not come easily and they will *require* U.S. leadership. But the United States alone is in a position to push the global market toward a more balanced structure that improves transparency and accountability and gives appropriate weight to labor protections, environmental concerns, and human rights. The United States was successful in foisting the Washington Consensus on the rest of the world because it controlled something that other nation's wanted—access to investment capital from the World Bank and private lenders. Because of the U.S. Treasury's disproportionate influence with the IMF, governments around the world were forced to dance to its tune.

When it comes to issues such as labor rights and environmental protections, the United States also controls access to a prize resource: the world's largest and most open consumer market. In a very real way, the U.S. economy serves as the world's "market of last resort," giving American political leaders a unique bargaining chip in global negotiations. No nation can realistically expect a rise to global economic prominence without access to the U.S. consumer market. It holds the key to most nations' balance of payments. When China has a trade deficit with Japan, for example, it generally does not finance the gap by selling products in Japan's heavily regulated and substantially closed economy, but by selling products in the United States to earn U.S. dollars to pay off the Japanese. The hegemony of the U.S. market allows the American president to speak softly in international negotiations but to wield a very big stick. Especially if the United States can form common cause with the European Union to strengthen environmental and labor protections, it will then be difficult, if not impossible, for the rest of the world to resist demands for reform.[80]

In his recent book, Joseph Stiglitz calls for similar structural reforms at the IMF and the World Bank. As he explicitly argues, "[W]hen there are externalities—when the actions of individuals have effects on others for which they neither pay nor are compensated—the market will typically result in the overproduction of some goods and the underproduction of others. Markets cannot be relied upon to produce goods that are essentially public in nature . . . and for a variety of reasons, markets are often not self-regulating."[81] To solve these problems, he calls for changing the governance of the IMF so that finance ministers are not the only ones heard and for an opening up of the internal procedures of the IMF to public scrutiny and transparency. He believes that ultimately such structural reforms will produce something more important, a change in the mindset of international institutions and the people who run them, prompting them to care about the environment and to consider the needs of the poor as well as the privileged. I wholeheartedly endorse Stiglitz's view that "promoting democracy and fair trade are necessary if the potential benefits of globalization are to be achieved."[82]

CHAPTER 6

Liberalism and Its Discontents

The foregoing chapters outline a liberal agenda intended to create and sustain a just political economy for the twenty-first century. Rather than concentrating economic and political power within a single bureaucratic structure and letting privileged officials make decisions on behalf of the people, it recognizes the market as the economic system that is not only most efficient but also most consistent with individual freedom and democracy. In a liberal society, the state acts on behalf of citizens to create markets that operate in the public interest. Markets rather than bureaucrats make most decisions about the production, consumption, and allocation of resources.

Rather than seeing markets as inevitable states of nature, however, liberals recognize them as human creations. By building competitive arenas, defining rules of play, and specifying media of exchange, governments necessarily regulate competition and constrain economic outcomes. In a democracy, it is the duty of citizens to understand markets and to monitor their performance to make sure that they continue to function in society's best interests. Citizens have a right to demand transparency about how markets work in practice and to obtain information about how, when, and where decisions are made by political actors to determine their operation. The public must assure itself that the process of market construction is not hijacked by a narrow conspiracy of owners and producers who skew it toward their selfish interests.

In any society, there are always a wide variety of possible markets and an infinite number of ways to structure each one. In a liberal society, the choice among alternative market structures is made openly and democratically, with full and accurate information. Having created the social, economic, and cultural institutions to support markets, citizens can then rely on their dynamism to create wealth and advance the material interests of society.

Always, however, a crucial input is human capacity, the sum total of individual capacities among a market's participants, and these generally must be cultivated with state assistance. Rather than viewing spending on health and education as frivolous, liberals view such expenditures as crucial *investments* that are *required* for future economic growth. Because the foundations of economic progress have shifted from land, labor, and capital to knowledge and information, societal resources devoted to science, technology, health, and education ultimately pay for themselves in the form of higher rates of economic growth and lower rates of social pathology.

A properly structured liberal society will be successful at creating wealth and distributing it widely, though not necessarily evenly. Because growth in a market economy has its ups and downs, liberal governments must protect citizens against market failures. Governments must also protect citizens from negative consequences stemming from the creative destruction of social institutions that inevitably accompanies growth under capitalism. In return for this protection, citizens are expected to engage, with suitable public support, in a lifelong process of learning, skill acquisition, and human capital formation. Because their material well-being is not tied to a particular industrial regime, citizens will not be threatened by institutional change and should not oppose innovation that promotes growth and structural change. Government must ensure that every citizen has an equal opportunity to acquire human capital and to apply it in creating and consuming wealth within unbiased and fair markets.

Obviously, in a well-functioning liberal society, social structures and cultural values will be in a constant state of evolution, as new technologies and the accumulation of knowledge continuously restructure the social institutions and categories of thought used by human beings. Although a liberal political economy is capable of generating great wealth and maximizing the material well-being of citizens, social change always threatens some people. Liberalism inevitably has its discontents, and it is important for liberals to understand them.

The discontents, of course, will always include the privileged few who, despite negligible personal effort and little individual initiative, derive a disproportionate share of power and wealth from existing social and economic arrangements. The discontents, however, also include people who subscribe to a worldview of unchanging values, eternal truths, and static (typically unequal) social relationships. Also among the discontents are those who resist extending full freedom and equality to racial and ethnic minorities; and more universally, they include men who are threatened by the cultivation of female capabilities, autonomy, and freedom.

The Fundamentalist Reaction

Those discontented with liberalism and its sequela have found their most potent expression in religious fundamentalism. Although originally thought to be a survival from an earlier period of faith and observance, fundamentalism is now recognized as a quintessentially modern phenomenon "with historical antecedents but no ideological precursors."[1] According to the leading scholars of fundamentalist movements, they are "specific religious phenomena that have emerged in the twentieth century, particularly in the wake of the success of modernization and secularization." They constitute "historical counterattacks mounted from those threatened religious traditions, seeking to hold ground against this spreading secular 'contamination,' and even to regain ground by taking advantage of the weaknesses of modernization."[2]

In the late 1980s, the American Academy of Arts and Sciences empaneled a group of investigators to undertake a systematic study of fundamentalist movements worldwide. Under the leadership of Professor Martin E. Marty of the University of Chicago and Professor R. Scott Appleby of the University of Notre Dame,

a diverse team of scholars joined together to create "The Fundamentalisms Project." Over the course of fifteen years and five
published volumes, they methodically investigated, catalogued,
and compared the attributes of fundamentalist movements among
Catholics, Protestants, Jews, Sunni and Shia Muslims, Hindus,
Sikhs, and Buddhists, seeking to identify and label the ideological
and organizational elements that were common to all of them.[3]

This painstaking work uncovered four broad ideological cur-
rents undergirding the world's fundamentalisms. The first is *se-
lectivity*: fundamentalists are, in fact, quite choosey about *which*
concepts and practices they adopt from religious tradition.[4] They
"select carefully from among the plethora of doctrines, practices,
and interpretations available in the tradition. However, the privileged past is defined with a keen eye on the particular challenges
of the present and the opportunities of the future. . . . Fundamentalists do not simply reaffirm the old doctrines; they subtly lift
them from their original context, embellish and institutionalize
them, and employ them as ideological weapons against a hostile
world."[5]

Fundamentalists likewise carefully select what they reject from
the modern, secular world. "In the strategies and methods these
leaders adopt in remaking the world, fundamentalists demonstrate a closer affinity to modernism that to traditionalism. . . .
They wish to best modernists at their own game . . . , [for] cou-
pled with this envy and resentment of modernity is a shrewd exploitation of its processes and instrumentalities. . . . Not only
[do] fundamentalists draw upon modern organization methods
and structures; they also . . . [take] advantage of the openness of
secular democracies."[6]

A second notable characteristic of fundamentalism is its
Manichean moralism, viewing the world as starkly divided between the forces of right and wrong, light and dark, good and evil,
God and the Devil.[7] Fundamentalists repudiate "secular-scientific
notions of progress and gradual historical evolution . . . [and] see
themselves as actors in an eschatological drama unfolding in the
mind of God and directing human history."[8] As a result, fundamentalists tend to "name, dramatize, and even mythologize their

enemies, situating the oppressive dictators or Westernized elites or compromising coreligionists within the same eschatological or mythic structure in which they see themselves."[9]

The third ideological trait of fundamentalist thought is *absolutism*. Even though fundamentalists carefully choose only some aspects of religious tradition to revere, they nonetheless insist on the absolute inerrancy of what they do select. "They steadfastly oppose hermeneutical methods developed by secularized philosophers or critics . . . [that] are not tied to sacred texts and traditions. This is not to say that fundamentalist interpretation itself is monolithic, only that it does not submit to the canons of critical rationality. Instead . . . fundamentalists employ their own distinctive strategies of interpretation, including 'hardened' and 'updated' traditional approaches designed in part to reify and preserve the absolutist character of the scared text or tradition."[10] To the outside world their dogmas often seem "intentionally scandalous" because they deliberately "violate the canons of the post-Enlightenment secular rationality that has characterized Western thought over the course of the past three centuries."[11]

The last ideological tenet of fundamentalism is *millenialism*, or the belief that history is moving toward a miraculous culmination, such as the coming of a messiah, the day of judgment, an Armageddon, or the end of days.[12]

> Fundamentalists seek to replace existing structures with a comprehensive system emanating from religious principles and embracing law, polity, society, economy, and culture.[13] [. . .] Religious identity . . . becomes the exclusive and absolute basis for a re-created political and social order that is oriented toward the future rather than the past. . . . Fundamentalists seek to remake the world in service of a dual commitment to the unfolding eschatological drama (by returning all things in submission to the divine) and to self-preservation (by neutralizing the threatening "Other").[14]

These ideological foundations are, in turn, associated with specific organizational features. *Sharp social boundaries* are drawn between an *elect membership* of adherents, and dividing lines are reinforced by *behavioral requirements* that prescribe certain clothing and practices and forbid others. These strictures are typically defined and breaches punished by a *centralized authoritarian organization*.[15] Not surprisingly, "[I]n the process of interpreting the tradition, evaluating modernity, and selectively retrieving salient elements of both, *charismatic and authoritarian male leaders* play a central role" (emphasis in the original).[16]

The fundamentalist impulse is clearly visible in numerous political-religious insurgencies throughout the world. Since September 11, considerable attention in the West has focused on Islamic fundamentalism. Al-Qaeda, of course, is a confederation of terrorist cells bound together by a radical Muslim ideology and committed to violence against what they see as corrupt leaders in the lands of Islam and their Western backers, notably the United States. Their goal is to force the economic and military withdrawal of the United States and its allies from Muslim territory, allowing fundamentalists to replace profane leaders, such as the House of Saud, and foreign interlopers, such as the Zionists in Palestine (and now the Americans in Iraq), with strict Islamic regimes.[17] Other prominent Muslim fundamentalist movements include the Islamic Brotherhood, Hammas, Hizbolah, the Taliban, and the Dakwah.[18]

Lesser known in the United States, but equally important in their own regions, are fundamentalist parties and movements associated with other religious traditions—the Hindu Bharatiya Janata Party of India,[19] the National Religious Party and the Block of the Faithful in Israel,[20] and the Buddhist Dharma Yuddhaya in Sri Lanka.[21] Wherever and whenever they occur, fundamentalist movements share a common critique of rational, secular, materialist society and seek to replace it with an absolutist, authoritarian regime based on religious laws divined and interpreted by an elite of male religious figures.

Varieties of American Fundamentalism

Fundamentalism arose in the nineteenth century as a response to the manifold social, economic, and cultural transformations introduced by the industrial revolution. As the pace of change accelerated over the course of the twentieth century, the size, power, and appeal of fundamentalist ideologies only grew, defying the predictions of secular philosophers ranging from Karl Marx to John Stuart Mill. Despite Nietzsche's famous dictum, God did not die. Religion did not wither away but transformed itself into a significant force that today offers a powerful challenge to liberalism.

Although the impulse to reject change and its accompanying moral relativism is most prominently expressed in religious terms, the fear and distrust of liberalism and the desire to return to "fundamentals" goes much deeper in the human psyche and is evident in other movements as well. In the United States, discontent with liberalism has coalesced around five broad ideological movements that adopt different fundamentals to venerate and specify somewhat different political goals, but that share a common antipathy, and often a visceral hatred, toward the liberal achievements of the twentieth century.

Theocrats

The most obvious of liberalism's discontents are the *theocrats*, who believe that America was founded as a Christian nation, that it enjoys a special dispensation from God under Jesus, and that American society and its institutions have been illegitimately taken over by godless heathens. It is therefore the duty of theocrats to reclaim state, local, and federal governments from the wicked Other in order to force a sinful American public back toward a fundamentalist version of Christian morality. Such morality comprises a deference to male authority, a subordinate status for women, patriarchal absolutism, and a puritanical attitude toward sex, which is typified by a hostility toward contraception, abortion, nonmarital intercourse, and, of course, homosexuality. These sexual strictures, however, are often honored more in the breach than in practice (as evidenced by the well-known infidelities, divorces, and out-of-wedlock children associated with many conservative figures).

American theocrats include evangelical ministers such as Pat Robertson, Jerry Falwell, and Donald Wildmon, along with paid skilled political operatives such as Ralph Reed (of the Christian Coalition), Gary Bauer (of the Family Research Council), and Phyllis Schlafly (of the Eagle Forum). At this late date, America's theocrats also include many people in government.[22] President George W. Bush believes he was divinely chosen for office, confiding to a Texas evangelist during the 2000 campaign that "I feel like God wants me to run for President."[23] Likewise, Supreme Court Justice Antonin Scalia holds that "government derives its moral authority from God" and that "the reaction of people of faith to the tendency of democracy to obscure the divine authority behind government should not be resignation to it, but the resolution to combat it as effectively as possible;"[24] and Representative Tom Delay (R., Texas) says his mission in government is to promote a "biblical worldview" and that he sought to impeach President Bill Clinton because he did not share that view.[25]

In recognition for his labors in the vineyards of the Lord, Representative Delay in 2002 was presented with the "Distinguished Christian Statesman Award" by the Center for Christian Statesmanship, whose mission is "to help reestablish the principles and practices of Christian statesmanship so prevalent at the birth of our nation . . . [and call] on our leaders to embrace America's heritage of Christian statesmanship and rebuild our nation's foundation for liberty."[26] Other recipients include John Ashcroft (then a Republican senator from Missouri and through 2004 U.S. Attorney General), representatives Dick Armey (R., Texas) and J. C. Watts (R., Oklahoma), along with senators Dan Coats (R., Indiana) and Sam Brownback (R., Kansas).[27]

According to investigations by journalist Jeffrey Sharlet, the planned, systematic infiltration of American government by theocrats goes back to1935 when a pious Norwegian immigrant in Seattle named Abraham Vereide decided that only Jesus could redeem the world from the twin threats of godless socialism and atheist communism and free America from the grip of radical labor unions allied with Roosevelt's New Deal.[28] He shared this vision with a group of business leaders at a weekly prayer breakfast, and with their support he promoted the candidacy of a city councilman who was willing to serve as God's instrument, getting him elected mayor of Seattle and then governor of the state of Washington. Emboldened by his success in the Northwest, in 1941 Vereide went to Washington, D.C., and began an effort to institutionalize Christianity at the highest levels of government.

The organization he began survives today as a little-known but powerful network of activist Christians located in and around the nation's capital. Known to members simply as "the Family," it includes people inside and outside of government who are, according to the current director's son, "here to learn to rule the world." Although the Family maintains a computerized list of associates, it collects no dues, issues no identification, has no office, and tells its members not to speak publicly about its activities. The Family's only visible event is the National Prayer Breakfast, which it has sponsored annually since 1953. Every February it convenes 3,000 people who pay $425 each to hear prominent politicians testify to their faith in Jesus and share their vision of a Christian America (for a total take of $1.275 million).[29]

At the 1990 Prayer Breakfast, President George H. W. Bush paid tribute to the organization's leader, Doug Coe, calling him "an ambassador of faith" and commended him for his "quiet diplomacy, I wouldn't say secret diplomacy."[30] The organization has its headquarters in a mansion in Arlington, Virginia, and it owns several other properties around the Washington metropolitan area, including a D.C. townhouse that serves as a dormitory and spiritual center for affiliates. Members of Congress who have resided in the townhouse include at least six representatives and one senator, and known associates of the Family include six other senators and five representatives,[31] all sharing a common desire to use the federal government to propagate conservative Christianity in the United States. Insofar as is politically possible, they seek to make the United States into a fundamentalist theocracy, and to date the theocrats have achieved remarkable success, occupying not only the White House (President Bush) but key positions in the executive branch (Attorney General Ashcroft), Congress (Representative DeLay, Senator Coats), and the Supreme Court (Justice Antonin Scalia).

Market Fundamentalists

The ideological roads traveled by conservatives generally lead back to the University of Chicago and to three varieties of Chicago Boys, each characterized by a distinctive brand of fundamentalism. The first and best known are the *market fundamentalists*, people who assume that markets exist by divine creation and proclaim an unshakeable faith in their miraculous powers to create material wealth and produce the greatest welfare for the greatest number—if only government can stay out of the way.[32] In their version of Manichean dualism, markets are the work of God and the angels, whereas governments represent the wages of sin and the devil, a parasitic demon against which true believers must constantly be on guard lest the forces of darkness triumph and humans descend into a collectivist hell.

The great prophet of market fundamentalism is Milton Friedman, formerly professor at the University of Chicago and lately high priest at capitalism's great temple—the Hoover Institution. He believes that governmental actions taken to accomplish any economic goal besides regulating the money supply constitute an unwarranted "intervention" in the "free market."[33] According to the gospel of Saint Milton, "[T]he government solution to a problem is usually as bad as the problem." Underscoring the association in his mind between government and forces of hades, he says that "hell hath no fury like a bureaucrat scorned."[34] The sacred canon of market fundamentalism, of course, was used to justify the Washington Consensus of the 1990s, a package of laissez-faire policies that were blindly and destructively imposed on countries by apostles at the IMF.[35]

Constitutional Fundamentalists

Closely associated with the market fundamentalists are *constitutional fundamentalists*, who follow the teachings of Professor Richard Epstein of the University of Chicago Law School.[36] In his gospel, the American legal system has a sacred obligation to promote economic efficiency, a creed that has been codified as the "law and economics" movement. He is perhaps best known for his sweeping interpretation of the "takings clause" of the Fifth Amendment to the U.S. Constitution (which states that private property shall not be taken for public use without fair compensation), extending it to argue "that most regulations, from zoning to pollution controls and nearly all federal transfer payments such as welfare, were 'takings' of someone else's property."[37] Accepting this premise, of course, invalidates the legal framework for most of the New Deal, Great Society, and the Civil Rights Era. Richard Posner, Epstein's colleague at the University of Chicago, summarizes the tenets of law and economics in his book *Economic Analysis of Law*, first published in 1972, which has become a kind of Holy Grail for the movement.[38]

Most of Reagan's and Bush's appointees to federal judgeships either went to the University of Chicago Law School or are unabashed followers of the law and economics movement, including Posner himself, along with Antonin Scalia, Robert Bork, Clarence Thomas, Danny J. Boggs, Frank Easterbrook, Bernard Siegan, Ralph Winter, and others.[39] Younger, less established acolytes tended to go to the upper echelons of the Department of Justice in Republican administrations. As the journalist Nina J. Easton has pointed out, "[L]ike the Religious Right, these young lawyers, too, were fundamentalists. But theirs was a fundamentalism of law, applied not to the Bible . . . but to the U.S. Constitution, a document they imbued with a patriotic air of sanctity."[40]

In 1982, students at the University of Chicago joined with like-minded fellows at other institutions, and after receiving support from prominent conservatives and professors, they founded the Federalist Society for Law and Public Policy Studies, which presently has an annual budget of $3 million and a membership of 25,000 practicing lawyers and 5,000 law students.[41] According to its website, the Federalist Society is "dedicated to reforming the current legal order" and is "founded on the principles that the state exists to preserve freedom, that the separation of governmental powers is central to our Constitution, and that it is emphatically the province and duty of the judiciary to say what the law is, not what it should be."[42]

Federalists take the Constitution as holy text, not to be modified or expanded, and to be applied according to the "original" intent of the divine prophets who wrote it, explicitly rejecting the view that the U.S. Constitution is a living document that must be amended and reinterpreted as society changes.[43] The fact that a goodly number of the Constitution's framers were slave holders whose primary motivation was to find a way to accommodate the institution of chattel servitude in a republic otherwise dedicated to personal liberty does not seem to trouble the fundamentalists; nor does the fact that the system of states' rights they devised was conceived mainly as a way to allow the systematic suppression and subordination of African Americans in the South.

Platonic Fundamentalists

Finally, the last of the Chicago Boys (and they *are* overwhelmingly male) are the *Platonic fundamentalists,* who trace their origins to the University of Chicago's Committee on Social Thought, a strange brew of classical philosophy and modern politics grounded in the teachings of Professor Leo Strauss, a faculty member of the committee from 1949 to 1967.[44] As noted by Nina Easton, "Strauss believed that the writings passed down by classical philosophers contained timeless truths that could only be unlocked with rigorous and imaginative reading of their works."[45] He also thought, however, that "the great classical thinkers knew, as he knew, that truth was dangerous to society and should not be circulated. Truth should only be accessible to a democratic aristocracy, one that by intellectual ability, interest, and character had devoted itself to the question for true knowledge."[46] In this sense, Straussian teachings represent a dogma of "radical elitism."

Strauss and the Committee on Social Thought labored mostly in obscurity until 1988, when *The Closing of the American Mind* became a bestseller.[47] Its author, Alan Bloom, was then a professor on the Committee on Social Thought and a longtime follower of Strauss. His book offered an extended albeit disjointed diatribe against the radicalism of the 1960s and the "political correctness" of the 1980s, decrying the shift of popular values away from classic notions of restraint, sacrifice, duty, and respect. As elitists, however, Straussians put little stock in religion for its own sake. Rather, they see it as important for cultivating appropriate values among the masses. To them, secularism is less a crisis of faith than one of virtue, and it was Straussians who led the charge in the "culture wars" of the 1990s, the rear-guard action mounted by conservatives during their years in the political wilderness of the Clinton administration.[48]

While William J. Bennett wrote popular tracts such as *The Book of Virtues* and *The Children's Book of Virtues* to provide moral instruction to the masses grounded in traditional Christian precepts, Irving Kristol (editor of *Commentary*), his wife Gertrude Himmelfarb (the author of *The De-Moralization of Society*), and their son William Kristol (editor of the *Weekly Standard*) produced more erudite prose for the conservative intelligentsia, many of them Jewish.[49] The younger Kristol has been particularly influential in spreading the Straussian message, serving as Chief of Staff to Secretary of Education William Bennett in the Reagan administration, principal advisor to Dan Quayle in the first Bush administration, and presently as a prominent editor and conservative pundit.

Straussian precepts achieved full flower in the neoconservative movement, recently described in an article by Irving Kristol published in the *Weekly Standard*. Kristol *père* states that the goal of neoconservatism is "to convert the Republican party, and American conservatism in general, against their respective wills, into a new kind of conservative politics . . . [that is] distinctly American. . . . Neoconservatism is the first variant of American conservatism in the past century that is in the 'American grain.'"[50] The pillars of neoconservative ideology are low taxes, limited government, the restoration of virtue, and a muscular foreign policy that derogates multilateral institutions and seeks to project U.S. power throughout the world in the service of American ideals (as defined by the neoconservatives, of course).

According to Kristol, "[T]he favorite neoconservative text on foreign affairs, thanks to professor Leo Strauss of Chicago . . . is

Thucydides on *The Peloponnesian War*."[51] Given that the United States is the only superpower, Kristol argues that "with power come responsibilities, whether sought or not, whether welcome or not. And it is a fact that if you have the kind of power we now have, either you will find opportunities to use it, or the world will discover them for you."[52] It is thus very much a Straussian perspective that underlies the militant, unilateralist foreign policy of George W. Bush.[53]

Although neoconservatism achieved its fullest expression after September 11, its rationale was laid out years earlier in a letter to President Clinton published in the *Washington Times* on January 26, 1998, and signed by eighteen prominent neoconservatives, including those who would go on to become architects of the Iraqi invasion and the Bush administration's war on terror: Elliot Abrams (member of the National Security Council), Richard Armitage (Deputy Secretary of State), John Bolton (Undersecretary of State), Richard Pearle (member and former chair of the Defense Policy Board), Peter Rodman (Assistant Secretary of Defense), Donald Rumsfeld (Secretary of Defense), and Paul Wolfowitz (Deputy Secretary of Defense).[54]

Although rationalized by the events of September 11, the plan for invading Iraq was in fact hatched in 1997 at a conservative Washington think tank known as the Project for the New American Century, an organization established "to make the case and rally support for American global leadership." It is the duty of the United States, the organization's adherents argue, "to shape a new century favorable to American principles and interests." It is therefore essential "to strengthen our ties to democratic allies and to challenge regimes hostile to our interests and values; . . . to promote the cause of political and economic freedom abroad; [and] . . . to accept responsibility for America's unique role in preserving and extending an international order friendly to our security, our prosperity, and our principles."[55]

The seeds for war were sown long before Bush came to power and discovered what he viewed as the grave threat posed by the regime of Saddam Hussein. The sad events of 9/11 only provided political cover for neoconservatives to implement a military intervention they had hoped to undertake long before they assumed office. As always, when people who are utterly convinced of their own virtue acquire vast military power, people die.

Libertarians

Coordinating much of the right-wing movement over the past decade has been a loosely knit group of *libertarians*, who worship at the altar of liberty and put the rights of the individual above all others. Possessed of a deep hatred of taxes and government, they seek to bring down the federal system created under the New Deal and Great Society, shrinking the size of the state, eliminating all taxes on wealth and income, and reducing other assessments to the barest minimum. They see no need for government to provide anything beyond public security and national defense.

The "field marshal" of the libertarian movement is Grover Norquist, who heads an antitax, antigovernment lobbying group known as Americans for Tax Reform.[56] He wields enormous power and influence in Washington. Every Wednesday he convenes a meeting of conservative leaders to discuss political strategy at which he browbeats those present into moving forward with additional tax cuts, irrespective of the state of the economy or the size of the federal deficit. Attendance at the meeting is mandatory, not voluntary, if one wishes to remain a player in Washington's conservative political circles.

Norquist's goal is, quite simply, to "de-fund the state" by reducing taxes and raising deficits to the point where further social spending will be impossible. As the journalist Robert Dreyfuss has noted, "[T]o Norquist, who loves being called a revolutionary, hardly an agency of government is not worth abolishing, from the Internal Revenue Service and the Food and Drug Administration to the Education Department and the National Endowment for the Arts."[57] In an interview broadcast on Pat Robertson's television show, *The 700 Club*, Norquist was candid about his long-term aspirations: "My goal is to cut government in half in twenty-five years."[58] Perhaps he was attempting to seem moderate to listeners of National Public Radio when he insisted that "I don't want to abolish government," but then he went on to say, "I simply want to reduce it to the size where I can drag it into the bathroom and drown it in the bathtub."[59]

Modern American libertarianism traces its roots to William F. Buckley, who in 1955 founded the conservative magazine the *National Review*, which he continues to edit; and in 1964 he joined with others to create the American Conservative Union, the nation's oldest conservative lobbying organization.[60] Although people of libertarian sentiment are mostly Republicans, there exists a separate political party for the purists. The Libertarian Party, founded in 1971 and operating in all fifty states, presently includes 500 office holders and in the 2002 elections fielded candidates in 255 of 435 elections for the House of Representatives. The party's goal is to "challenge the cult of the omnipotent state and defend the rights of the individual," and, like Professor Epstein, the party opposes "all government interference with private property, such as confiscation, nationalization, and eminent domain."[61]

Fellow Travelers

To a greater extent than most Americans realize, the coming to power of George W. Bush represents the culmination of a fundamentalist revolution in U.S. politics. The ideological interests that put Bush into the White House, and which now dominate his administration, represent a tenuous coalition of Christian theocrats and secular fundamentalists who worship the market (acolytes of Saint Milton), the constitution (federalists), classical texts (Straussians), or the ideal of unrestrained freedom (libertarians). In the administration of George W. Bush, there has been a little something for everyone in the coalition: Christians control social policy, Friedmanites run the economy, Straussians dominate in foreign and military affairs, and libertarians and federalists populate the Department of Justice and the federal courts.

Yet these true believers could not and did not win the elections of 2000 and 2002 by themselves, for even taken all together, the Friedmanites, Straussians, libertarians, and federalists comprise a rather small and rarefied group. Although fundamentalist Christians are larger in number and more plebeian in origin, they amount to no more than 20 percent of the electorate. The winning Republican coalition thus relied upon several fellow travelers who joined the revolution less for reasons of faith than for motives of self-interest and expediency.

Cronies

Essential to the success of the Republican party have been a cadre *crony capitalists* who have either sought to use the government and the resources it controls as a feeding trough, or to gain control of the federal regulatory apparatus to rewrite the rules of competition in their favor.[62] The former category includes large multinational construction firms such as Bechtel and Halliburton, along with defense contractors such as Raytheon and General Dynamics, which make their living from federal contracts and spending. The latter category includes energy firms such as Enron, communications giants such as Worldcom, media conglomerates such as Rupert Murdoch's News Corporation and Clear Channel Communications, as well as a host of lesser-known firms in extractive industries such as coal, oil, and natural gas, which benefit greatly from deregulation.

A record $3 billion was spent on U.S. elections in the year 2000 cycle.[63] Nearly all of this money came from a very small group of wealthy donors and corporate interests. In the 2002 elections, for example, less than one-tenth of 1 percent of all Americans accounted for 83 percent of all campaign contributions.[64] Among donors to the congressional elections of 1996, 20 percent had incomes of $500,000 or greater; 26 percent had incomes from $250,000 to $500,000; and 35 percent had incomes between $100,000 and $250,000. In contrast, only 5 percent had incomes under $50,000 in a year when the median income was around $35,000.[65] The Bush campaign, in

particular, cultivated a wealthy elite of 242 large donors who collectively became known as "the Pioneers," each of whom raised at
least $100,000 in campaign donations; another 310 individuals
participated in the pioneer network but did not reach the
$100,000 threshold.[66]

It is difficult to believe that hard-nosed businessmen would be
willing to invest such large sums in a political campaign without
anticipating some return on their investments. The most obvious
return came in the form of a huge reduction in the amount and
share of taxes paid by the richest 1 percent of the population. The
tax cut was accompanied by a deliberate redistribution of IRS auditing efforts away from the wealthy and toward the poor. Whereas
11.4 percent of taxpayers reporting income over $100,000 were au-
dited in 1988, only 1.2 percent of such people were audited in 1999.
In contrast, the percentage of taxpayers with incomes under
$25,000 who were audited *rose* slightly, going from 1.0 to 1.4 per-
cent over the same period.[67]

But the foregoing actions represent only a general payoff to
the wealthy and affluent. More specific payoffs accrued to particular high rollers in the election sweepstakes, and they were even
more impressive. In 2003 the public lobbying group Common
Cause published a study that described the campaign contributions made by fourteen Bush Pioneers and the favors they received in return.[68] The results of that study are summarized in
table 1. As can be seen, large donors reaped a bonanza of special
favors from Republicans once the latter acquired power. The
array of government concessions included leases to federal
property, favorable terms for the exploitation of federal resources, the easing of EPA restrictions, influence and sometimes
outright control over industry regulators, targeted tax breaks,
subsidies for production, and access to lucrative no-bid government contracts. Although wealthy interests are fond of lecturing
the poor about the virtues of self-sufficiency and independence,
they are as fond as anyone of feeding from the federal trough.

The quintessential example of crony capitalism is the Carlyle
Group, a seventeen-billion-dollar private equity firm made up of
"300 investment professionals working in offices in 12 coun-

TABLE 1
Profile of Money Raised and Favors Received by Fourteen "Bush Pioneers" from the 2000 Elections

Name	Firm or Interest	Amount Raised	Favor Received
Anthony Alexander	First Energy Corp	$108,000	Exemptions from EPA regulations
Charles Cawley	MBNA Corp	$396,000	Support for overhaul of bankruptcy laws
J. Nelson Fairbanks	U.S. Sugar Corp	$100,000+	Subsidies for sugar production
Wayne Berman	Flo-Sun	$104,000	Subsidies for sugar production
James Harless	International Industries	$250,000	Subsidies for "clean coal" technology
			Easing of air-water emission restrictions
Roger Hirl	Occidental Petroleum	$100,000+	Govt-funded security for oil operations in Colombia
Don Jordan	Reliant Energy	$114,000	Meeting with Dick Cheney's Energy Task Force
Kenneth Lay	Enron Corp	$308,000	Key role in shaping Bush energy policy
Thomas Loeffler	Loeffler, Jonas & Tuggey	$185,000	Access to Bush White House for Saudi clients of lobbying firm
Dennis Nixon	Bancshares Corp	$100,000+	Less prosecution of money-laundering networks
Tony Sanchez	Sanchez Oil & Gas	$100,000+	Support for energy tax breaks
Frederick Webber	Am. Chemistry Council	$206,000	Opposition to chemical security bill
			Easing of EPA security requirements

Source: Common Cause. 2003. *Prospecting for Access: How the Bush Pioneers Shaped Public Policy.* Washington, D.C.: Common Cause.

tries."[69] Established in 1987, it is one of the most powerful, well-connected, and secretive companies in the world and makes money by using its impressive personal connections to steer government spending around the globe to firms in which its members have invested.[70] Until recently it was chaired by Frank Carlucci (former Secretary of Defense) and it includes as board members former President George H. W. Bush, former Secretary of State James Baker, former Head of the Office of Management and Budget Richard Darman, former head of the Securities and Exchange Commission Arthur Leavitt, former British Prime Minister John Major, and, until September 11, 2001, several members of the Bin Laden family.

The ideological predisposition to privatize also provides Republicans with unique opportunities to combine business with pleasure in the realm of elections. By privatizing the tasks of running an election and turning them over to private firms controlled by conservative businessmen, Republicans have created new levers of power and new ways of controlling voter behavior. A good example is a firm known as ChoicePoint, "the leading provider of identification and credential verification services for business and government"[71] and the owner of a subsidiary known as Database Technologies (DBT). The board of ChoicePoint is filled with prominent Republican fundraisers, including, for example, former New York Mayor Rudy Giuliani's finance chief.[72] In 1999, the Florida Department of Elections, supervised by Secretary of State Katherine Harris in coordination with her boss, Governor Jeb Bush, awarded DBT a $2.3 million no-bid contract to "purge" voter rolls of unauthorized voters—specifically, convicted felons—in preparation for the 2000 election. Curiously, the firm that had previously held the contract for this work, which simply requires cross-referencing governmental databases, received a mere $5,700 for its services.[73] So there seems to have been a rich load of "gravy" in the contract for ChoicePoint stockholders—not a bad business!

In addition to enjoying good business, considerable political pleasure came to Republicans from the job that DBT accomplished during the 2000 elections. By skillful programming, DBT was able to purge from the voter list any *black* voter who might *conceivably* have been convicted of a felony, no matter how shaky the computerized evidence, but *not purging* a *white* voter unless a variety of more stringent criteria were met. Although DBT was required by contract to verify manually any decision to strike a voter from the list, the mandated verifications were never done. Indeed, Katherine Harris lied to the U.S. Commission on Civil Rights under oath by insisting that the terms of the contract stated that hand verification was up to county election supervisors and not the contractors.[74]

As a result of DBT's work, Secretary Harris removed 57,000 voters from the registration list, thus preventing them from voting in the year 2000. Some 54 percent of those on the list were minorities and thus likely Democratic voters; and at least 90 percent of the names included on the "scrub list" were *not*, in fact, felons and were inappropriately purged from the voter rolls and denied the right to vote. Later investigations showed that because of DBT's actions, another 40,000 voters were prevented from registering in the first place.[75] Given that George W. Bush officially won Florida by a few hundred votes to become president of the United States, it is absolutely clear that the business deal with ChoicePoint DBT cost Al Gore the presidency. A sweet business deal for Republicans indeed!

Neo-confederates

The foregoing episode of "Jim Crow in Cyberspace"[76] dovetails with the interests of a second group of fellow travelers who were also happy to join their fundamentalist friends in a jihad against liberalism: the *neo-confederates*, whose goal is to overturn the accomplishments of the civil rights era and to reimpose a system of racial subordination, not just in the South but throughout the United States. The rise of the neo-confederate movement coincides with the backlash against federal actions taken to enforce racial equality and the "southernization" of the Republican party.[77]

As is well known, following the defeat of the South in 1865, the Confederacy stubbornly refused to die. As described in chapter 2, during the years of Reconstruction (1865–75), former rebels engaged in a systematic campaign of civil disobedience, guerilla warfare, and violent terrorist actions until federal troops finally left and turned civil institutions back to the former slave holders, who promptly created a new system of racial subordination known as Jim Crow, which was then ratified by the U.S. Supreme Court in the infamous *Plessy* decision of 1896. This system prevailed throughout the South until the civil rights era, which renewed black enfranchisement to the point that some have it called the "Second Reconstruction."[78]

The restoration of white supremacy after 1875 was accompanied by an upsurge in Confederate patriotism. The United Daughters of the Confederacy was established in 1894 and the Sons of Confederate Veterans in 1896 to preserve the legacy of the Southern Cause and glorify its heroes.[79] The latter organization insists that "the preservation of liberty and freedom was the motivating factor in the South's decision to fight the Second American Revolution."[80] These organizations worked politely and publicly in civil society to legitimize the Jim Crow system, while the Ku Klux Klan (founded in 1866 by former Confederate General Nathan Bedford Forrest) employed violence, intimidation, and other less seemly means to enforce the color line.

These paleo-confederate organizations were eclipsed by the civil rights movement of the 1960s and 1970s; but beginning in the 1980s the United States began to experience a neo-confederate revival that not only restored the older Confederate organizations to new respectability but also led to the formation of brand new organizations that cultivated a membership and political agenda outside the South.[81] The Council of Conservative Citizens, for example, was organized in 1985 as the "true voice of the American right" (the initials CCC being a softer way of writing KKK). In its newsletter, the *Citizen's Informer* (circulation around 20,000), the CCC espouses an unabashed ideology of white supremacy, opposing all government-sponsored affirmative action programs and standing "against the tide of nonwhite, Third World immigrants swamping this country."[82]

Another neo-confederate group, the League of the South, was founded in 1984 and currently has around 8,000 members seeking "to advance the cultural, social, economic, and political wellbeing and independence of the southern people by all honourable [sic] means."[83] The Jefferson Davis society was established more recently, in 1994, "to preserve the memory and protect the honor of Jefferson Davis, president of the Confederate States of America" so that his name will "inspire the hearts of young and old with patriotic thoughts, deeds of heroism, noble endurance, and Christian kindness, and will shine in the firmament of history to all generations to come."[84] One has to wonder why, in the mid-1990s, it became politically acceptable to honor a treasonous slave holder who took up arms against his own country and directed an armed rebellion that took the lives of at least 600,000 Americans in what still stands as the nation's most lethal war.

The leading outlet for the expression of neo-confederate ideology is the magazine *Southern Partisan*, founded in 1979 and published quarterly with a circulation of nearly 10,000.[85] Patrick Buchanan has been a frequent columnist, and numerous conservative politicians and right-wing activists have given interviews to its correspondents, including Representative Dick Armey (R., Texas) and senators John Ashcroft (R., Missouri), Thad Cochran (R., Mississippi), Phil Gramm (R., Texas), Jesse Helms (R., North Carolina), and Trent Lott (R., Mississippi), along with prominent right-wing activists such as Pat Robertson, Jerry Falwell, and Phyllis Schlafly.

In an interview with *Southern Partisan* published in 1984, for example, Senator Trent Lott expressed his admiration for the president of the Confederacy, stating that "a lot of the fundamental principles that Jefferson Davis believed in are very important to people across the country, and they apply to the Republican Party." In an irony that seemed to escape him, he then went on to link the Party of Lincoln to the ideals of the Confederacy: "The platform we had in Dallas, the 1984 Republican platform, all the ideas we supported there . . . are things that Jefferson Davis and his people believed in."[86]

What is most shocking is not that Trent Lott said such a thing, but that no one took him to task for it at the time and that he got away with uttering—and legislatively acting upon—such sentiments for another two decades. In the wake of the civil rights movement, a public official who expresses admiration for an infamous traitor should be called upon to defend what it is about the man's principles that he so admires: His conviction that African Americans were inherently inferior? The view that states have the right to authorize chattel slavery? The precept that in order to protect states' rights an armed rebellion against the U.S. government is legitimate?

Eventually, of course, Trent Lott paid a political price for his racist sentiments—he was forced to resign as Senate Majority Leader (though not much of a price, to be sure: he is still in the senate). But what is perhaps more disturbing is that liberals sat back and allowed an avowed neo-confederate to become Attorney General of the United States and thus in charge of enforcing the nation's civil rights laws. In a 1998 interview with *Southern Partisan*, John Ashcroft gushed, "[Y]our magazine also helps set the record straight. You've got a heritage of doing that, of defending Southern patriots like [Robert E.] Lee, [Stonewall] Jackson and [Confederate President Jefferson] Davis. Traditionalists must do more. I've got to do more. We've all got to stand up and speak in this respect, or else we'll be taught that these people were giving their lives, subscribing their sacred fortunes and their honor to some perverted agenda."[87] It seems that in contemporary Republican circles, taking up arms against the federal government to preserve a state's right to slavery is not a "perverted agenda."

Belly of the Beast: The VARWICON

We are now in a position to see the lineup of conservative discontents that worked to hobble the Clinton presidency and then stole the office for themselves in 2000. The passion in the coalition of interests that brought George W. Bush to power is provided by a collection of true believers seeking to challenge liberalism's ethos of social change through expanded rights and investment in human capabilities. They seek to promote a "return" to fundamentals that they discern through a privileged, selective reading of the Bible, economics texts, the Constitution, or ancient Greek and Roman works. They are joined by a wealthy elite of crony capitalists, who bankrolled the fundamentalists in order to rewrite the rules of the political economy in their favor while channeling federal resources toward their companies. Neo-confederates hopped onto the bandwagon to promote their agenda of racial subordination and white privilege.

The fact remains, however, that voters supporting these interests do not add up to a majority of the electorate. Indeed, to a considerable extent they overlap one another: Christian fundamentalists are also market fundamentalists and many are also neo-confederates or crony capitalists. The small number and overlapping characteristics of people pursuing these various conservative agendas would ordinarily leave radical Republicans a minority party with little hope of electoral success.

To gain control of Congress, the presidency, and the judiciary with views that lie well outside the mainstream of U.S. public opinion, they have relied on a well-organized, highly interrelated, and substantially coordinated set of private institutions. These organizations were founded largely during the 1970s and 1980s with the express goal of overturning the legacy of the New Deal and Great Society. It was Hillary Clinton who named this organizational behemoth, and the name has stuck. Upon being informed by ex-conservative writer David Brock of a long-standing, institutionalized effort to dig up and at times fabricate dirt on her husband, she complained to the press about a "Vast Right-Wing Conspiracy" (known for short a VARWICON) that was out to destroy the Clinton presidency.[88] The VARWICON indeed exists; it is a rapacious beast created by conservatives to hound liberals personally, demean their views ideologically, destroy their credibility publicly, and ultimately to bring them, their politics, and their vision of government to the ground.

The most visible face of the VARWICON is the conservative "punditocracy," a legion of commentators, editorialists, talk show hosts, and regular program "guests" who have turned the talking heads of yesterday's news format into the brainless, shouting heads of today's twenty-four-hour news culture. Telegenic pundits such as Rush Limbaugh, John McLaughlin, George Will, Bill O'Reilly, Sean Hannity, Ann Coulter, Laura Ingraham, and Chris Matthews dominate the airwaves and the headlines and increasingly determine the public "spin" afforded any issue or event.[89] To be sure, there are liberal voices in the punditocracy—such as Jim Hightower, Molly Ivins, Al Franken, George Stephanopolous, and (in a remarkable reversal of roles) Kevin Phillips—but in general they are far less visible, especially on television and radio, and reach far fewer households. Liberals get TV air time mostly as foils for right-wing hosts on conservative talk shows, serving as well-paid props whose assigned role is to sputter ineffectively or defend extreme positions that are willful caricatures of liberal positions.[90]

Despite the notoriety of the shouting heads, however, the public in general and liberals in particular know relatively little about the web of conservative individuals and institutions who underlie them, who own the media that broadcasts their words, who fund the institutions that create their ideas, who pay for the research that market-tests their slogans, and who groom candidates to lead the conservative revolution. These people and institutions comprise the VARWICON, and until liberals wake up to the threat posed by this monster and undertake serious countermeasures, they will continue to be devoured in the field of American politics.

Table 2 lists some of the key people who lead and fund the conservative movement and thus provide the VARWICON with its money and organizational capacities. First, there are theocrats such as Donald Wildmon, Louis Sheldon, Paul Weyrich, and Beverly LaHaye, who are famous in conservative circles but largely unknown to the public. Others such as Pat Robertson, Phyllis Schlafly, Ralph Reed, and Jerry Falwell are better known by virtue of their frequent media appearances.

Some of the theocrats—notably Marlin Maddoux, Larry Burkett, and Pat Robertson—are wealthy in their own right, often because of business enterprises linked to Christian consumers such as International Christian Media, Christian Financial Concepts, and the Christian Broadcasting Network; but others are of modest

TABLE 2
Key Players in the Vast Right-Wing Conspiracy

Name	Importance
Theocrats	
Donald Wildmon	Founder, American Family Association
Pat Robertson	Founder, Christian Coalition, 700 Club
Jerry Falwell	Founder, Moral Majority
Bill Bright	Founder, Campus Crusade for Christ and Alliance Defense Fund
Larry Burkett	Founder, Christian Financial Concepts
Rev. James Dobson	Founder, Focus on the Family
Rev. D. James Kennedy	Founder, Coral Ridge Ministries
Marlin Maddoux	President, International Christian Media
Ralph Reed	Former President, Christian Coalition
Gary Bauer	Founder, Campaign for Working Families
Beverly LaHaye	Founder, Concerned Women for America
Phyllis Schlafly	Founder, Eagle Forum
Paul Weyrich	Founder, Free Congress Research and Education Foundation
Kenneth L. Connor	Founder, Family Research Council
Michael Farris	Founder, Madison Project
Rev. Louis Sheldon	Founder, Traditional Values Coalition
Libertarians, Federalists, and Capitalists	
William F. Buckley	Founder, American Conservative Union
Grover Norquist	Founder, Americans for Tax Reform
Edward Crane	Founder, Cato Institute
Charles G. Koch	Founder, Cato Institute
Steve Moore	Founder, Club for Growth
Joseph Coors	Founder, Heritage Foundation
Clint Bolick	Founder, Institute for Justice
William Mellor	Founder, Institute for Justice
Morton C. Blackwell	Founder, Leadership Institute
David Nolan	Founder, Libertarian Party
Thomas Roe	Founder, State Policy Network
Rupert Murdoch	President and CEO, News Corporation
Richard Mellon Scaife	Person behind Scaife Foundations
David and Charles Koch	Persons behind Koch Family Foundations
Roger Ailes	Conservative Media Consultant, CEO of Fox News
Conservative Media Outlets	
Fox News Channel	Owned by Rupert Murdoch
Washington Times	Owned by Unification Church
Weekly Standard	Owned by Rupert Murdoch
National Review	Edited by William F. Buckley
Christian Broadcasting Network	Founded and Run by Pat Robertson
International Christian Media	Owned by Marlin Maddoux
Drudge Report	Core of conservative internet rumor mill

Source: Website of People for the American Way. Right Wing Watch: Right Wing Organizations. At http://www.pfaw.org/pfaw/general/default.aspx?oid=3147 and organization websites.

socioeconomic status and contribute mostly their time and energy to the fundamentalist movement.

The second section in table 2, which groups together libertarians, federalists, and capitalists, includes people who represent the serious money behind the VARWICON, such as Joseph Coors (the beer magnate), Richard Scaife (a Mellon heir), Charles and David Koch (major industrialists), and Rupert Murdoch (the media mogul). This list also includes important organizers such as Grover Norquist (founder of Americans for Tax Reform) as well as intellectuals such as Clint Brolick (founding member of the Federalist Society and the Institute for Justice).

The last section presents leading media outlets for the conservative movement. The Christian Broadcasting Network and International Christian Media offer programming that reflects fundamentalist family values, presents national and international news from a Christian viewpoint, and offers editorial commentary to advance the theocratic aims of the movement. The Fox News Channel, owned by Rupert Murdoch and run by Roger Ailes, a media-savvy political operative formerly in the employ of presidents Reagan and George H. W. Bush, sponsors conservative staples such as the crossfire-like program *Hannity and Colmes* and *The O'Reilly Factor*, a political talk show. Its news programs cheer on the conservative revolution. They have played an especially prominent role in beating the drums for the war in Iraq. The *Weekly Standard* is a magazine of conservative news and opinion that is owned by Murdoch and edited by William Kristol. It attracts a highbrow audience similar to that of William F. Buckley's *National Review*, whereas the *Washington Times*, owned by the Reverend Sun Myung Moon's Unification Church, generally takes a lower path editorially, often repeating allegations and fabrications introduced to the world via internet-based rags such as the *Drudge Report* or other rumor-mongering sources.

Some of the institutions mentioned in table 2 will be familiar to readers because of their high public profile, but others may be quite obscure to people unfamiliar with the anatomy of the conservative movement. The next three tables therefore profile key institutions in the VARWICON, noting the date of their founding, their approximate size, the annual resources at their disposal, and their general purpose or activity. Table 3, for example, lists the leading theocratic organizations in the United States.

The relatively recent founding dates of these institutions suggest their reactionary nature. They dates range from 1972 to 1996 with a median of 1982. Six of the organizations were created in the three-year period between 1977 and 1980, on the eve of the Republican ascendancy. In addition to spreading Christian theology, these organizations to a remarkable degree concern themselves with the regulation of sexuality and the maintenance of traditional male authority within the family. In a very real way, they constitute a reaction to the political, social, and sexual revolutions of the 1960s. Their annual budgets vary considerably, but in total they yield a remarkable accumulation of resources in the service of fundamentalist Christianity. A rough summation of the budgets listed in the fourth column of the table reveal that at least $228 million is available in any given year to promote conservative family values and fundamentalist mores in the United States.

Table 4 focuses on those organizations devoted to advancing libertarian, federalist, or laissez-faire principles. Their more diverse founding dates suggest the more principled and less reactionary nature of these institutions. The founding dates range from 1919 to 1999, with a median of 1979. The two oldest (the Hoover Institution, founded in 1919) and the American Enterprise Institute (1943) were founded to advance the principles of free market economics. Among the older institutions, those taking principled stands likewise tend to dominate, such as the American Conservative Union (1964) and the Libertarian Party (1971).

As time advances, however, the nature and goals of the institutions grow more reactionary. Groups such as Americans for Tax Reform (1982), the National Center for Policy Analysis (1983), the National Taxpayers Union (1969) are basically reactions to the expansion of government during the Great Society; and American Legislative Exchange Council (1973), the Federalist Society (1982), the Center for Individual Rights (1989), and the Institute for Justice (1991) are essentially reactions to federal post-1960s civil rights enforcement and "judicial activism." Together the organizations listed

TABLE 3
The Leading Theocratic Organizations in the Vast Right-Wing Conspiracy

Organization	Founding	Size	Resources	Purpose or Activity
Eagle Forum	1972	80,000 members	$2.3 million	Opposes sex education, reproductive rights, AIDS education, sexual harassment legislation, federal support for daycare, U.S. involvement with UN, affirmative action, bilingual education, diversity education, gay and lesbian rights, evolution
National Right to Life Committee	1973	3,000 chapters	$12.4 million	Lobbies congress and organizes activists on anti-abortion agenda
Free Congress Foundation	1977	Not available	$11.4 million	Leader of fight in culture wars. Goal is for cultural conservatives to dominate all aspects of American culture and politics
American Family Association	1977	500,000 members	$11.4 million	Promotes God and Christianity in American Life
Focus on the Family	1977	2.3 mil. subscribers 1,300 employees	$129 million	Multi-media empire dedicated to disseminate the gospel of Jesus and preserve traditional values
Concerned Women for America	1979	500,000 members	$12.7 million	To protect values that support the biblical design of the family; feminism is anti-god, anti-family
American Life League	1979	300,000 members	$6.9 million	To end all forms of abortion with no exceptions
Traditional Values Coalition	1980	43,000 churches	Not available	Largest church lobby in the United States. Seeks to "restore America's cultural heritage" by opposing gay and lesbian civil rights, reproductive freedom, teaching of evolution, and sex education

Organization	Year	Members/Staff	Budget	Description
Family Research Council	1983	455,000 members	$10 million	Conservative think tank championing "traditional family values." Promotes the Judeo-Christian world view as basis for a just, free, stable society
Institute for American Values	1987	20 staff & fellows	$163,000	Seeks to contributing intellectually to the renewal of marriage and family life
Christian Coalition	1989	350,000 members	$3 million	Controls the agenda of the Republican party by training and electing pro-family, Christian candidates to public office
Am. Center for Law and Justice	1990	50 employees	$12.1 million	Supports funding of faith-based social services, public expression of religion, and family values
American Renewal	1992	Not available	Not available	Arm of the Family Research Council. Seeks to renew monotheism and Judeo-Christian morality
Alliance Defense Fund	1994	400+ lawyers	$15.4 million	Christian legal firm established to help defend "family values," and work against ACLU
The Madison Project	1994	Not available	Not available	Political Action Committee was established to support conservative family values, pro-life candidates
Campaign for Working Families	1996	Not available	$800,000	Endorses and financially supports anti-choice, anti-gay candidates for political office

Source: Website of People for the American Way. Right Wing Watch: Right Wing Organizations. At http://www.pfaw.org/pfaw/general/default.aspx?oid=3147 and organizational websites.

TABLE 4

The Leading Libertarian, Federalist, and Free-Market Organizations in the Vast Right-Wing Conspiracy

Organization	Founding	Size	Resources	Purpose or Activity
Hoover Institution	1919	250 fellows & staff	$25 million	Seeks to promote individual, economic, and political freedom; private enterprise through scholarship
American Enterprise Institute	1943	50 fellows	$24.4 million	Think tank dedicated to limited government, private enterprise, vital cultural and political institutions, and a strong foreign policy and national defense
Hudson Institute	1961	70 fellows & staff	$7.3 million	Promotes applied research on public policy issues from a viewpoint of free markets, individual responsibility, respect for culture and religion, and national security
American Conservative Union	1964	Not available	$4.5 million	Rates congressional voting records; hosts annual Conservative Political Action Conference
National Taxpayers Union	1969	335,000 members	$1.2 million	Fund that endorses candidates and distributes information to voters on the tax records of office seekers
Libertarian Party	1971	500 office-holders	Not available	Seeks to challenge the cult of the omnipotent state and defend the rights of the individual

Organization	Year	Size	Budget	Description
American Legislative Exchange Council	1973	2,400 legislators	$5.4 million	Creates model legislation to roll back civil rights, ease pollution restrictions, limit government regulations, and private public services
Cato Institute	1977	76 scholars/fellows	$17.6 million	A libertarian public policy organization that pushes for privatization, free markets, limited government
Manhattan Institute	1978	30 fellows & staff	$5 million	Dedicated to producing books, reviews, interviews, speeches, articles, and op-ed pieces to promote greater economic choice and individual responsibility
Leadership Institute	1979	54 employees	$8.2 million	Recruits, trains, and finds jobs for right-wing activists in public policy
Americans for Tax Reform	1982	14 employees	$1.2 million	Opposes all tax increases as a matter of principle
Federalist Society for Law and Public Policy Studies	1982	25,000 lawyers	$3 million	Dedicated to overturning current legal order by developing and promoting conservative positions and influencing who will become judges, top government officials, and leading decision-makers. FS is "dedicated to reforming the current legal order"
National Center for Policy Analysis	1983	22 employees	$5.2 million	Seeks to privatize social security, medicare, health care, criminal justice, environment, education, and welfare

(continued)

TABLE 4 (Contd.)

Organization	Founding	Size	Resources	Purpose or Activity
Center for Individual Rights	1989	10 employees	$1.9 million	Dedicated to ending affirmative action in higher education
Institute for Justice	1991	12 employees	$5.4 million	Public interest law firm that opposes affirmative action and supports faith-based public services
State Policy Network	1992	40 state groups	$391,000	Network of conservative organizations in 37 states and nation-wide
Club for Growth	1999	9,000 members	$453,000	Organization that seeks to cut taxes and reduce size of federal government by closing several cabinet-level departments

Source: Website of People for the American Way. Right Wing Watch: Right Wing Organizations. At http://www.pfaw.org/pfaw/general/default.aspx?oid=3147 and organization websites.

TABLE 5

The Leading Foundations Supporting the Vast Right-Wing Conspiracy

Foundation	Founding	Assets	Annual Disbursements
JM Foundation	1924	$29 million	$1.2 million
Smith Richardson Foundation	1935	$494 million	$23 million
Pioneer Fund	1937	NA	$500,000
Bradley Foundation	1942	$532 million	$33 million
Olin Foundation	1953	$90 million	$3 million
Heritage Foundation	1973	$107 million	$38 million
Coors Foundation	1975	$770 million	$2.5 million
Koch Family Foundations	1980	$60 million	$9 million
Castle Rock Foundation	1993	$67 million	$3 million
Earhart Foundation	NA	$95 million	$5.9 million
Scaife Family Foundations	NA	$320 million	$22 million

Sources: Website for Media Transparency, The Money Behind the Media, at http://www.mediatransparency.org/. Website of People for the American Way, Right Wing Watch: Buying a Movement, at http://www.pfaw.org/pfaw/general/default.aspx?oid=2052.

in table 4 can marshal in the neighborhood of $116 million per year in the service of conservative causes, reactionary or principled.

Much of the money supporting the foregoing institutions comes from a small set of private foundations chartered by wealthy individuals and families to promote a distinctly right-wing political agenda. Eleven of the most important such foundations are listed in table 5. The largest and most important are the Coors Foundation (with assets of $770 million), the Bradley Foundation ($532 million in assets), the Smith Richardson Foundation ($494 million in assets), and the Scaife Family Foundations ($320 million in four separate funds). Smaller, but nonetheless active foundations include the Olin Foundation, Castle Rock Foundation, Earhart Foundation, and Pioneer Fund. The latter has been a key contributor to research on eugenics and propaganda supporting an ideology of black inferiority.[91]

The people and institutions just described operate in a coordinated, synergistic fashion to maximize their effect and make the
VARWICON equal to much more than the sum of its parts.[92] For
example, Richard Scaife contributed large sums of personal and
Scaife Foundation funds to the effort to uncover, fabricate, and
otherwise produce unflattering information on former President
Bill Clinton's sex life and financial dealings and to diminish the
status, respectability, and credibility of his supporters. Salacious
bits of information coming out of these investigations were then
made public through less respectable journalistic sources such as
the *Drudge Report* or the *Washington Times*, where annoying journalistic conventions such as fact checking and corroboration are
not allowed to get in the way of a good story.

Once the nasty news appeared in these sources, it could then be
picked up and reported by "respectable" organizations such as the
Washington Post, New York Times, and National Public Radio, which
insulated themselves from the dirt by claiming that they were reporting not the allegations, but the "controversy" surrounding
them. The multiplication of stories in the print media then served
as fodder for commentary on right-wing talk radio shows, whose
hosts typically begin with the premise that the allegations are true
and move on to add their own embellishments (maybe that's why
Rush Limbaugh calls his listeners "dittoheads"). Newspaper and
magazine stories then contribute debating points for the shouting
heads to use as props in shows such as *The McLaughlin Group,
Hannity and Colmes*, and *Hardball*, whose hosts are fed additional
material from thinkers at conservative think tanks such as the Heritage Foundation. Representatives from think tanks also serve as
guest commentators on news and discussion programs.

The charges set forth by this juggernaut never need to be substan-
tiated. To serve their political purpose they need only be repeated, for
once the media frenzy is in gear, the target of the allegations will be
forced to devote time, money, and emotional energy to the tasks of
damage control and legal defense, leaving significantly less of each
resource to advance a liberal political agenda. Although some foundations (such as the Ford Foundation) and certain institutions (such
as the Brookings Institution) are said to be "liberal," in most cases

they actually support nonpartisan scientific research on social issues. But such is the degree to which conservatives have been able to frame the debate that logic and data contradicting their ideological rantings is labeled as "liberal." In the end, liberals do not have anything remotely comparable to the interconnected nexus of people, institutions, money, and media that are routinely accessible to liberalism's discontents through the VARWICON.

CHAPTER 7

Liberalism Unbound

By describing the source, nature, and organization of the discontent roiling on the right in the last chapter, my intent was not to demoralize liberals with the daunting power of the conservative forces lined up against them. On the contrary, the political record of the past decade contains clear signs that a liberal realignment is in the offing. We must remember that in 2000 George W. Bush lost the popular election and that more than 51 percent of all votes cast were for one of two left-leaning candidates. If Ralph Nader had cut a last-minute deal with Al Gore to support him in return for being named head of the Environmental Protection Agency in a Gore administration, and if only half of Nader's votes had gone to Gore as a result, then Gore would have won the electoral college in a landslide. As it turned out, even if the votes in Florida had been accurately counted, or if Jeb Bush and his minions had not prevented voting by so many likely Democrats, or if the U.S. Supreme Court had allowed a full and complete recount across all of Florida's counties, Al Gore still would have won.

The fact that so much money, organization, and effort, and all the many resources of the VARWICON had to go into the 2000 campaign to achieve even a hair's breadth of electoral success testifies more to the weakness of the conservative position than its strength. After all, as John B. Judis and Ruy Teixeira point out in *The Emerging Democratic Majority*, "[I]n the three presidential elections from 1992 to 2000, the Democrats won twenty states and the District of Columbia all three times. These represented a total of 267 electoral votes, just three short of a majority."[1]

More important than the electoral numbers, however, is the fact that conservatives no longer have a salable political message. The radicals now in charge of the Republican party offer economic policies what work against the material interests of four-fifths of the American people. They seek to impose repressive moral policies that are wildly out of synch with the relatively tolerant sentiments of the American public. Moreover, despite continued ambivalence and some backsliding, Americans show no desire to turn back the clock on race. Instead they seek some way forward that is consistent with fundamental American values. If liberals play their cards right, a realignment is indeed possible, perhaps even likely.

Elements of a Realignment

A liberal realignment won't just happen, of course. It will require considerable effort, and a stable restructuring must be woven from sound ideological material and organizational strands if it is to hold. First and foremost, liberals need to articulate a coherent program that sets a clear agenda for the nation and specifies its place in a globalizing world. Second, liberals must convince voters that a progressive political agenda is in their individual and collective self-interest as private citizens and as Americans. Finally, liberals must develop a blueprint for a political coalition composed of specific, identifiable segments of the electorate that can be assembled into a working majority.

The Vision Thing

One thing liberals have lacked to this point is a coherent political and ideological message, and this is what I have attempted to provide in this book, grounding liberalism in a social scientific understanding of the origins, structure, and nature of markets, and connecting this understanding to a liberal political tradition stretching back two centuries. The brand of liberalism that I have sketched out has more in common with the progressive Republican politics of Theodore Roosevelt than the angry, moralistic Republicanism of Pat Buchanan, John Ashcroft, or George Bush.[2]

In their book, John B. Judis and Ruy Teixeira outline a salable liberal vision that is consistent with views held by a majority of Americans.[3] According to their reading of public opinion data, Americans view government as an instrument of public good, to be used to nurture science and technology in the service of progress. Americans seek to use the *visible hand* of government to supplement the *invisible hand* of the market and through government policies to make sure that the broad public interest is being served—that competition is open and fair; that the environment is protected; that the safety of products is ensured; that investors are shielded against fraud and deceit; and that security and health in the workplace are maintained. Citizens look to the state to subsidize education and job training, and to maintain a safety net to protect them from the fluctuations of the market. In short, Americans want a government that manages markets effectively, provides insurance against economic shocks, and equips them to participate fully in a postindustrial economy. They do not seek a government that guarantees jobs through public spending or provides open-ended transfers to able but idle workers.

As the last chapter revealed, the conservatives of the Republican party seek to implement a program that is radically at odds with these desiderata. Rather than using government as an instrument of progress, they seek to defund it by creating deficits so large that social spending becomes impossible, enabling them to "drown it in the bathtub," as Grover Norquist so quaintly put it. In their preferred world, tax rates will be high for the middle class and low for the rich; the social security system will be scrapped in favor of private investment accounts; medicare and medicaid will be dismantled and replaced by for-profit insurance schemes; education will be privatized and public involvement limited to the provision of vouchers; unemployment insurance will end; and publicly subsidized loans and fellowships for education and training will be curtailed. Military spending will increase and access to public resources will be granted to private concessions at bargain prices.

The United States will withdraw its support from the international institutions that have maintained peace and prosperity for the past fifty years, and U.S. military power will be deployed unilaterally and preemptively to advance American interests and "virtue" throughout the world.

As Paul Krugman points out in *The Great Unraveling*, the enactment of these policies by the Bush administration should not have come as a surprise—they were announced years in advance for anyone who cared to listen.[4] The people who implemented them are revolutionaries who consider the institutions, rules, and norms of the postwar political economy to be illegitimate and feel justified in destroying them by any means necessary, whether or not their actions obey the rules of the system itself. Where liberals went wrong was in not taking the radicals at their word. By seeking to cooperate with conservatives to "moderate" their program, they only served as handmaidens to the conservative revolution.

In ideological terms, the challenge facing liberals is two-fold. First, they must make voters see the true face of the modern Republican party, telling them in a plain and simple way what the radical Republicans really are doing and the sort of world they seek to construct. Until now, their stated goals seemed so extreme and so far-fetched that many liberals simply failed to believe them; but the radicals' aims are very real indeed, and under the presidency of George W. Bush they have been substantially implemented, leaving Democrats gaping in disbelief. Liberals should now have more than enough concrete evidence to expose the radical, un-American, and ultimately unpopular nature of the conservative revolution that has been wrought under the Republican Congress, presidency, and judiciary.

The ultimate fact is that 80 percent of the electorate have derived few, if any, material benefits from the political economy over the past three decades. Voters need to understand that continued support for the radical Republicans will not only enable the rich to squeeze the middle class further, but will also allow libertarian radicals to realize their dream of killing off the New Deal, dismantling its social protections, and intimidating the rest of the world militarily. People need to understand that it will be the sons and daughters

of middle- and working-class parents—not those of the corporate
and political elite—who will be killed and maimed on foreign bat-
tlefields fighting in the name of American virtue.

A Return to Materialist Politics

The second challenge facing liberals is to present a compelling
political program to the public, one grounded in the concrete
interests of voters. Beginning in the 1970s, liberals undertook a
disastrous shift away from a materialist to a postmaterialist politics, focusing on values and rights rather than concrete economic
outcomes.[5] In his study of liberalism, Jeffrey M. Berry reports that
"in 1963 six of ten bills designed to reduce economic inequality
passed; in 1979 four of seven, and in 1991 two of seven. Over time,
Congress has come to consider less legislation designed to reduce
economic inequality, consider fewer bills designed to raise wages
or improve job skills when it does take up such legislation, and
pass a smaller proportion of all these economic inequality bills
reaching the agenda stage."[6]

Rather than addressing the economic hopes and pecuniary
fears of American citizens, liberals instead focused on the extension of rights and the promotion of "correct" values, using the
heavy hand of the state and other positions of privilege to brow-
beat laggard citizens into submission. Liberal groups mobilized
in Washington and concentrated on issues they thought would
appeal to the liberal intelligentsia—the environment, personal ful-
fillment, lifestyle, rights, self-actualization, progressive values—
"issues," Berry writes, that are "unconnected to the problems of
the poor, the disadvantaged, or even the working class. The data . . .
indicate unequivocally that as the new left grew and grew, the old
left was left increasingly isolated."[7] A year before the third-party
candidacy of Ralph Nader cost Al Gore the presidency, Berry
prophetically wrote that "Ralph Nader liberalism helped to crowd
out Hubert Humphrey liberalism."[8]

The shift to a moral rather than a material politics achieved
many legislative successes, owing to a well-organized network of

citizen groups working the halls of Congress;[9] but it also triggered a fundamentalist backlash and brought about the desertion of the Democratic party by the white working class. Unfortunately, morality never makes for a stable or lasting political coalition. Self-interest does. Group interest does. It's not that rights and values are unimportant; but they must be presented and justified as part of a broader package to improve the material well-being of citizens, not to punish some and reward others in the service of ideology.

The central message articulated by liberals should be that by ensuring the freedoms and capabilities of all citizens, and by making sure that markets operate fairly and openly, everyone benefits—more wealth is created, and it is more equally distributed. Voters must be made to see that curtailing the freedoms and capabilities of some not only reduces the efficiency of markets, but also needlessly limits the wealth they create, lowering the standard of living for all Americans and reducing the nation's influence on the world stage.

Rather than making such a case, liberals have engaged in an internecine identity politics to test the correctness of one another's values and unmask the closet racists, homophobes, bigots, and elitists in their midst. In a curious reversal of history, liberals ceded the sobriquet of "class warfare" to the rhetoric of the right. At present, when a liberal politician rises to decry the unfairness of tax cuts for the wealthy, and the rising inequalities of income and wealth, he or she will be accused of "waging class warfare" by conservatives. In the face of this charge, liberals do not stand firm. Typically they backpedal, as if it were a sin to represent the material interests of one's constituents. In the future, the response of liberals to the charge of class warfare should be: "You're damn right it's class warfare. You started the war and we're fighting back."

A New Liberal Coalition

As already mentioned, there are concrete signs that a political alignment is on the horizon and that we are on the verge of a new liberal majority. According to Judis and Teixeira, the new majority coalition will include four key constituencies.[10] The first is professionals, the fastest growing class in the postindustrial knowledge economy, currently comprising around 15 percent of the work force. This constituency includes people earning a range of incomes and working in a variety of industries—architects, engineers, scientists, computer specialists, lawyers, physicians, nurses, teachers, social workers, therapists, designers, artists, and actors—not just the affluent elite. What unites them is the fact that they create, manipulate, and deploy symbolic knowledge to generate value in a knowledge-based service economy.[11] As a group, professionals have become increasingly liberal, supporting Democrats by at least 52 to 40 percent in the past five presidential elections, as compared to the more conservative class of corporate managers, who voted Republican by 49 to 41 percent.[12]

The second element of the liberal constituency is women, who in 2000 supported Al Gore by 54 to 43 percent.[13] Female labor force participation has steadily increased over the past several decades to the point where the large majority of women—and even majorities of those with young children—are gainfully employed.[14] As they have moved into the work force, often in sole support of their families, they have become more responsive to bread-and-butter economic issues and are attuned to issues of inequality and discrimination. At the same time, as primary care givers for children and the elderly, they strongly support public investments in health, education, and daycare, and are wary of reckless militarism that puts the lives of their sons and daughters at risk.

The third element in the liberal coalition consists of minorities, notably African Americans and Latinos, but also Asians. The hostility of the radical Republicans to civil rights, the prominent position of neo-confederates in the party, and the animus they continue to express toward minorities in general and immigrants in particular has not been lost on this constituency. In the 2000 and 2004 elections, some 90 percent of African Americans delivered their votes to the Democratic candidate for president, while around 62 percent of Latinos and 55 percent of Asian Americans supported his candidacy.[15]

The foregoing constituencies represent the demographic present and future of the United States. Given their higher life expectancies, women constitute an absolute majority of the U.S. population; and the higher up the age distribution one goes, the more the sex ratio is skewed toward women and the higher the rates of voting and political participation.[16] Owing to the globalization and the rapid expansion of the postindustrial economy, professionals and immigrants have also been rising as a share of the U.S. population, and their fraction will continue to grow in the future.[17] Moreover, both of the latter groups are concentrated in states that are rich with electoral votes.[18]

Though not a group characterized by rapid growth, the white working class nonetheless represents a key constituency that liberals need to cultivate by bringing inequality front and center as a campaign issue and pridefully taking up the gauntlet of class warfare thrown down by the radical right. That the current leaders of the Republican party, along with their shills in the media, are mostly millionaires closely allied with corporate interests needs to be hammered home in campaign rhetoric, and Republicans must be held accountable for shifting the tax burden away from the wealthy and placing it on the middle class. That liberals have been unable to take advantage of the fact that 80 percent of the electorate has been ravaged economically by Republican policies over the past three decades speaks volumes about the fecklessness of the their past politics.

Roadblocks

Naturally, a successful liberal politics involves more than having a clear vision that can be contrasted to that of conservatives and sold to a working majority of American voters. No matter what they offer ideologically and programmatically, liberals must ultimately face and defeat the VARWICON. Liberals cannot expect the radical conservatives, who have come this far in achieving their political goals, simply to step aside and cede power to a coalition they consider to be immoral and illegitimate. Rather, they will use all available means to prevent such a transfer of power from occurring. Liberal political leaders must therefore gird themselves for an onslaught of negative and dirty politics. There will be well-financed investigations of their sex lives; intensive scrutiny of their financial dealings; a fine-tooth combing of public utterances to find words that can be lifted out of context in misleading ways; and rumor-mongering of the crassest sort. Nothing will be too far-fetched or fantastic to find a home on some right-wing web page or scandal sheet.

At the same time, the conservative idea factory will go into high gear to develop new slogans to discredit liberal positions, and, using surveys, focus groups, and test panels, they will turn the concepts and slogans into effective sound bites. In the same way that the inheritance tax became the "death tax," liberals can expect their positions to be caricatured and served up for public consumption in misleading ways. Great money and effort will go into creating new phrases and ideas that can be passed on to conservative pundits.

In elections themselves, liberals should be prepared for Republican attempts to suppress voting by liberal constituencies, employing now-familiar tactics such as the selective purging of registration lists, the creation and re-creation of gerrymandered districts, and the systematic allocation of older, error-prone voting machines to liberal precincts. It is not beyond the realm of possibility that the efforts at electoral reform will themselves be hijacked. According to Walden O'Dell, the chief executive of Diebold, the leading manufacturer of the touch-screen voting systems that are now being touted as replacements for error-prone manual punch card-systems, "I am committed to helping Ohio deliver its electoral votes to the president next year."[19] Of course, he did just that—delivering the state to Bush by a slim margin amid accusations of fraud and a remarkable lack of transparency.

In service of this goal, Diebold voting machines are programmed *not* to leave a paper trail and the company has refused to make its software available for public inspection. Fortunately, the company mistakenly left a copy of its source code on a public file server, enabling academic investigators to take a close look. They concluded that the program was unreliable and subject to abuse, a conclusion subsequently confirmed by election officials in the state of Maryland.[20] Liberals would do well to support legislation that has been introduced by Representative Rush Holt of New Jersey to *require* that computerized voting systems make their software available for public inspection and leave paper records. Nothing is out of bounds to revolutionaries who see the political system itself as corrupt and themselves as answering to a higher authority.

Liberals need to be ready, not just to react to such radical tactics, but to go on the offensive themselves, making conservatives acknowledge and defend their own words and policies. Ask George Bush why, like his strong supporter Grover Norquist, he wants to drown the government in the bathtub, John Ashcroft what he likes so much about Jefferson Davis, Tom Delay what he means by seeking to impose a biblical worldview, Dick Cheney why he lets energy companies write their own rules and regulations, and Bill Frist why total taxes are higher for people in the middle of the income distribution than at the top. Inquiring minds want to know.

However successful the political mobilization of liberals, and no matter how vulnerable the program of the radical conservatives is to exposure and critique, liberals face two important structural barriers to electoral success, for on the road to a liberal realignment conservatives can rely on two important barriers to slow down the drift of the electorate leftward. These two roadblocks to liberalism merit close attention from liberal politicians and the public, and must be made into campaign issues themselves. They are the self-interested and deleterious role of the media in the current political system, and the corrupt system of campaign financing that allocates disproportionate power to dollars rather than votes.

The Media

The news is not what it used to be. Until well into the 1980s, broadcast news was generally considered as part of a network's public service mission, something executives and managers contributed to the citizenry in return for access to public airwaves, which were regulated as a natural monopoly.[21] Profits came from the commercial air time that filled the screen most of the day and during prime time. News programs were not really expected to make much money, and there was little competition for viewers. During the hour set aside for news each evening, networks and stations offered basically the same lineup of local and national news. If viewers turned on their televisions, they likely watched essentially the same information being imparted in the same way on one of the three networks—ABC, CBS, or NBC. Substantial sums might be devoted to network news operations, but more for reasons of public service and prestige—not because executives anticipated a high profit.

In the 1980s, however, the world of broadcast news changed.[22] Cable replaced airwaves as the medium by which TV was delivered, and the number of channels available and the variety of programs offered exploded. In the new environment, a slowly growing number of viewers was divided among a larger and rapidly growing number of programs and channels. As competition for customers and ratings intensified, profit margins fell and viewing habits segmented. Fewer TV viewers watched any single program at any point in time, and those who did watch a particular show tended to share basic social, economic, and demographic characteristics, which producers quickly recognized, and they quickly tailored their programming so as to attract more of the same viewers and steer others away.[23] Increasingly, Americans of different classes, races, and ethnicities were seeing entirely different worlds reflected on their television screens.

To capitalize on the new media possibilities, in 1980, Ted Turner founded CNN as the first twenty-four-hour all-news network, and rival 24-7 news operations soon followed. Viewers at 6 PM soon had numerous options besides standard network news. In addition to the three traditional broadcast networks, viewers could select from two new networks (WB and Fox) and several cable networks as well as a host of entertainment programming: sports events, sitcoms, cartoons, TV reruns, classic movies, new movies, pay-per-view films, and music television. By the 1990s it was possible, even likely, that a viewer would turn on the television at 6 PM and *not* watch the news.[24]

Rather than *broad*-casting to a mass market of American consumers, the media found itself increasingly *narrow*-casting to specific population clusters defined by particular socioeconomic and demographic characteristics.[25] To make a profit, a television programmer no longer had to attract the largest possible number of viewers, but to draw in a smaller number of specific kinds of viewers, access to whom could then be sold to advertisers eager to reach that particular segment of the population. In this new world, television news ceased to be a public service; it simply became one more show expected to earn a profit.[26]

The demand that news be profitable has, in turn, markedly affected the size and quality of news operations and the sorts of topics they cover. Reporters have become entertainers rather than journalists, and they cover happenings that provide colorful, graphic images, not issues and events that are important for citizens to understand.[27] Real journalism requires a relatively intelligent, educated person finding a story and digging up facts—both of which are necessarily time-intensive. True journalism is thus expensive to produce and a drag on the bottom line. It makes much more sense, economically, to hire a good-looking person who knows little but has an appealing on-camera personality and then send that person to do stand-up coverage at the scene of murders, robberies, fires, natural disasters, and traffic accidents, all of which provide good visuals. This formula explains local TV news in a nutshell.[28]

The new media environment also transformed national and international news gathering and reporting. Permanent news bureaus staffed by knowledgeable people familiar with local issues were closed down and replaced by superstar swat teams of celebrity reporters who travel the world and swoop in to cover "breaking news stories" such as wars, genocides, terrorist attacks, and the odd high-profile sex scandal, with disproportionate attention given, of course, to any event that involves Americans, no matter how few or how unimportant they might be—but the more tragic the better.[29]

Thus, during the invasion of Iraq, Americans received an endless stream of transmissions from reporters "embedded" with American troops and exhaustive coverage of the capture and rescue of Private Jessica Lynch; but they received little information relevant to understanding the roots of the war, the nature of the Baath regime, prior U.S. involvement with Saddam Hussein, the history of the region, or the structure and composition of modern Iraq and the prospects for a stable political solution. To American television viewers, the international scene increasingly appears to be one of violent actions taken against well-intentioned Americans for no apparent reason, and the domestic scene is one of random crime, disorder, and violence.[30]

The economic imperatives of the new media environment have also brought about a proliferation of political talk shows based on a confrontational format of extreme positions argued by predictable, colorful personalities.[31] The last thing a talk-show programmer wants to see is on-camera consensus or a thoughtful discussion of a complicated issue. What sells is conflict, and the louder the shouting, the more outrageous the insults, and the more incredible and mendacious the claims, the better. Political talk shows are cheap to produce, as they require no news organization, no staff of knowledgeable reporters, no intellectual preparation, no fact checking, no sources, and no time-consuming effort to piece together a verifiable story. Like local TV news, they require no actual journalism, just willing pundits with extreme views, bad manners, and a willingness to prostitute themselves for the entertainment of a hard core of news junkies and political operatives.

One final but crucial aspect of the transformation of the news media is the concentration of ownership that has taken place.[32] The various media are not only connected technologically but also through common ownership. Huge media conglomerates have emerged to determine the content and ultimately the access of citizens to newspapers, magazines, radio, television, cable, and the Internet. As Eric Alterman points out in his acerbic critique *What Liberal Media?*, when AOL took over TimeWarner, it also took over, wholly or partially, "Warner Brothers Pictures . . . , Warner

Brothers Animation, Little Brown & Company . . . , Time Life Books . . . , Sunset Books, Warner Books, the Book of the Month Club . . . , Atlantic Records, Warner Audio Books, Elektra, Warner Brothers Records, Time-Life Music, Columbia House . . . , *Time* magazine, *Fortune, Life, Sports Illustrated, Vibe, People, Entertainment Weekly, Money, In Style, Martha Stewart Living, Sunset, Asia Week, Parenting, Weight Watchers, Cooking Light,* DC Comics, . . . HBO, Cinemax, Warner Borthers Television . . . , Comedy Central, E!, Black Entertainment Television, Court TV, the Sega channel, the Home Shopping Network, Turner Broadcasting, the Atlanta Braves and Atlanta Hawks, World Championship Wrestling, Hanna-Barbera Cartoons, New Line Cinema, Fine Line Cinema, Turner Classic Movies, Turner Pictures, Castle Rock Productions, CNN, CNN Headline News, CNN International, CNN/SI, CNN Airport Network, CNNfi, CNN radio, TNT, WTBS, and the Cartoon Network."[33]

The transformation of the media is of great importance to liberals because the news media is, in effect, a political institution.[34] Only through the news media can political leaders reach and address the public, and through reporters, commentators, and pundits the positions and programs of politicians are ultimately presented and interpreted. In a liberal world, the media should be managed to offer Americans a true marketplace of ideas and information, but under the watch of the radical conservatives, the regulatory apparatus has moved in the opposite direction. Consolidation of ownership has reduced the number of players in the media market and allocated disproportionate power and influence to a very few individuals and corporations who are unrepresentative of the population at large: they are far richer and much more conservative.

A key goal of liberal politics should be the re-regulation of the mass media, particularly the broadcast media. Rather than managing the media to enable owners to maximize their profits, it should be structured to maximize diversity and to prevent monopolies of news and information by breaking up the media conglomerates and increasing the number of owners who participate in competitive but profitable markets. In a liberal world, citizens

do not grant access to communications channels and public airwaves simply to allow a few people and firms to make immense
profits. Rather, they constitute media markets so that they, the citizens, gain access to as much information as possible from a variety of sources and viewpoints that are independent from one
another and the government. The interests of a democratic republic lie in maximizing information and debate, not in maximizing
profits for a few. Profits are simply the incentive that citizens rely
on to make media markets work, but as a public creation they
should always be structured and supervised to promote the general interest.

At the same time, the punditocracy of commentators, writers,
and reporters has grown in wealth and influence to become a class
in and of itself.[35] Journalists are generally well educated, enjoy
high incomes, travel in international circles, and live in areas of
concentrated affluence within sophisticated metropolitan centers.
The punditocracy plays a crucial role in presenting and interpreting political messages yet its members remain wholly unaccountable to the public for any prejudices or biases they might have.
Naturally, pundits and reporters, like everyone else, share certain
preferences specific to their social and economic circumstances.

An essential liberal reform is thus for government to require reporters, editorialists, and commentators to report the sources and
amounts of the income that they earn. They are more than just
private citizens. They are public figures with important responsibilities in a democratic polity. It is thus fitting and appropriate for
citizens to ask, in return for giving them the chance to become
rich and famous using public resources, that members of the punditocracy report from whom they are receiving their money. As
Washington Post Editor Ben Bradlee commented to the journalist
James Fallows in his book on "why Americans hate the media,"
"[I]f the Insurance Institute of America . . . pays [you] $10,000 to
make a speech, don't tell me you haven't been corrupted. You can
say you haven't and you can say you will attack insurance issues in
the same way, but you won't. You cant."[36]

While deconcentrating media ownership and demanding transparency from those who deliver and interpret news are important

long-term goals in the liberal agenda, it also important to understand the structure and organization of the today's media for a more immediate and practical purpose: winning elections. The segmentation of broadcast media has rewritten the rules of the political game in an important way. Rather than crafting a single message to sell to all voters through mass broadcasts, the task is now to develop a series of messages designed to appeal to specific sociodemographic groups through carefully tailored narrow-casts, placing them in channels and programs where they will be seen by targeted segments of the population, who can then be combined into a winning electoral coalition. For liberals, this strategy obviously involves developing campaigns aimed at professionals, women, minorities, and the working class.

Finally, liberals need to do a better job of managing the media, which for better or worse now stands between them and the realization of their agenda. The main thing for liberals to understand is that for all their assertions of independence, the media are really a pack of sheep who set and follow a very small number of scripts or frames,[37] and which frame becomes the master narrative for a political campaign can determine a candidate's success or failure, as Al Gore discovered to his dismay in the 2000 election. Reporters took a strong dislike to Gore because he was aloof, cerebral, and most threatening of all, *he thought he knew more than they.*[38] They took their revenge by inventing the script of Al Gore as inveterate liar and exaggerator, and then took small mistakes he made completely out of context and blew them out of proportion to illustrate his supposed braggadocio and mendacity, at times going so far as to deliberately and willfully misquote him.[39]

In contrast, reporters and the media generally liked George Bush because he didn't presume to be smarter than they were and he invented playful nicknames to make each person feel like he or she was part of his inner circle. They assigned him the script of the bumbling but well-intentioned regular guy, the compassionate conservative who did not understand all the details but had a good heart and could connect with the common person. This script remained in force up until September 11, which transformed his role into Commander-in-Chief in the War on Terror.

Under both scripts, however, the press gave him a free pass to re-peat an outrageous litany of half-truths, distortions, and bald-face lies without calling his character or integrity into question.[40]

For liberals, the lesson from this experience is to be constantly aware of the power of the national press corps and its unique abil-ity to frame issues and people. Liberals should take care to butter up and stroke the egos of pundits and reporters at every turn, and work assiduously to influence their framing of a campaign in ways that accurately reflect liberal viewpoints and that sympathetically portray their candidates. Although no one elected him as political gatekeeper, the ads for Chris Matthew's *Hardball* program like to say, "The road to the White House goes through him."

One Dollar, One Vote

Moving hand-in-glove with the concentration of wealth over the past several decades has been a growing concentration of political power among the wealthy.[41] Those with access to wealth and in-come not only vote in larger numbers than the poor; they make more campaign contributions in higher amounts, and they are more likely to become involved personally with candidates and campaigns. Not surprisingly, they also enjoy far greater access to elected representatives, who inevitably tend to sympathize with and act upon their interests.[42] Such has always been the case in American politics, but the tide of plutocracy has ebbed and flowed over time. During the last decade of the twentieth century, how-ever, the United States entered a reprise of the gilded age. In what Kevin Phillips has called "millennial plutographics," the system of one person, one vote gave way to a new calculus of one dollar, one vote.[43]

The rise of television as the primary instrument of public com-munication in U.S. political campaigns, combined with the dereg-ulation of the media, dramatically inflated the cost of running for office, leading elected officials to spend ever-larger portions of their time raising money rather than attending to their public du-ties. The system of campaign finance that emerged during the

1990s basically functioned as a system of institutionalized bribery and legalized influence peddling.[44] Politicians needed ever greater amounts of cash to finance campaign ads and buy media time, and they relied increasingly on a small pool of wealthy people and institutions to provide most of the funds. Is it any wonder that the policies of the past two decades have benefited the top of the income distribution?

Despite claims to serve the interest of the markets and freedom, the plutocratic policies of the radical Republicans actually led to an unprecedented wave of financial scandals, swindles, and frauds in the first years of the new century. As always, when the rich are given unbridled control of the regulatory apparatus of government, they inevitably abuse it to ruin markets, destroy wealth, and squander the public's money. Turning markets over to producers to run is almost always bad for the markets and the public. By avoiding regulatory scrutiny and helping George W. Bush rewrite energy policy, officials at Enron brought about major disruptions in energy markets that caused serious power shortages and ultimately destroyed billions of dollars of wealth.[45]

Although recent efforts at campaign finance and corporate reform begin to move American policy away from the plutocracy it has become, the power of money politics will not be checked until the process of selecting our public officials is freed from the corrupting effect of having to raise huge sums of money from private donors. A critical element in the liberal program of progressive politics should not simply be campaign finance reform, but *federalizing the process of electing national officials.* Elections are the most important and fundamental process of democratic government, the primary means by which the people express their will. The process of campaigning and electing should therefore be open and free from the taint of private money.

A final campaign issue for liberals and a central element of their political program should thus be the creation of a Federal Bureau of Elections to supervise and administer elections for the House of Representatives, the United States Senate, the presidency, and vice presidency. Such an agency could organize and monitor voting through a network of computerized polling stations located in post office branches, backed up by paper records that are available for inspection by the media, the courts, and the public. All campaign funds would be publicly provided and equalized among competitors in any particular district. Candidates running for the House, Senate, and the presidency would be prohibited from raising campaign funds privately and third parties would be prohibited from campaigning for or against candidates during the month prior to the election. Finally, elections would be moved to the first weekend in November to facilitate participation and maximize public involvement.

Taking a Stand

For the past two decades, the radicals of the Republican party have been playing political hardball with corked bats while liberals have showed up to play a friendly game of slow-pitch with a 16-inch ball and no mitts. Liberals completely underestimated the tenacity, organization, and will of the radical right; they refused to believe that conservatives actually sought to achieve their stated aims; they failed to organize themselves to fight on matters of principle; and they offered no coherent program other than to position themselves as "Republicans lite." As a result of liberal weakness, the political economy of the United States is in disarray and its stature on the world stage is compromised.

In recent years, the idea that "liberals can't win" somehow became established in progressive circles, and the Democratic party ceased to be a party of opposition. Democrats sold themselves as competent technocrats who could deliver political pork and moderate the radical side of Republicanism, but they offered no coherent ideological platform of their own. They could muster no alternative liberal vision for American society, and, bereft of a message to sell to voters, they ran from the label "liberal" as the kiss of political death. In doing so, they allowed a radical right to assume power and implement a conservative agenda that is far more politically off-center than anything liberals ever envisioned.

The politicians who are out of touch with America at this point are the radical conservatives who run the Republican party, and the time has come to hoist them on their own petard, give them a match, and let them blow themselves up. Liberals can accomplish this goal only if they vigorously assert their own liberalism, articulate a compelling alternative vision, and engage in a true partisan politics of opposition. Rather than running from the label "liberal," progressive politicians need to be able to look voters straight in the eye and say, "Yes I am a liberal; this is what I stand for; this is how my program will improve your lives; and this is how the radical conservatives have screwed you royally over the past three decades."

American politics increasingly seems like the "Emperor's New Clothes," with no one willing to utter obvious truths about the U.S. political economy. Silence and timidity on the left have permitted the forces of the right to restructure U.S. economic and political institutions so as to lower the standard of living for most Americans, leave them vulnerable to shocks from the market, expose them to greater risks in the environment and at work, and abridge their civil liberties. Virtually all indicators of social and economic well-being show the American public to be worse off now than before the conservative ascendance.

Mounting a serious liberal opposition to what conservatives have done and are still doing will not be easy, and success is by no means guaranteed. In this book, however, I have endeavored to outline a way forward by offering a coherent liberal ideology and a practical program of politics that is consistent with the values and aspirations of Americans, by making liberals aware of the array of people, institutions, and resources lined up against them on the right, and by highlighting likely roadblocks on the road to a liberal realignment, while offering suggestions for how to overcome them.

The history of liberalism is one of short periods of reform followed by longer periods of stasis and retreat. The liberal moment of the nation's founding during 1776–89 was followed by seven decades in which a nation dedicated to liberty tolerated the institution of chattel slavery. The Civil War and Reconstruction from 1860 to 1876 eliminated slavery and extended civil rights to former slaves, but it was followed by a reassertion of conservative hegemony, the imposition of a new system of racial subordination, and a gilded age of rapacious, destructive capitalism. The Progressive Era from 1900 to 1920 brought corporate reform, women's suffrage, and further extensions of democracy, but was followed by a twelve-year period of retrenchment that very nearly destroyed the market system itself.

The New Deal saved capitalism from its excesses, and while Franklin Roosevelt's New Deal of 1932–45 grew into Harry Truman's Fair Deal of 1945–52, most of the great achievements came during the first Roosevelt Administration (1932–36). The full realization of many liberal dreams had to await the New Frontier and Great Society enacted by presidents Kennedy and Johnson from 1960 to 1968, which expanded the social safety net, ended legalized segregation in the South, and made minority political rights a reality throughout the country. In achieving these ends, however, liberals paid a high price by triggering a conservative counterattack that reached its culmination in the administration of George W. Bush.

The world is once again at a critical turning point, and decisions made by the United States and its citizens will inevitably play a crucial role in determining the evolution of global society, the future of its economy, and perhaps even the fate of humanity itself. The challenges are daunting: rising inequalities within nations; the stagnation of vast parts of the developing world; spreading fundamentalism; and a shift toward nihilistic ideologies. Attention has focused too much on the failures of past liberal policies and globalism rather than their remarkable record of success: continued material advancement in North America, Europe, and Japan, and Oceania; the expansion of economic development to other nations in Asia and Latin America; the extension of markets and freedoms to all parts of the globe; and the avoidance of global warfare despite a long nuclear standoff between ideologically opposed superpowers.

The negative focus has led some political movements to forsake the liberal principle that the role of government is to uphold freedom and invest in the capabilities of all citizens. Whereas fundamentalists seek to re-create imagined social orders of the past, with their built-in asymmetries of power along the lines of age, gender, race, and ethnicity, a revived anarchist movement seeks to bring the whole system of global capitalism crashing down. Neither vision offers much hope for the future. Neither is capable of preserving the rights and expanding the freedoms of the world's citizens while securing their social well-being and material improvement.

In the year 2005 we stand at a crossroads much like that faced by decision-makers in 1914, when the first round of globalism and trade produced unprecedented wealth and great opportunities but also led to daunting challenges. Then, as now, the world was a cauldron of economic inequalities, unfulfilled aspirations, left-wing revolutions, and right-wing counter-revolutions marked by a rising tide of civil disorder and terrorist violence. Rather than building on the institutional frameworks that people of good will had created to manage the global political economy and resolve disputes, however, decision-makers turned their backs on peace and progress and chose war instead.

In 1914, one great power chose a course of unilateral military action to combat an international terrorist threat; but this sparked a chain reaction of violence that destroyed the global system of trade, investment, and stability that for a century had brought peace and prosperity to millions. In the aftermath of this destruction, the United States had a unique opportunity to put things right, to reconstitute the system while attending to its defects, but despite a bold liberal blueprint advanced by President Woodrow Wilson, conservatives in the U.S. Senate triumphed, not only rejecting U.S. participation in the World Court and League of Nations, but raising new barriers to the international movement of people, capital, goods, and ideas. This program of withdrawal led to the collapse of both the global and the American economies and set the stage for World War II, which was bloodier and more destructive than the first.

In the ashes of that conflict, however, the United States did not falter but took the lead in putting together a new international political economy that substantially solved the problems of its predecessor and produced a host of social, economic, and political marvels. Despite ample evidence of continued progress, however, over time the limitations and defects of the international system it created have become apparent, and it is increasingly under attack. Let us hope that American leaders and voters today have the wisdom to move forward rather than backward, to face squarely the problems and limitations of the global political economy and to fix them through institutional evolution and innovation rather than fundamentalist repression, nihilistic destruction, or self-centered withdrawal. The liberal vision of society that I have outlined views our current problems as remediable and the future potentially unbounded; but the destructive power now at our disposal means that the stakes are even higher than they were in the past century. Let us hope we choose better.

Notes

★ ★ ★ ☆ ★ ★ ★

Chapter 1: Return of the "L" Word

1. For a sample of the worldview of conservatives, see the following sources: Coulter, Ann. 2003. *Treason: Liberal Treachery from the Cold War to the War on Terrorism.* New York: Crown. Coulter, Ann. 2003. *Slander: Liberal Lies about the American Right.* New York: Crown. Charen, Mona. 2003. *Useful Idiots: How Liberals Got It Wrong in the Cold War and Still Blame America First.* Washington, D.C.: Regnery. Bruce, Tammy. 2003. *The Death of Right and Wrong: Exposing the Left's Assault on Our Culture and Values.* New York: Prima Lifestyles. Hannity, Sean. 2003. *Let Freedom Ring: Winning the War of Liberty.* New York: Harper Collins. Ingraham, Laura. 2003. *Shut Up and Sing: How Elites from Hollywood, Politics, and the UN are Subverting America.* Washington, D.C.: Regnery.

2. See Bloom, Allan. 1988. *The Closing of the American Mind.* New York: Simon and Schuster. Kimball, Roger. 1991. *Tenured Radicals: How Politics Has Corrupted Our Higher Education.* New York: Harper Collins. D'Souza, Dinesh. 1998. *Illiberal Education: The Politics of Race and Sex on Campus.* New York: Free Press.

3. Brock, David. 2003. *Blinded by the Right: The Conscience of an Ex-Conservative.* New York: Three Rivers.

4. Smelser, Neil J., and Richard Swedberg, eds. 1994. *The Handbook of Economic Sociology.* Princeton and New York: Princeton University Press and the Russell Sage Foundation. Swedberg, Richard. 2003. *Principles of Economic Sociology.* Princeton: Princeton University Press. Guillén, Mauro F., Randall Collins, Paula England, and Marshall Meyer, eds. 2002. *The New Economic Sociology: Developments in an Emerging Field.* New York: Russell Sage Foundation. Carruthers, Bruce G., and Sarah L. Babb. 2000. *Economy/Society: Markets, Meanings, and Social Structure.* Thousand Oaks, Calif.: Pine Forge.

Chapter 2: Where Liberalism Went Wrong

1. Smith, Rogers M. 1997. *Civic Ideals: Conflicting Visions of Citizenship in U.S. History.* New Haven: Yale University Press.

2. Rusk, Jerrold G. 2001. *A Statistical History of the American Electorate.* Washington, D.C.: Congressional Quarterly Press. P. 50.

3. Ibid.

4. Higginbotham, A. Leon, Jr. 1996. *Shades of Freedom: Racial Politics and Presumptions of the American Legal Process.* New York: Oxford University Press.

5. Phillips, Kevin. 2002. *Wealth and Democracy: A Political History of the American Rich.* New York: Broadway. P. 38.

6. Ibid., 232–48.

7. Rusk, *A Statistical History,* 50.

8. Phillips, *Wealth and Democracy,* 59.

9. Galbraith, John Kenneth. 1958. *The Affluent Society.* 4th ed. New York: Houghton-Mifflin.

10. Terkel, Studs. 1986. *The Good War: An Oral History of World War Two.* New York: Pantheon.

11. Higginbotham, *Shades of Freedom.*

12. Caro, Robert A. 2002. *Master of the Senate: The Years of Lyndon Johnson.* New York: Knopf.

13. Massey, Douglas S., and Nancy A. Denton. 1993. *American Apartheid: Segregation and the Making of the Underclass.* Cambridge: Harvard University Press. Pp. 186–216.

14. Lemann, Nicholas. 1992. *The Promised Land: The Great Black Migration and How It Changed America.* New York: Vintage. Pp. 109–222.

15. Califano, Joseph A., Jr. 1999. "What Was Really Great about the Great Society: The Truth behind the Conservative Myths." *Washington Monthly,* October.

16. Rusk, *A Statistical History,* 50.

17. Califano, "What Was Really Great."

18. Quadagno, Jill. 1994. *The Color of Welfare: How Racism Undermined the War on Poverty.* New York: Oxford University Press.

19. Phillips, Kevin. 1969. *The Coming Republican Majority.* New York: Arlington.

20. Lind Michael, 2003. *Made in Texas: George W. Bush and the Southern Takeover of American Politics.* New York: Basic.

21. Edsall, Thomas B., and Brian Faler. 2002. "Lott Remarks on Thurmond Echoed 1980 Words: Criticism Unabated Despite Apology for Comment on Former Dixiecrat's Presidential Bid." *Washington Post,* December 11, p. A6.

22. "Interview with Trent Lott." 1984. *Southern Partisan* 5 (4):44.

23. Edsall, Thomas Byrne, and Mary D. Edsall. 1991. *Chain Reaction: The Impact of Race, Rights, and Taxes on American Politics.* New York: Norton.

24. Brady, Joseph. 1996. *Bad Boy: The Life and Politics of Lee Atwater.* New York: Perseus.

25. Phillips, Kevin. 1990. *The Politics of Rich and Poor: Wealth and the American Electorate in the Reagan Aftermath.* New York: Random House.

26. Phillips, *Wealth and Democracy,* 96.

27. Ibid., 137.

28. Levy, Frank. 1998. *The New Dollars and Dreams: American Incomes and Economic Change.* New York: Russell Sage Foundation. Pp. 38–48.

Handwritten marginalia: RETO : The Federal Bull DOZER.

29. Wolff, Edward. 1996. *Top Heavy: The Increasing Inequality of Wealth in America and What Can Be Done about It.* New York: New Press.

30. Phillips, *Wealth and Democracy,* 149.

31. Ibid., 120, 123.

32. Ibid., 153.

33. Ibid., 166, 343–46.

34. Conason, Joe. 2003. *Big Lies: The Right-Wing Propaganda Machine and How It Distorts the Truth.* New York: St. Martin's. Pp. 13–28.

35. Moynihan, Daniel Patrick. 1970. *Maximum Feasible Misunderstanding: Community Action in the War on Poverty.* New York: Free Press.

36. Bauman, John F. 1987. *Public Housing, Race, and Renewal: Urban Planning in Philadelphia, 1920–1974.* Philadelphia: Temple University Press. White, Michael J. 1980. *Urban Renewal and the Residential Structure of the City.* Chicago: Community and Family Studies Center. Gans, Herbert J. 1982. *Urban Villagers: Group and Class in the Life of Italian-Americans.* New York: Free Press.

37. Hirsch, Arnold R. 1983. *Making the Second Ghetto: Race and Housing in Chicago, 1940–1960.* New York: Cambridge University Press.

38. Quadagno, *The Color of Welfare,* 61–88.

39. Danziger, Sheldon, and Peter Gottschalk. 1995. *America Unequal.* New York: Russell Sage. Pp. 39–68.

40. Inglehart, Ronald. 1977. *The Silent Revolution: Changing Values and Political Styles among Western Publics.* Princeton: Princeton University Press. Inglehart, Ronald. 1990. *Culture Shift in Advanced Industrial Society.* Princeton: Princeton University Press.

41. Dallek, Robert. 1998. *Flawed Giant: Lyndon B. Johnson, 1960–1973.* New York: Oxford University Press.

42. Phillips, *Wealth and Democracy,* 108–67.

43. Schrag, Peter. 1998. *Paradise Lost: California's Experience, America's Future.* Berkeley: University of California Press. Pp. 27–126.

44. Ibid., 129–87.

45. Appy, Christian G. 1993. *Working-Class War: American Combat Soldiers and Vietnam.* Chapel Hill: University of North Carolina Press.

46. Kuttner, Robert. 2002. "Republicans' Favorite Democrats." *The American Prospect* 13 (12). Available at http://www.prospect.org/print/V13/12/kuttner-r.html.

47. Nash, Gary B., Ross E. Dunn, and Charlotte A. Crabtree. 2000. *History on Trial: Culture Wars and the Teaching of the Past.* New York: Vintage.

48. Brock, David. 2002. *Blinded by the Right: The Conscience of an Ex-Conservative.* New York: Crown. Pp. 1–21.

49. Bloom, Alan. 1988. *The Closing of the American Mind.* New York: Simon and Schuster. Dinesh D'Souza. 1998. *Illiberal Education: The Politics of Race and Sex on Campus.* New York: Free Press. Bork, Robert H. 1996. *Slouching Towards Gomorrah: Modern Liberalism and American Decline.* New York: Regan.

Kimball, Roger. 1991. *Tenured Radicals: How Politics Has Corrupted Our Higher Education*. New York: Harper Collins.

50. Best, Steven, and Douglas Kellner. 1991. *Postmodern Theory*. New York: Guilford.

51. Skrentny, John David. 2002. *The Minority Rights Revolution*. Cambridge: Belknap.

52. Louglin, Sean, and Robert Yoon. 2003. "Millionaires Populate U.S. Senate: Kerry, Rockefeller, Kohl among the Wealthiest." CNN.com/Inside Politics, June 13. Available at http://www.cnn.com/2003/ALLPOLITICS/06/13/senators.finances/.

Chapter 3: Liberalism and the Market

1. This chapter draws upon insights from the burgeoning field of economic sociology, which studies how markets are embedded in broader social institutions. For summaries see the following: Smelser, Neil J., and Richard Swedberg, eds. 1994. *The Handbook of Economic Sociology*. Princeton and New York: Princeton University Press and the Russell Sage Foundation. Swedberg, Richard. 2003. *Principles of Economic Sociology*. Princeton: Princeton University Press. Guillén, Mauro F., Randall Collins, Paula England, and Marshall Meyer, eds. 2002. *The New Economic Sociology: Developments in an Emerging Field*. New York: Russell Sage Foundation. Carruthers, Bruce G., and Sarah L. Babb. 2000. *Economy/Society: Markets, Meanings, and Social Structure*. Thousand Oaks, Calif.: Pine Forge.

2. Massey, Douglas S. 2002. "A Brief History of Human Society: The Origin and Role of Emotions in Social Life." *American Sociological Review* 67:1–29.

3. Sanderson, Stephen K. 1999. *Social Transformations: A General Theory of Historical Development*. Lanham, Md.: Roman and Littlefield. Fiske, Alan Page. 1991. *Structures of Social Life: The Four Elementary Forms of Human Relations*. New York: Free Press. Pp. 371–408.

4. Massey, "A Brief History of Human Society," 1–10; Sanderson, *Social Transformations*, 20–52. Kelly, Robert L. 1995. *The Foraging Spectrum: Diversity in Hunter-Gatherer Lifeways*. Washington, D.C.: Smithsonian Press.

5. Weber, Max. 1981. *General Economic History*. New Brunswick, N.J.: Transaction. Also see the following: Collins, Randall. 1992. "Weber's Last Theory of Capitalism: A Systematization." In *The Sociology of Economic Life*, edited by Mark Granovetter and Richard Swedberg. Boulder, Colo.: Westview. Pages 85–109. Carruthers and Babb, *Economy/Society*, 7–8.

6. Fiske, *Structures of Social Life*, 13–39.

7. Zelizer, Viviana. *The Social Meaning of Money*. New York: Basic. Williams, Jonathan, ed, 1998. *Money: A History*. New York: St. Martin's. Davies, Glyn. 2002. *A History of Money from Ancient Times to the Present Day*. Cardiff: University of Wales Press.

8. Goody, Jack. 1986. *The Logic of Writing and the Organization of Society.* Cambridge: Cambridge University Press.

9. Massey, "A Brief History of Human Society," 1–28.

10. Wallerstein, Immanuel. 1974. *Modern World-System I: Capitalist Agriculture and the Origins of European World-Economy in the 16th Century.* New York: Academic. Wallerstein, Immanuel. 1980. *Modern World-System II: Mercantilism and the Consolidation of the European World-Economy, 1600–1750.* New York: Academic.

11. Hobsbawm, Eric J. 1989. *The Age of Empire 1875–1914.* New York: Vintage. O'Rourke, Kevin H., and Jeffrey G. Williamson. 1999. *Globalization and History: The Evolution of a Nineteenth-Century Atlantic Economy.* Cambridge: MIT Press.

12. James, Harold. 2001. *The End of Globalization: Lessons from the Great Depression.* Cambridge: Harvard University Press.

13. Heilbroner, Robert L., and William Milberg. 2001. *The Making of Economic Society.* Englewood Cliffs, N.J.: Prentice Hall.

14. Peterson, William. 1969. *Population.* 2nd ed. New York: Macmillan. Pp. 630–96.

15. Esping-Anderson, Gøsta. 1990. *The Three Worlds of Welfare Capitalism.* Princeton: Princeton University Press.

16. Olson, Mancur. 1984. *The Rise and Decline of Nations: Economic Growth, Stagflation, and Social Rigidities.* New Haven: Yale University Press.

17. Castells, Manuel. 1998. *End of Millennium.* Malden, Mass.: Basil Blackwell. P. 469.

18. Greider, William. 1997. *One World, Ready or Not: The Manic Logic of Capitalism.* New York: Touchstone.

19. Friedman, Thomas L. 2000. *The Lexus and Olive Tree.* New York: Farrar Straus and Giroux.

20. Sen, Amartya. 1999. *Development as Freedom.* New York: Anchor.

21. Smelser and Swedberg, eds. *The Handbook of Economic Sociology,* 183–367; Swedberg, *Principles of Economic Sociology,* 131–56.

22. Madrick, Jeff. 2002. *Why Economies Grow: The Forces That Shape Prosperity and How We Can Get Them Working Again.* New York: Basic. Pp. 115–32.

23. Kapstein, Ethan B., and Branko Milanovic. 2002. *When Markets Fail: Social Policy and Economic Reform.* New York: Russell Sage Foundation.

24. Jackson, Kenneth T. 1985. *Crabgrass Frontier: The Suburbanization of the United States.* New York: Oxford University Press. Hays, R. Allen. 1985. *The Federal Government and Urban Housing: Ideology and Change in Public Policy.* Albany: State University of New York Press.

25. Lea, Michael J. 1996. "Innovation and the Cost of Mortgage Credit: A Historical Perspective." *Housing Policy Debate* 7:147–74. Hays, *The Federal Government and Urban Housing.*

26. U.S. Bureau of the Census. 1975. *Historical Statistics of the United States: Colonial Times to 1970,* vol. 2. Washington, D.C.: U.S. Government Printing

Office. P. 646. U.S. Bureau of the Census. 2003. *Statistical Abstract of the United States: 2002.* Washington, D.C.: U.S. Government Printing Office. P. 600.

27. Massey, Douglas S., Joaquin Arango, Graeme Hugo, Ali Kouaouci, Adela Pellegrino, and J. Edward Taylor. 1998. *Worlds in Motion: Understanding International Migration at the End of the Millennium.* Oxford: Oxford University Press.

28. Carruthers and Babb, *Economy/Society,* 1–14, 45–100. Swedberg, *Principles of Economic Sociology,* 53–73. Granovetter, Mark. 1985. "Economic Action and Social Structure: The Problem of Embeddedness," *American Journal of Sociology* 91 (1985): 481–510; Swedberg, Richard. 1994. "Markets as Social Structures." Pp. 255–82 in *The Handbook of Economic Sociology,* edited by Smelser and Sweberg.

29. Coleman, James S. 1990. *Foundations of Social Theory.* Cambridge: Belknap.

30. Davis, Mike. 1990. *City of Quartz: Excavating the Future in Los Angeles.* New York: Verso. Davis, Mike. 1998. *Ecology of Fear: Los Angeles and the Imagination of Disaster.* New York: Metropolitan.

31. Becker, Gary S. 1991. *A Treatise on the Family.* Cambridge: Harvard University Press.

32. Davies, *A History of Money,* 1–33.

33. Williamson, Oliver E. 1994. *Transaction Cost Economics and Organization Theory.* Pp. 77–107 in *The Handbook of Economic Sociology,* edited by Smelser and Swedberg.

34. Davies, *A History of Money,* 34–110.

35. Ibid., 110–284.

36. Ibid., 367–456, 549–95.

37. Friedman, Milton. 1956. *A Restatement of the Quantity Theory of Money.* Chicago: University of Chicago Press.

38. Davies, *A History of Money,* 457–548.

39. Jackson, *Crabgrass Frontier,* 208. Massey, Douglas S., and Nancy A. Denton. 1993. *American Apartheid: Segregation and the Making of the Underclass.* Cambridge: Harvard University Press. Pp. 36–37.

40. Filvaroff, David B., and Raymond E. Wolfinger. 2000. "The Origin and Enactment of the Civil Rights Act of 1964." In *Legacies of the 1964 Civil Rights Act,* edited by Bernard Grofman. Charlottesville: University of Virginia Press.

41. Klinker, Philip A., and Rogers M. Smith. 1999. *The Unsteady March: The Rise and Decline of Racial Equality in America.* Chicago: University of Chicago Press. Pp. 268–75.

42. Metcalf, George R. 1988. *Fair Housing Comes of Age.* New York: Greenwood. Pp. 101–14. Massey and Denton, *American Apartheid,* 186–217.

43. Klinker and Smith, *The Unsteady March,* 242–316.

44. Barry, Brian. 1989. *Theories of Justice.* Berkeley: University of California Press.

45. Rawls, John. 1971. *A Theory of Justice*. Oxford: Oxford University Press.

46. Hochschild, Jennifer L. 1981. *What's Fair? American Beliefs about Distributive Justice*. Cambridge: Harvard University Press. Kluegel, James R., and Eliot R. Smith. 1986. *Beliefs about Inequality: Americans' Views of What Is and What Ought to Be*. New York: Aldine de Gruyter. Hochschild, Jennifer L. 1995. *Facing Up to the American Dream: Race, Class, and the Soul of the Nation*. Princeton: Princeton University Press. Lamont, Michèle. 2000. *The Dignity of Working Men: Morality and the Boundaries of Race, Class, and Immigration*. Cambridge: Harvard University Press.

47. Schuman, Howard, Charlotte Steeh, Lawrence Bobo, and Maria Krysan. 1998. *Racial Attitudes in America: Trends and Interpretations*. Cambridge: Harvard University Press.

48. For Johnson's 1965 speech at Howard University, see http://www.lbjlib.utexas.edu/johnson/archives.hom/speeches.hom/650604.asp.

49. Glazer, Nathan. 1975. *Affirmative Discrimination: Ethnic Inequality and Public Policy*. New York: Basic. Walkowski, Paul J., and Adolph Caso. 1999. *Affirmative Action, Affirmative Discrimination*. Wellesley, Mass.: Branden.

50. This section draws heavily on the work of Amartya Sen and Martha Nussbaum. See the following: Sen, Amartya. 1992. *Inequality Reexamined*. Cambridge: Harvard University Press. Sen, Amartya. 1999. *Development as Freedom*. New York: Random House. Sen, Amartya, and Jean Dreze. 1999. *The Amartya Sen and Jean Dreze Omnibus: Comprising Poverty and Famines, Hunger and Public Action, and India: Economic Development and Social Opportunity*. New York: Oxford University Press. Nussbaum, Martha C. 2000. *Women and Human Development: The Capabilities Approach*. New York: Cambridge University Press.

51. Cherlin, Andrew J. 1999. *Public and Private Families*. New York: McGraw Hill. Cheal, David J. 2002. *Sociology of Family Life*. New York: Palgrave Macmillan. Folbre, Nancy. 2001. *The Invisible Heart: Economics and Family Values*. New York: New Press. Casper, Lynne M., and Suzanne M. Bianchi. 2001. *Continuity and Change in the American Family*. Newbury Park, Calif.: Sage.

52. Aries, Philippe. 1965. *Centuries of Childhood: A Social History of Family Life*. New York: Random House. Stone, Lawrence. 1990. *The Family, Sex and Marriage in England 1500–1800*. London: Penguin.

53. Bianchi, Suzanne M., and Daphne Spain. 1986. *American Women in Transition: The Population of the United States in the 1980s*. New York: Russell Sage Foundation. Spain, Daphne, and Suzanne M. Bianchi. 1996. *Balancing Act: Motherhood, Marriage, and Employment among American Women*. New York: Russell Sage Foundation.

54. Ehrenreich, Barbara, and Arlie R. Hochschild. 2003. *Global Woman: Nannies, Maids, and Sex Workers in the New Economy*. New York: Metropolitan.

55. Reich, Robert B. 1992. *The Work of Nations: Preparing Ourselves for 21st-Century Capitalism*. New York: Vintage. Bell, Daniel. 1999. *The Coming of Post-Industrial Society*. New York: Basic. Thurow, Lester C. 2002. *Building Wealth: The*

New Rules for Individuals, Companies, and Nations in a Knowledge-Based Economy. New York: Harper Collins.

56. Massey, Douglas S. 2000. "Higher Education and Social Mobility in the United States, 1940–1998." Pp. 45–66 in *America's Research Universities: Quality, Innovation, Partnership*, edited by Ann Leigh Speicher. Washington, D.C.: Association of American Universities.

57. Green, Gareth M., and Frank Baker. 1991. *Work, Health, and Productivity.* New York: Oxford University Press. Folland, Sherman. 2002. *The Economics of Health and Health Care.* New York: Prentice Hall.

58. Lino, Mark. 2002. *Expenditures on Children by Families, 2001 Annual Report.* Washington, D.C.: Center for Nutrition Policy and Promotion, U.S. Department of Agriculture.

59. James, *The End of Globalization.* Kapstein and Milanovic, *When Markets Fail.*

60. McElvaine, Robert S. 1994. *The Great Depression: America 1929–1941.* New York: Times Books. Watkins, T. H. 1995. *The Great Depression: America in the 1930s.* Boston: Back Bay.

61. Capelli, Peter. 1999. *The New Deal at Work: Managing the Market-Driven Workforce.* Cambridge: Harvard Business School Press. Reagan, Patrick D. 2000. *Designing a New America: The Origins of New Deal Planning, 1890–1943.* Amherst: University of Massachusetts Press.

62. Inglehart, Ronald. 1989. *Culture Shift in Advanced Industrial Society.* Princeton: Princeton University Press. Kluegel and Smith, *Beliefs about Inequality.* Hochschild, *Facing Up to the American Dream.*

63. Esping-Anderson, *The Three Worlds of Welfare Capitalism.*

64. Kornblum, Allan N. 1976. *The Moral Hazards: Police Strategies for Honesty and Ethical Behavior.* Boston: Lexington. Parker, Hermione. 1982. *Moral Hazard of Social Benefits: A Study of the Impact of Social Benefits and Income Tax on Incentives to Work.* Oxford: Transatlantic Arts.

65. Skocpol, Theda. 1995. *Protecting Soldiers and Mothers: The Political Origins of Social Policy in the United States.* Cambridge: Harvard University Press. Katz, Michael B. 1997. *In the Shadow of the Poorhouse: A Social History of Welfare in America.* New York: Basic. Katz, Michael B. 2002. *The Price of Citizenship: Redefining the American Welfare State.* New York: Henry Holt.

66. Glasberg, Davita S., and Dan Skidmore. 1997. *Corporate Welfare Policy and the Welfare State: Bank Deregulation and the Savings and Loan Bailout.* New York: Aldine de Gruyter.

67. Calavita, Kitty, Henry N. Pontell, and Robert H. Tillman. 1997. *Big Money Crime: Fraud and Politics in the Savings and Loan Crisis.* Berkeley: University of California Press. Rosoff, Stephen M., Robert Tillman, and Henry Pontell. 1997. *Profit Without Honor: White Collar Crime and the Looting of America.* New York: Prentice Hall. Fox, Loren. 2002. *Enron: The Rise and Fall.* New York: John Wiley. McLean, Bethany, and Peter Elkind. 2003. *Smartest*

Guys in the Room: The Amazing Rise and Scandalous Fall of Enron. New York: Portfolio.

68. Palast, Greg. 2002. *The Best Democracy Money Can Buy: An Investigative Reporter Exposes the Truth about Globalization, Corporate Cons, and High Finance Fraudsters.* London: Pluto. Huffington, Arianna. 2003. *Pigs at the Trough: How Corporate Greed and Political Corruption Are Undermining America.* New York: Crown. Ivins, Molly, and Lou Dubose. 2003. *Bushwhacked: Life in George W. Bush's America.* New York: Random House. Hightower, Jim. 2003. *Thieves in High Places: They've Stolen Our Country—And It's Time to Take It Back.* New York: Viking.

69. See Halliburton Corporation's website at http://www.halliburton.com/about/index.jsp.

70. See the task force's website at http://www.nrdc.org/air/energy/taskforce/tfinx.asp.

71. Krugman, Paul. 2003. *The Great Unraveling: Losing Our Way in the New Century.* New York: Norton.

72. Palast, *The Best Democracy Money Can Buy.* McLean and Elkind, *Smartest Guys in the Room.*

Chapter 4: Domestic Policies

1. Phillips, Kevin. 1990. *The Politics of Rich and Poor: Wealth and the American Electorate in the Reagan Aftermath.* New York: Random House. Wolff, Edward. 1996. *Top Heavy: The Increasing Inequality of Wealth in America and What Can Be Done About It.* New York: New Press. Levy, Frank. 1998. *The New Dollars and Dreams: American Incomes and Economic Change.* New York: Russell Sage Foundation. Bernhardt, Annette D., Martina Morris, Mark S. Handcock, and Marc A. Scott. 2001. *Divergent Paths: Economic Mobility in the New American Labor Market.* New York: Russell Sage.

2. Phillips, *The Politics of Rich and Poor.* Danziger, Sheldon, and Peter Gottschalk. 1997. *America Unequal.* Cambridge: Harvard University Press. Wolff, *Top Heavy.* Levy, *The New Dollars and Dreams.* Bernhardt et al., *Divergent Paths.*

3. Schrag, Peter. 1998. *Paradise Lost: California's Experience, America's Future.* Berkeley: University of California Press.

4. Phillips, *The Politics of Rich and Poor.* Danziger and Gottschalk, *America Unequal.* Wolff, *Top Heavy.* Levy *The New Dollars and Dreams.* Bernhardt et al., *Divergent Paths.*

5. Galster, George C., and Edward W. Hill. 1992. *The Metropolis in Black and White: Place, Power, and Polarization.* New Brunswick, N.J.: Rutgers University Press. Brooks-Gunn, Jeanne, Greg J. Duncan, and J. Lawrence Aber. 1997. *Neighborhood Poverty: Context and Consequences for Children.* New York: Russell

Sage Foundation. Polednak, Anthony P. 1997. *Segregation, Poverty, and Mortality in Urban African Americans*. New York: Oxford University Press. Fitzpatrick, Kevin M., and Mark LaGory. 2000. *Unhealthy Places: The Ecology of Risk in the Urban Landscape*. New York: Routledge.

6. Hays, R. Allen. 1985. *The Federal Government and Urban Housing: Ideology and Change in Public Policy*. Albany: State University of New York Press. Danziger and Gottschalk, *America Unequal*.

7. Dolbeare, Cushing N. 2001. "Changing Priorities: The Federal Budget and Housing Assistance, 1976–2006." Available at http://www.nlihc.org/pubs/appendixbtable4.htm.

8. Massey, Douglas S., and Mitchell L. Eggers. 1993. "The Spatial Concentration of Affluence and Poverty During the 1970s." *Urban Affairs Quarterly* 29: 299–315. Jargowsky, Paul A. 1997. *Poverty and Place: Ghettos, Barrios, and the American City*. New York: Russell Sage Foundation. Massey, Douglas S., and Mary J. Fischer. 2003. "The Geography of Inequality in the United States 1950–2000." Pp. 1–40 in *Brookings-Wharton Papers on Urban Affairs 2003*, edited by William G. Gale and Janet Rothenberg Pack. Washington, D.C.: Brookings Institution.

9. Simon, Julian. 1981. *The Ultimate Resource*. Princeton: Princeton University Press.

10. Barro, Robert J. 1998. *Determinants of Economic Growth: A Cross-Country Empirical Study*. Lionel Robbins Lectures. Cambridge: MIT Press. O'Rourke, Kevin H., and Jeffrey G. Williamson. 1999. *Globalization and History: The Evolution of a Nineteenth Century Atlantic Economy*. Cambridge: MIT Press. Madrick, Jeff. 2002. *Why Economies Grow: The Forces that Shape Prosperity and How to Get Them Working Again*. New York: Basic.

11. Sen, Amartya. 1999. *Development as Freedom*. New York: Random House. Sen, Amartya, and Jean Dreze. 1999. *The Amartya Sen and Jean Dreze Omnibus: Comprising Poverty and Famines, Hunger and Public Action, and India: Economic Development and Social Opportunity*. Oxford: Oxford University Press. Sen, Amartya, and Martha C. Nussbaum. 1993. *The Quality of Life*. Oxford: Oxford University Press. Nussbaum, Martha C. 2000. *Women and Human Development: The Capabilities Approach*. New York: Cambridge University Press.

12. Krugman, Paul. 1997. *Development, Geography, and Economic Theory*. Ohlin Lectures. Cambridge: MIT Press. Ben-David, Dan, Hakan Nordstrom, and Alan Winters. 1999. *Trade, Income, Disparity, and Poverty*. Geneva: World Trade Organization. Milanovic, Branko. 2002. "True World Income Distribution, 1988 and 1993: First Calculations Based on Household Surveys Alone." *The Economic Journal* 112:51–92. Della Paolera, Gerardo, and Alan M. Taylor. 2003. *A New Economic History of Argentina*. New York: Cambridge University Press.

13. Palast, Greg. 2003. *The Best Democracy Money Can Buy: The Truth about Corporate Cons, Globalization, and High-Finance Fraudsters*. New York: Plume.

Corn, David. 2003. *The Lies of George W. Bush: Mastering the Politics of Deception.* New York: Crown. Conason, Joe. 2003. *Big Lies: The Right-Wing Propaganda Machine and How It Distorts the Truth.* New York: St. Martin's.

14. Yinger, John. 1993. *Closed Doors, Opportunities Lost: The Continuing Costs of Housing Discrimination.* New York: Russell Sage Foundation. Turner, Margery Austin, Stephen L. Ross, George Galster, and John Yinger. 2002. *Discrimination in Metropolitan Housing Markets: National Results from Phase I of HDS2000.* Washington, D.C.: Urban Institute Press.

15. Ross, Stephen L., and John Yinger. 2002. *The Color of Credit: Mortgage Discrimination, Research Methodology, and Fair-Lending Enforcement.* Cambridge: MIT Press. Turner, Margery Austin, Fred Freiberg, Erin B. Godfrey, Carla Herbig, Diane Levy, Robin E. Smith. 2002. *All Other Things Being Equal: A Paired Testing Study of Mortgage Lending Institutions.* Washington, D.C.: Urban Institute Press.

16. Turner, Margery Austin, Michael E. Fix, Raymond J. Struyk. 1991. *Opportunities Denied, Opportunities Diminished.* Washington, D.C.: Urban Institute Press. Bertrand, Marianne, and Sendhil Mullainathan. 2002. "Are Emily and Brendan More Employable than Lakisha and Jamal? A Field Experiment on Labor Market Discrimination." *Capital Ideas: Research Highlights from the University of Chicago Graduate School of Business* 4 (4):1–2.

17. Fix, Michael E., and Margery Austin Turner. 1998. *A National Report Card on Discrimination in America: The Role of Testing.* Washington, D.C.: Urban Institute Press. Smelser, Neil, William Julius Wilson, and Faith Mitchell, eds. 2001. *America Becoming: Racial Trends and Their Consequences,* vols. I and II. Washington, D.C.: National Academies Press.

18. Schuman, Howard, Charlotte Steeh, Lawrence Bobo, and Maria Krysan. 1998. *Racial Attitudes in America: Trends and Interpretations.* Cambridge: Harvard University Press.

19. Metcalfe, George R. 1988. *Fair Housing Comes of Age.* New York: Greenwood. Schwemm, Robert G. 1990. *Housing Discrimination: Law and Litigation.* New York: Boardman.

20. Fix, Michael, Raymond J. Struyk. 1992. *Clear and Convincing Evidence: Measurement of Discrimination in America.* Lanham, Md.: Rowman and Littlefield.

21. Galster, George C. 1990. "Racial Discrimination in Housing Markets in the 1980s: A Review of the Audit Evidence." *Journal of Planning Education and Research* 9:165–75. Massey, Douglas S., and Nancy A. Denton. 1993. *American Apartheid: Segregation and the Making of the Underclass.* Cambridge: Harvard University Press.

22. Kushner, James A. 1988. "An Unfinished Agenda: The Fair Housing Enforcement Effort." *Yale Law and Policy Review* 6:348–60. Galster, George C. 2001. "Progress in Integration HAS Been Made." Pp. 70–71 in *Challenges to Equality,* edited by Chester Hartman. Armonk, N.Y.: Sharpe. Galster, George C. 1996.

"Future Directions in Mortgage Discrimination Research and Enforcement." Pp. 679–716 in *Mortgage Lending, Racial Discrimination, and Public Policy*, edited by John Goering and Ronald Wienk. Washington, D.C.: Urban Institute Press.

23. House, James S., Karl R. Landis, and Debra Umberson. 1988. "Social Relationships and Health." *Science* 241:540–45. Waite, Linda J., and Maggie Gallegher. 2001. *The Case for Marriage: Why Married People Are Happier, Healthier, and Better Off Financially.* New York: Broadway.

24. Rogers, Richard G, Robert A. Hummer, and Charles B. Nam. 2000. *Living and Dying in the USA: Behavioral, Health, and Social Differentials of Adult Mortality.* San Diego: Academic. Lantz, Paula M., John W. Lynch, James S. House, et al. 2001. "Socioeconomic Disparitites in Health Change in a Longitudinal Study of U.S. Adults: The Role of Health Risk Behaviors." *Social Science and Medicine* 53:29–40.

25. Coale, Ansley J. 1974. "The History of the Human Population." Pp. 15–28 in *The Human Population.* San Francisco: Freeman. Preston, Samuel H. 1995. "Human Mortality Throughout History and Prehistory." Pp. 30–36 in *The State of Humanity*, edited by Julian Simon. London: Blackwell. Riley, James C. 2001. *Rising Life Expectancy: A Global History.* Cambridge: Cambridge University Press. Preston, Samuel H., and Kevin M. White. 1996. How Many Americans Are Alive Because of Twentieth-Century Improvements in Mortality?" *Population and Development Review* 22:415–29.

26. See American Association for the Advancement of Science Website, *R&D Budget Policy Program*, at www.aaas.org/spp/rd.

27. Crimmins, Eileen. 1981. "The Changing Pattern of American Mortality Decline, 1947–1977." *Population and Development Review* 7:229–54. Crimmins, Eileen. 1997. "Trends in Mortality, Morbidity and Disability: What Should We Expect for the Future of Our Aging Population." Pp. 317–25 in *International Population Conference: Beijing, 1997.* Liege, Belgium: International Union for the Scientific Study of Population. Wilmoth, John R. 2003. "Mortality Decline." Pp. 654–62 in *Encyclopedia of Population*, edited by Paul Demeny and Geoffrey McNicoll. New York: Macmillan.

28. Olson, Mancur. 1971. *Logic of Collective Action: Public Goods and the Theory of Groups.* Cambridge: Harvard University Press. Samuelson, Paul A., and William H. Norhaus. 2001. *Economics.* 17th ed. New York: McGraw Hill.

29. Nozick, Robert. 1977. *Anarchy, State and Utopia.* New York: Free Press. Boaz, David. 1998. *Libertarianism: A Primer.* New York: Free Press. Murray, Charles. 1998. *What It Means to Be a Libertarian: A Personal Interpretation.* New York: Broadway.

30. McNeill, William H. 1998. *Plagues and Peoples.* New York: Anchor. Diamond, Jared. 1999. *Guns, Germs, and Steel: The Fates of Human Societies.* New York: Norton. Oldstone, Michael B. A. 2000. *Viruses, Plagues, and History.* Oxford: Oxford University Press.

31. Olson, Mancur. 1982. *The Rise and Decline of Nations: Economic Growth, Stagflation, and Social Rigidities.* New Haven: Yale University Press.

32. Ivins, Molly, and Lou Dubose. 2003. *Bushwhacked: Life in George W. Bush's America.* New York: Random House. Krugman, Paul. 2003. *The Great Unraveling: Losing Our Way in the New Century.* New York: Norton. Corn, *The Lies of George W. Bush.*

33. Kozol, Jonathan. 1991. *Savage Inequalities: Children in America's Schools.* New York: Crown.

34. Gatto, John Taylor. 2003. "Against School: How Public Education Cripples Our Kids, and Why." *Harper's* 307 (September).

35. National Commission on Excellence in Education. 1994. *A Nation at Risk: The Full Account.* Washington, D.C.: USA Research. Wong, Kenneth K., James W. Guthrie, and Douglas N. Harris. 2003. *A Nation at Risk: A Twenty-Year Reappraisal.* Mahwah, N.J.: Erlbaum.

36. Brinton, Mary C. 1993. *Women and the Economic Miracle: Gender and Work in Postwar Japan.* Berkeley: University of California Press. Folbre, Nancy. 2001. *The Invisible Heart: Economics and Family Values.* New York: New Press.

37. Davis, Kingsley, and Pietronella van den Oever. 1982. "Demographic Foundations of New Sex Roles." *Population and Development Review* 8: 495–511.

38. Fischer, Claude S. 1975. "Toward a Subcultural Theory of Urbanism." *American Journal of Sociology* 80:1319–41. Fischer, Claude S. 1995. "The Subcultural Theory of Urbanism: A Twentieth-Year Assessment." *American Journal of Sociology* 101:543–77.

39. Jameson, Fredric, and Masao Miyoushi. 1998. *The Cultures of Globalization.* Durham, N.C.: Duke University Press. Urban, Greg. 2001. *Metaculture: How Culture Moves Through the World.* Minneapolis: University of Minnesota Press.

40. Toffler, Alvin. 1984. *Future Shock.* New York: Bantam. Hann, C. M. 1994. *When History Accelerates: Essays on Rapid Social Change, Complexity and Creativity.* London: Althone.

41. Rifkin, Jeremy. 1995. *The End of Work: The Decline of the Global Labor Force and the Dawn of the Post-Market Era.* New York: Putnam. Cappelli, Peter, Laurie Bassi, Harry Katz, David Knoke, Paul Osterman, and Michael Useem. 1997. *Change at Work.* New York: Oxford University Press. Walsham, Geoff. 2001. *Making a World of Difference: IT in a Global Context.* New York: Wiley. Kennedy, Paul. 1993. *Preparing for the Twenty-First Century.* New York: Random House.

42. Block, Fred, and Gene A. Burns. 1986. "Productivity as a Social Problem: The Uses and Misuses of Social Indicators. *American Sociological Review* 51:767–80.

43. Olson, Mancur. 1982. *The Rise and Decline of Nations: Economic Growth, Stagflation, and Social Rigidities.* New Haven: Yale University Press.

44. Krugman, *The Great Unraveling.*

45. Preston, Samuel H. 1984. "Children and the Elderly: Divergent Paths for America's Dependents." *Demography* 21:435–57.

46. *United Nations Demographic Yearbook.* 2000. New York: United Nations.

47. National Center for Educational Statistics. 2003. *The Condition of Education 2003: Indicator 40—International Comparisons of Expenditures for Education.* Washington, D.C.: U.S. Government Printing Office.

48. U.S. Immigration and Naturalization Service. 1991. *1990 Statistical Yearbook of the Immigration and Naturalization Service.* Washington, D.C.: U.S. Government Printing Office. U.S. Immigration and Naturalization Service. 2001. *2000 Statistical Yearbook of the Immigration and Naturalization Service.* Washington, D.C.: U.S. Government Printing Office.

49. Ibid.

50. Kuh, Charlotte. 2001. "Reflecting America? Immigrants, Women, and Minorities in the S&T Workforce," in *Making Strides.* Washington, D.C.: American Association for the Advancement of Science.

51. Brinton, *Women and the Economic Miracle.*

52. College Board. 1998. *The 1998 College-Bound Seniors, National Report.* New York: College Board.

53. Western, Bruce, and Becky Pettit. 2000. "Incarceration and Racial Inequality in Men's Employment." *Industrial and Labor Relations Review* 54:3–16. Western, Bruce, Jeffrey R. Kling, and David F. Weiman. 2001. "The Labor Market Consequences of Incarceration." *Crime and Delinquency* 47:410–27. Beckett, Katherine, and Bruce Western. 2001. "Governing Social Marginality: Welfare, Incarceration, and the Transformation of State Policy." Pp. 35–50 in *Mass Imprisonment: Social Causes and Consequences,* edited by David Garland. London: Sage.

54. Western, Bruce and Katherine Beckett. 1999. "How Unregulated Is the U.S. Labor Market? The Penal System as a Labor Market Institution." *American Journal of Sociology* 104:1030–60.

55. Justice Policy Institute. 2002. *Cellblocks or Classrooms? The Funding of Higher Education and Corrections and Its Impact on African American Men.* Washington, D.C.: Justice Policy Institute.

56. Tonry, Michael. 1995. *Malign Neglect: Race, Crime, and Punishment in America.* New York: Oxford University Press. Gainsborough, Jenni, and Marc Mauer. 2001. *Diminishing Returns: Crime and Incarceration in the 1990s.* Washington, D.C.: The Sentencing Project.

Chapter 5: Global Policies

1. O'Rourke, Kevin H., and Jeffrey G. Williamson. 1999. *Globalization and History: The Evolution of a Nineteenth-Century Atlantic Economy.* Cambridge: MIT

Press. James, Harold. 2001. *The End of Globalization: Lessons from the Great Depression.* Cambridge: Harvard University Press. Aghion, Philippe, and Jeffrey G. Williamson. 1999. *Growth, Inequality, and Globalization: Theory, History, and Policy.* Cambridge: Cambridge University Press.

2. Hatton, Timothy J., and Jeffrey G. Williamson. 1994. *Migration and the International Labour Market, 1850–1939.* London: Routledge. Hatton, Timothy J., and Jeffrey G. Williamson. 1998. *The Age of Mass Migration: Causes and Economic Impact.* Oxford: Oxford University Press. Massey, Douglas S., and J. Edward Taylor. 2004. "Back to the Future: Immigration Research, Immigration Policy, and Globalization in the Twenty-First Century." Pp. 375–94 in *International Migration: Prospects and Policies,* edited by J. Edward Taylor and Douglas S. Massey. Oxford: Oxford University Press.

3. Thomas, Dorothy Swaine. 1941. *Social and Economic Aspects of Swedish Population Movements, 1750–1933.* New York: Macmillan. Thomas Brinley. 1973. *Migration and Economic Growth: A Study of Great Britain and the Atlantic Economy.* Cambridge: Cambridge University Press.

4. Kenwood, A. George, and Alan L. Lougheed. 1999. *The Growth of the International Economy 1820–2000.* London: Routledge.

5. McGillivray, Fiona, Iain McLean, Robert Pahre, and Cheryl Schonhardt-Bailey. 2002. *International Trade and Political Institutions: Instituting Trade in the Long 19th Century.* London: Edward Elgar. Hobsbawm, Eric J. 1997. *Age of Empire: 1875–1914.* London: Peter Smith.

6. Williamson, Jeffrey. 1997. *Industrialization, Inequality and Economic Growth.* London: Edward Elgar.

7. Strachan, Hew. 2003. *The First World War: To Arms.* Oxford: Oxford University Press.

8. Gilbert, Martin. 1994. *The First World War: A Complete History.* New York: Henry Holt. Tuchman, Barbara W. 1994. *Guns of August.* New York: Ballentine. Keegan, John. 1999. *The First World War.* New York: Knopf. Ferguson, Niall. 2000. *The Pity of War: Explaining World War I.* New York: Basic.

9. "I remember that a fortnight or so before the last war, the Kaiser's friend Herr Ballin, the great shipping magnate, told me that he had heard Bismarck say towards the end of his life, 'If there is ever another war in Europe, it will come out of some damned silly thing in the Balkans.'" Winston Churchill, House of Commons, 16 August 1945.

10. Nicholson, Colin. 2001. *The Longman Companion to the First World War.* Saddle River, N.J.: Longman.

11. Aaronson, Susan Ariel. 2001. *Taking Trade to the Streets: The Lost History of Public Efforts to Shape Globalization.* Ann Arbor: University of Michigan Press.

12. Gilbert, Martin. 1991. *The Second World War: A Complete History.* New York: Henry Holt. Taylor, A.J.P. 1996. *The Origins of the Second World War.* New York: Touchstone.

13. Times of London. *The Times Atlas of the Second World War*. London: Times of London.

14. Schlesinger, Stephen. 2003. *Act of Creation: The Founding of the United Nations: A Story of Superpowers, Secret Agents, Wartime Allies and Enemies, and Their Quest for a Peaceful World*. Boulder, Colo.: Westview.

15. Fasulo, Linda. 2003. *An Insider's Guide to the UN*. New Haven: Yale University Press.

16. De Vries, Margaret G. 1986. *The IMF in a Changing World, 1945–85*. Washington, D.C.: International Monetary Fund. Peet, Richard. 2003. Polak, Jacques J., and Catherine Gwin. 1994. *The World Bank and the International Monetary Fund: A Changing Relationship*. Washington, D.C.: Brookings Institution. Kapur, Devesh, John P. Lewis, and Richard C. Webb. 1997. *The World Bank: Its First Half Century*. Washington, D.C.: Brookings Institution.

17. Aaronson, *Taking Trade to the Streets*, 30–84.

18. Gordon, David M. 1994. "Chickens Come Home to Roost: From Prosperity to Stagnation in the Postwar U.S. Economy." Pp. 34–76 in *Understanding American Economic Decline*, edited by Michael A. Bernstein and David E. Adler. New York: Cambridge University Press. Halberstam, David. 1986. *The Reckoning*. New York: Morrow.

19. Massey, Douglas S. 2003. "Mondialisation et Migrations: L'Exemple des Etat-Unis." *Futuribles* 284:1–9.

20. Melchior, Arne, Kjetil Telle, and HenrikWiig. 2000. "Globalisation and Inequality: World Income Distribution and Living Standards 1960–1998." *Studies on Foreign Policy Issues*, Report 6b, Norwegian Ministry of Foreign Affairs. World Bank. 1998. *1997 Human Development Report*. Washington, D.C.: World Bank. Lindert, Peter, and Jeffrey G. Williamson. 2003. "Does Globalization Make the World More Unequal?" Pp. 227–71 in *Globalization in Historical Perspective*, edited by Michael Bordo, Allan M. Taylor, and Jeffrey G. Williamson. Chicago: University of Chicago Press.

21. Sen, Amartya. 1999. *Development as Freedom*. New York: Random House. Dowrick, Steve, and J. Bradford DeLong. 2003. "Globalization and Convergence." Pp. 110–18 in *Globalization in Historical Perspective*, edited by Michael Bordo, Allan M. Taylor, and Jeffrey G. Williamson. Chicago: University of Chicago Press.

22. Madrick, Jeff. 2002. *Why Economies Grow: The Forces That Shape Prosperity and How to Get Them Working Again*. New York: Basic. Krauss, Melvyn. 1997. *How Nations Grow Rich: The Case for Free Trade*. Oxford: Oxford University Press.

23. Aaronson, *Taking Trade to the Streets*, 64.

24. Williamson, John. 2000. "What Should the World Bank Think About the Washington Consensus?" *World Bank Research Observer* 15 (August): 251–64. Washington, D.C.: The International Bank for Reconstruction and Development. Williamson, John. 2003. "An Agenda for Restarting Growth and Reform."

Pp. 1–19 in *After the Washington Consensus: Restarting Growth and Reform in Latin America*, edited by Pedro-Pablo Kuczynski and John Williamson. Washington, D.C.: Institute for International Economics.

25. Stiglitz, Joseph E. 2002. *Globalization and Its Discontents*. New York: Norton. Nam, Moises. 2000. "Washington Consensus or Washington Confusion?" *Foreign Policy* (spring).

26. Einhorn, Jessica. 2001. "The World Bank's Mission Creep." *Foreign Affairs* (September/October). Hockett, Robert. 2002. "From Macro to Micro to Mission Creep: Defending the IMF's Emerging Concern with Infrastructural Prerequisites to Global Financial Stability." *Columbia Journal of Transnational Law* 41:152–93.

27. Stiglitz, *Globalization and Its Discontents*, 14.

28. Ibid., 35.

29. Collier, Simon, and William F. Sater. 1996. *A History of Chile, 1808–1994*. New York: Cambridge University Press. Salces, Alejandra Mizala. 2003. *Financial Market Liberalization in Chile, 1973–1982*. New York: Garland. Bouzas, Roberto, and Saúl Keifman. 2003. "Making Trade Liberalization Work." Pp. 157–79 in *After the Washington Consensus*, edited by Kuczynski and Williamson. Centeno, Miguel A., and Alejandro Portes. 2004. "The Informal Economy in the Shadow of the State." Forthcoming in *Out of the Shadows: The Informal Economy and Political Movements in Latin America*, edited by Patricia Fernandez Kelly and Jon Sheffner. Princeton: Princeton University Press.

30. Palast, Greg. 2003. *The Best Democracy Money Can Buy: The Truth about Corporate Cons, Globalization, and High Finance Fraudsters*. New York: Plume.

31. Loveman, Brian. 2001. *Chile: The Legacy of Hispanic Capitalism*. Oxford: Oxford University Press. Valdes, Juan Gabriel. 2003. *Pinochet's Economists: The Chicago School of Economics in Chile*. Cambridge: Cambridge University Press.

32. Stiglitz, *Globalization and Its Discontents*, 73–78.

33. Hall, Peter A., and David W. Soskice. 2001. *Varieties of Capitalism: The Institutional Foundations of Comparative Advantage*. Oxford: Oxford University Press. Fligstein, Neil. 2001. *The Architecture of Markets: An Economic Sociology of Twenty-First Century Capitalist Societies*. Princeton: Princeton University Press. Whitley, Richard. 2000. *Divergent Capitalisms: The Social Structuring and Change of Business Systems*. Oxford: Oxford University Press. Guillén, Mauro. 2001. *The Limits of Convergence: Globalization and Organizational Change in Argentina, South Korea, and Spain*. Princeton: Princeton University Press.

34. De Soto, Hernando. 2000. *The Mystery of Capital: Why Capitalism Triumphs in the West and Fails Everywhere Else*. New York: Basic.

35. Friedman, Thomas L. 2000. *The Lexus and the Olive Tree: Understanding Globalization*. New York: Farrar Straus and Giroux.

36. Stiglitz, *Globalization and Its Discontents*, 62–67.

37. Ibid., 89–132. Healey, Mark Alan, and Ernesto Seman. 2002. "Down, Argentine Way: How the IMF's Darling Collapsed." *The American Prospect*, January 28.

38. Agénor, Pierre-Richard, Marcus Miller, David Vines, and Axel Weber, eds. 2000. *The Asian Financial Crisis: Causes, Contagion and Consequences.* Cambridge: Cambridge University Press. Noble, Gregory W., and John Ravenhill, eds. 2002. *The Asian Financial Crisis and the Architecture of Global Finance.* Cambridge: Cambridge University Press. Garcia, Valeriano F. 1997. *Black December: Banking Instability, the Mexican Crisis, and Its Effect on Argentina.* Washington, D.C.: World Bank. Ferrer, Aldo, and Pablo Ariel Grinspun. 2003. *Crisis Argentina y Globalizacion.* Buenos Aires: Nuevo Hacer.

39. Kaplan, Robert D. 1997. *The Ends of the Earth: From Togo to Turkmenistan, from Iran to Cambodia, a Journey to the Frontiers of Anarchy.* New York: Vintage. Ayittey, George B. N. 1999. *Africa in Chaos.* New York: St. Martin's. Van de Walle, Nicolas. 2001. *African Economies and the Politics of Permanent Crisis, 1979–1999.* New York: Cambridge University Press.

40. Sachs, Jeffrey D., and Katharina Pistor. 1997. *The Rule of Law and Economic Reform in Russia.* Boulder, Colo.: Westview. Mason, David S. 1997. *Revolution and Transition in East-Central Europe.* Boulder, Colo.: Westview. Hoffman, David E. 2002. *The Oligarchs: Wealth and Power in the New Russia.* New York: Perseus.

41. Poznanski, Kazimierz. 1997. *Poland's Protracted Transition: Institutional Change and Economic Growth, 1970–1994.* Cambridge: Cambridge University Press. Lucas, Robert E. B., and Donald Verry. 1999. *Restructuring the Malaysian Economy: Development and Human Resources.* New York: Macmillan. Walter, Carl E., and Fraser J. T. Howie. 2001. *To Get Rich Is Glorious: China's Stock Markets in the '80s and '90s.* New York: Macmillan. Karadeloglou, Pavlos. 2002. *Enlarging the EU: The Trade Balance Effects.* New York: Macmillan. Webber, Michael, Mark Wang, and Zhu Ying. 2003. *China's Transition to a Global Economy.* New York: Macmillan. Bhagwati, Jagdesh. 2004. *In Defense of Globalization: How the New World Economy Is Helping Rich and Poor Alike.* New York: Oxford University Press.

42. Tonelson, Alan. 2002. *The Race to the Bottom: Why a Worldwide Worker Surplus and Uncontrolled Free Trade Are Sinking American Living Standards.* Boulder, Colo.: Westview. "Pat Buchanan on Free Trade & Immigration." *Issues 2000: Every Presidential Candidate's Views on Every Issue.* At www.issues2000.org/2000/Pat_Buchanan_Free_Trade_&_Immigration.htm.

43. Singer, Peter. 2002. *One World: The Ethics of Globalization.* New Haven: Yale University Press.

44. Goldenberg, Suzanne. 2003. "Up to 15,000 People Killed in Invasion, Claims Think Tank." *The Guardian,* October 29. Global Security. "Casualties in Iraq." At http://www.globalsecurity.org/index.html.

45. Dunn, Timothy. 1996. *The Militarization of the U.S.-Mexico Border, 1978–1992: Low-Intensity Conflict Doctrine Comes Home.* Austin: University of Texas Press. Baum, Dan. 1997. *Smoke and Mirrors: The War on Drugs and the Politics of Failure.* Boston: Back Bay. Andreas, Peter. 2000. *Border Games: Policing*

the U.S. Mexico Divide. Ithaca, NY: Cornell University Press. Massey, Douglas S., Jorge Durand, and Nolan J. Malone. 2002. *Beyond Smoke and Mirrors: Mexican Immigration in an Era of Economic Integration*. New York: Russell Sage Foundation.

46. Ewing, Alphonse B. 2003. *The USA Patriot Act*. Hauppauge N.Y.: Nova Science.

47. Gills, Barry K. 2000. *Globalization and the Politics of Resistance*. New York: Macmillan.

48. Cavanaugh, John, Jerry Mander, et al. 2002. *Alternatives to Globalization: A Better World Is Possible*. San Francisco: Barrett-Koehler. Danaher, Kevin, and Jason D. Mark. 2003. *Insurrection: Citizen Challenges to Corporate Power*. London: Routledge.

49. Solnit, David, and David E Kyvig. 2004. *Globalize Liberation: How to Uproot the System and Build a Better World*. San Francisco: City Lights Foundation Books. Sklair, Leslie. 2002. *Globalization: Capitalism and Its Alternatives*. Oxford: Oxford University Press.

50. Held, David, and Anthony McGrew. 2002. *Globalization/Anti-Globalization*. London: Polity. Held, David, and Anthony G. McGrew. 2002. *Governing Globalization: Power, Authority, and Global Governance*. London: Polity. Nye, Joseph S., and John D. Donahue. 2000. *Governance in a Globalizing World*. Washington, D.C.: Brookings Institution. Plattner, Marc F., and Aleksander Smolar. 2000. *Globalization, Power, and Democracy*. Baltimore: Johns Hopkins University Press.

51. Smith, Jackie G., and Hank Johnston. 2002. *Globalization and Resistance: Transnational Dimensions of Social Movements*. Lanham, Md.: Rowman and Littlefield. Brecher, Jeremy, Tim Costello, and Brendan Smith. 2000. *Globalization from Below*. Cambridge, Mass.: South End.

52. Kovel, Joel. 2002. *The Enemy of Nature: The End of Capitalism or the End of the World?* London: Zed. Ewald, Shawn. 2003. *Anarchism in Action: Methods, Tactics, Skills, and Ideas*. Online book at http://www.radio4all.org/aia/. Powell, William. 2003. *The Anarchist Cookbook*. Fort Lee, N.J.: Barricade.

53. Freeman, Derek. 1983. *Margaret Mead and Samoa: The Making and Unmaking of an Anthropological Myth*. Cambridge: Harvard University Press.

54. Burke, James. 2000. *Connections*. New York: St. Martin's. Burke, James. 2003. *Twin Tracks: The Unexpected Origins of the Modern World*. New York: Simon and Schuster.

55. Barber, Benjamin R. 1995. *Jihad vs. McWorld: How the Planet Is Both Falling Apart and Coming Together and What This Means for Democracy*. 1995. New York: Times Books. Gray, John. 1998. *False Dawn: The Illusions of Global Capitalism*. London: Granta. Jameson, Frederic. 2000. "Globalization and Strategy." *New Left Review* 4:49–68.

56. Iyer, Pico. 1988. *Video Night in Kathmandu: And Other Reports from the Not-so-far East*. London: Bloomsbury. Orvell, Miles. 1995. *After the Machine: Visual*

Arts and the Erasing of Cultural Boundaries. Jackson: University of Mississippi Press. Hannurz, Ulf. 1996. *Transnational Connections: Culture, People, Places.* London: Routledge.

57. Cowen, Tyler. 2002. *Creative Destruction: How Globalization Is Changing the World's Cultures.* Princeton: Princeton University Press. Pp. 47–72.

58. Ibid., 73–101.

59. Patterson, Orlando. 1987. "The Emerging West Atlantic System: Migration, Culture, and Underdevelopment in the U.S. and the Caribbean." Pp. 227–60 in *Population in an Interacting World*, edited by William Alonso. Cambridge: Harvard University Press. Patterson, Orlando. 1994. "Ecumenical America: Global Culture and the American Cosmos." *World Policy Journal* 11:103–17. Urban, Greg. 2001. *Metaculture: How Culture Moves Through the World.* Minneapolis: University of Minnesota Press.

60. McNeil, William H. 1976. *Plagues and Peoples.* New York: Anchor Press. Diamond, Jared. 1997. *Guns, Germs, and Steel: The Fates of Human Societies.* New York: Norton.

61. Cowen, *Creative Destruction*, 1–18, 128–52.

62. Hammel, Eugene A. 1990. "A Theory of Culture for Demography." *Population and Development Review* 16:455–85.

63. Goody, Jack, et al., eds. 1977. *The Domestication of the Savage Mind.* Cambridge: Cambridge University Press.

64. Singer, *One World*, 56–77.

65. Aaronson, *Taking Trade to the Streets*, 165.

66. Ibid., 178–79.

67. Nader, Ralph. 1993. *The Case Against Free Trade: GATT, NAFTA and the Globalization of Corporate Power.* New York: North Atlantic.

68. Singer, *One World*, 59–63.

69. Aaronson, *Taking Trade to the Streets*, 58–83.

70. Ibid., 174–89.

71. Singer, *One World*, 66.

72. Ibid., 58.

73. Aaronson, *Taking Trade to the Streets*, 150.

74. World Trade Organization. 2002. *Ten Common Misunderstandings about the WTO.* Geneva: World Trade Organization. At www.wto.org/english/thewto_e/whatis_e/inbrief_e/inbro3_e.htm, and cited in Singer, *One World*, 57.

75. Aaronson, *Taking Trade to the Streets*, 174–89.

76. Ibid., 174–76.

77. National Research Council Committee on Monitoring International Labor Standards. 2004. *Monitoring International Labor Standards: Toward Better Techniques and More Reliable Sources of Information.* Washington, D.C.: National Academies Press.

78. Stiglitz, *Globalization and Its Discontents*, 214–52.

79. Singer, *One World,* 75–77, 96–105, 145.

80. Nye, Joseph S. 2003. *The Paradox of American Power: Why the World's Only Superpower Can't Go It Alone.* New York: Oxford University Press.

81. Stiglitz, *Globalization and Its Discontents,* 222.

82. Ibid., 217.

Chapter 6: Liberalism and Its Discontents

1. Lawrence, Bruce. 1992. *Defenders of God: The Fundamentalist Revolt against the Modern Age.* San Francisco: Harper and Row. P. 100.

2. Almond, Gabriel A., Emmanuel Sivan, and R. Scott Appleby. 1995. "Fundamentalism: Genus and Species." Pp. 399–424 in *Fundamentalisms Comprehended,* edited by Martin E. Marty and R. Scott Appleby. Chicago: University of Chicago Press. P. 403.

3. The five volumes of the Fundamentalisms Project are as follows: Marty, Martin E., and R. Scott Appleby, eds. 1991. *Fundamentalisms Observed.* Chicago: University of Chicago Press. Hardacre, Helen, Everett Mendelsohn, and Majid Tehranian, eds. 1993. *Fundamentalisms and Society: Reclaiming the Sciences, the Family, and Education.* Chicago: University of Chicago Press. Garvey, John H., Timur Kuran, and David C. Rapoport, eds. 1993. *Fundamentalisms and the State: Remaking Polities, Economies, and Militance.* Chicago: University of Chicago Press. Almond, Gabriel A., R. Scott Appleby, and Emmanuel Sivan, eds. 1993. *Strong Religion: The Rise of Fundamentalisms around the World.* Chicago: University of Chicago Press. Ammerman, Nancy T., Robert E. Frykenberg, Samuel C. Heilman, and James Piscatori, eds. 1994. *Accounting for Fundamentalisms: The Dynamic Character of Movements.* Chicago: University of Chicago Press. Marty, Martin E. and R. Scott Appleby, eds. 1995. *Fundamentalisms Comprehended.* Chicago: University of Chicago Press.

4. Almond, Sivan, and Appleby, "Fundamentalism: Genus and Species," 406.

5. Marty, Martin E., and R. Scott Appleby. 1993. "Conclusion: An Interim Report on a Hypothetical Family." Pp. 825–26 in *Fundamentalisms Observed,* edited by Marty and Appleby.

6. Ibid., 827–28.

7. Almond, Sivan, and Appleby, "Fundamentalism: Genus and Species," 406–7.

8. Marty and Appleby, "Conclusion: An Interim Report on a Hypothetical Family," 819.

9. Ibid., 820.

10. Almond, Sivan, and Appleby, "Fundamentalism: Genus and Species," 407.

11. Marty and Appleby, "Conclusion: An Interim Report on a Hypothetical Family," 818.

12. Almond, Sivan, and Appleby, "Fundamentalism: Genus and Species," 407.

13. Marty and Appleby, "Conclusion: An Interim Report on a Hypothetical Family," 824.

14. Ibid., 825.

15. Almond, Sivan, and Appleby, "Fundamentalism: Genus and Species," 407–9.

16. Marty and Appleby, "Conclusion: An Interim Report on a Hypothetical Family," 826.

17. Burke, Jason. 2003. *Al-Qaeda: Casting a Shadow of Terror*. London: I. B. Taurus. Williams, Paul L. 2002. *Al Qaeda: Brotherhood of Terror*. New York: Alpha.

18. Sidahmed, Abdel Salam, and Anoushiravan Ehteshami, eds. 1996 *Islamic Fundamentalism*. Boulder, Colo.: Westview. Ojeda, Auriana. 2002. *Islamic Fundamentalism*. Farmington Hills, Mich.: Greenhaven. Hoveyda, Fereydoun. 2002. *The Broken Crescent: The "Threat" of Militant Islamic Fundamentalism*. Westport, Conn.: Praeger.

19. Sarkar, Sumit. 2002. *Beyond Nationalist Frames: Postmodernism, Hindu Fundamentalism, History*. Bloomington: Indiana University Press.

20. Shahak, Israel, and Norton Mezvinsky. 1999. *Jewish Fundamentalism in Israel*. London: Pluto.

21. Bartholomeusz, Tessa J. 2002. *In Defense of Dharma: Just-War Ideology in Buddhist Sri Lanka*. London: Routledge.

22. Easton, Nina J. 2000. *Gang of Five: Leaders at the Center of the Conservative Ascendancy*. New York: Simon and Schuster. Harding, Susan Friend. 2000. *The Book of Jerry Falwell: Fundamentalist Language and Politics*. Princeton: Princeton University Press. Brock, David. 2002. *Blinded by the Right: The Conscience of an Ex-Conservative*. New York: Crown. Conason, Joe. 2003. *Big Lies: The Right-Wing Propaganda Machine and How It Distorts the Truth*. New York: St. Martin's.

23. Mansfield, Stephen. 2003. *The Faith of George W. Bush*. 2003. Lake Mary, Fla.: Charisma House.

24. Conason, *Big Lies*, 99.

25. Krugman, Paul. 2003. *The Great Unraveling: Losing Our Way in the New Century*. New York: Norton. P. 7.

26. Center for Christian Statesmanship. At http://www.statesman.org/.

27. Ibid.

28. Sharlet, Jeffrey. 2003. "Jesus Plus Nothing: Undercover among America's Secret Theocrats." *Harper's* 306:53–64.

29. Ibid., 54.

30. Ibid., 55.

31. Ibid., 54, 56. According to the author, the members of Congress who have stayed at the townhouse include representatives Mike Doyle (D., Pennsylvania), Ed Bryant (R., Tennessee), John Baldacci (D., Maine), Bart Stupak

(R., Pennsylvania), and Senator John Ensign (R., Nevada). Others in Congress who are reportedly affiliates of the Family include senators Don Nickles (R., Oklahoma), Charles Grassley (R., Iowa), Pete Domenici (R., New Mexico), James Inhofe (R., Oklahoma), Bill Nelson (D., Florida), and Conrad Burns (R., Montana), as well as representatives Jim De Mint (R., South Carolina), Frank Wolf (R., Virginia), Jospeh Pitts (R., Pennsylvania), Zack Wamp (R., Tennessee), and Bart Tupak (D., Michigan).

32. Stiglitz, Joseph E. 2002. *Globalization and Its Discontents*. New York: Norton. P. 14. See also Frank, Thomas. 2001. *One Market Under God: Extreme Capitalism, Market Populism, and the End of Economic Democracy*. New York: Anchor.

33. Friedman, Milton, and Rose Friedman, 1980. *Free to Choose: A Personal Statement*. New York: Harcourt, Brace, Javanovich. Butler, Eamonn. 1985. *Milton Friedman: A Guide to His Economic Thought*. New York: Universe. Friedman, Milton, and Rose Friedman. 2002. *Capitalism and Freedom*. Chicago: University of Chicago Press.

34. John Petrie's Collection of Milton Friedman Quotes. At http://www.arches.uga.edu/~jpetrie/friedman.html.

35. Stiglitz, *Globalization and Its Discontents*, 58, 102, 114.

36. Easton, Nina J. 2000. *Gang of Five: Leaders at the Center of the Conservative Ascendancy*. New York: Simon and Schuster. P. 64.

37. Ibid., 67.

38. Posner, Richard A. 1972. *Economic Analysis of Law*. Boston: Little, Brown.

39. Easton, *Gang of Five*, 66.

40. Ibid., 188.

41. Ibid., 67–69.

42. Website of Federalist Society for Law and Public Policy Studies. At http://www.fed-soc.org/ourpurpose.htm.

43. Easton, *Gang of Five*, 66.

44. Drury, Shadia B. 1997. *Leo Strauss and the American Right*. New York: Macmillan.

45. Easton, *Gang of Five*, 40.

46. Ibid., 38, 40.

47. Bloom, Allan. 1988. *The Closing of the American Mind*. New York: Simon and Schuster.

48. Hunter, James Davison. 1992. *Culture Wars: The Struggle to Define America*. New York: Basic.

49. See Bennett, William J. 1993. *The Book of Virtues*. New York: Simon and Schuster. Bennett, William J. 1995. *The Children's Book of Virtues*. New York: Simon and Schuster. Himmelfarb, Gertrude. 1996. *The De-Moralization of Society: From Victorian Virtues to Modern Values*. New York: Vintage. Kristol, William. *The Neoconservative Imagination: Essays in Honor of Irving Kristol*. Washington, D.C.: American Enterprise Institute.

50. Kristol, Irving. 2003. "The Neoconservative Persuasion: What It Was and What It Is," *Weekly Standard* 8 (August 25). Also at www.weeklystandard.com/Content/Public/Articles/000/000/003/000tzmlw.asp?, p. 1

51. Ibid., 2.

52. Ibid.

53. Daalder, Ivo H., and James M. Lindsay. 2003. *America Unbound: The Bush Revolution in Foreign Policy.* Washington, D.C.: Brookings Institution.

54. Abrams, Elliot, Richard L. Armitage, William J. Bennett, Jeffrey Bergner, John Bolton, Paula Dobriansky, Francis Fukuyama, Robert Kagan, Zalmay Khalilzad, William Kristol, Richard Pearle, Peter W. Rodman, Donald Rumsfeld, William Schneider, Jr., Vin Weber, Paul Wolfowitz, R. James Woolsey, and Robert B. Zoelick. 1998. "Speaking of Iraq." *Washington Times*, January 26, p. A 21.

55. Website of the Project for a New American Century. Statement of Principles. At http://www.newamericancentury.org/statementofprinciples.htm.

56. Easton, *Gang of Five*, 60–88, 158–76, 359–74.

57. Dreyfuss, Robert. 2001. "Grover Norquist: 'Field Marshal' of the Bush Plan." *The Nation*, May 14.

58. Website of People for the American Way. "Right Wing Watch." At http://www.pfaw.org/pfaw/general/default.aspx?oid=3147.

59. Website of Americans for Tax Reform. At www.atr.org/atrnews/052501npr.html.

60. Website of People for the American Way. "Right Wing Watch." At http://www.pfaw.org/pfaw/general/default.aspx?oid=3147.

61. Website of Libertarian Party: The Party of Principle. "Statement of Principles." At http://www.lp.org/issues/platform/sop.html.

62. Palast, Greg. 2003. *The Best Democracy Money Can Buy: The Truth about Corporate Cons, Globalization, and High Finance Fraudsters.* New York: Plume. Hightower, Jim. 2003. *Thieves in High Places: They've Stolen Our Country—And Its Time to Take It Back.* New York: Viking.

63. Public Campaign. 2003. "The Road to Clean Elections." Public Campaign Website. At http://www.publicampaign.org/publications/index.htm.

64. Ivans, Molly, and Lou Dubose. 2003. *Bushwhacked: Life in George W. Bush's America.* New York: Random House. P. 283.

65. Phillips, Kevin. 2002. *Wealth and Democracy.* New York: Broadway. P. 328.

66. Texans for Public Justice. The Bush Pioneer-Ranger Network: View Profiles of the Bush Pioneers and Rangers. Texans for Public Justice Website. At http://www.tpj.org/page_view.jsp?pageid=203.

67. Phillips, *Wealth and Democracy*, 327.

68. Common Cause. 2003. *Prospecting for Access: How the Bush Pioneers Shaped Public Policy.* Washington, D.C.: Common Cause.

69. Carlyle Group Website. At http://www.carlylegroup.com/eng/company/index.html.

70. Baer, Robert. 2003. *Sleeping with the Devil: How Washington Sold Our Soul for Saudi Crude.* New York: Crown. Conason, *Big Lies.* Briody, Dan. 2003. *The Iron Triangle: Inside the Secret World of the Carlyle Group.* New York: Wiley.

71. Website for ChoicePoint. At http://www.choicepoint.com/.

72. Palast, *The Best Democracy Money Can Buy*, 21.

73. Ibid., 44.

74. Ibid., 11–81.

75. Ibid., 12, 35.

76. Ibid., 11.

77. Lind, Michael. 2003. *Made in Texas: George W. Bush and the Southern Takeover of American Politics.* New York: Basic.

78. Marable, Manning. 1984. *Race, Reform and Rebellion: The Second Reconstruction in Black America, 1945–1982.* New York: Macmillan. Donaldson, Gary A. 2000. *The Second Reconstruction: A History of the Modern Civil Rights Movement.* New York: Krieger.

79. Website for Temple of Democracy, maintained by Edward H. Sebesta and Professor Euan Hague at DePaul University, Chicago. At http://www.temple ofdemocracy.com/.

80. Website for Sons of Confederate Veterans. At http://www.scv.org/.

81. Website for Temple of Democracy. At http://www.templeofdemoc racy.com/.

82. Website for Council of Concerned Citizens. At http://www.cofcc.org/.

83. Website for League of the South. At http://www.dixienet.org/.

84. Website for the Jefferson Davis Society. At http://www.state.ga.us/civilwar/ davis.html.

85. Website for Temple of Democracy. At http://www.templeofdemoc racy.com/.

86. "Interview with Trent Lott." 1984. *Southern Partisan* 5 (4):44.

87. "Interview with John Ashcroft." 1998. *Southern Partisan* 20 (2).

88. Brock, *Blinded by the Right.*

89. Alterman, Eric. 2003. *What Liberal Media? The Truth about Bias and the News.* New York: Basic.

90. Franken, Al. 2003. *Lies, and the Lying Liars Who Tell Them.* New York: Dutton.

91. Tucker, William H. 2002. *The Funding of Scientific Racism: Wickliffe Draper and the Pioneer Fund.* Urbana: University of Illinois Press.

92. My account of the operation of the Vast Right Wing Conspiracy is based on my reading of the following: Brock, *Blinded by the Right.* Alterman, *What Liberal Media?* Conason, *Big Lies.* Fallows, James. 1996. *Breaking the News: How the Media Undermine American Democracy.* New York: Pantheon. Cook, Timothy E. 1998. *Governing with the News: The News Media as a Political Institution.* Chicago: University of Chicago Press. I also spent much time perusing the websites of conservative organizations.

Chapter 7: Liberalism Unbound

1. Judis, John B., and Ruy Teixeira. 2002. *The Emerging Democratic Majority.* New York: Scribner. P. 4.

2. Dionne, E. J. 1996. *They Only Look Dead.* New York: Simon and Schuster.

3. Judis and Teixeira, *The Emerging Democratic Majority*, 37–68.

4. Krugman, Paul. 2003. *The Great Unraveling: Losing Our Way in the New Century.* New York: Norton. Pp. 1–10.

5. Inglehart, Ronald. 1977. *The Silent Revolution.* Princeton: Princeton University Press. Inglehart, Ronald. 1997. *Modernization and Postmoderization.* Princeton: Princeton University Press.

6. Berry, Jeffrey M. 1999. *The New Liberalism: The Rising Power of Citizen Groups.* Washington, D.C.: Brookings Institution. P. 56.

7. Ibid., 57.

8. Ibid., 60.

9. Ibid., 61–86.

10. Judis and Teixeira, *The Emerging Democratic Majority*, 37–68.

11. Ibid., 42.

12. Reich, Robert B. 1991. *The Work of Nations: Preparing Ourselves for 21st Century Capitalism.* New York: Knopf. Florida, Richard. 2002. *The Rise of the Creative Class: And How It's Transforming Work, Leisure, Community and Everyday Life.* New York: Basic.

13. Judis and Teixeira, *The Emerging Democratic Majority*, 50.

14. Bianchi, Suzanne M., and Daphne Spain. 1986. *American Women in Transition.* New York: Russell Sage Foundation. Spain, Daphne, and Suzanne M. Bianchi. 1996. *Balancing Act: Motherhood, Marriage, and Employment among American Women.* New York: Russell Sage Foundation. Casper, Lynne M., and Suzanne M. Bianchi. 2001. *Continuity and Change in the American Family.* Newbury Park, Calif.: Sage.

15. Judis and Teixeira, *The Emerging Democratic Majority*, 56–62.

16. Anderton, Douglas L., Richard E. Barrett, and Donald J. Bogue. 1997. *The Population of the United States.* New York: Free Press. Pp. 85–88, 402–442.

17. Bogue, Donald. 1984. *The Population of the United States: Historical Trends and Future Projections.* New York: Free Press.

18. Judis and Teixeira, *The Emerging Democratic Majority*, 69–116.

19. Krugman, Paul. 2003. "Hack the Vote." *New York Times.* Op-Ed, December 2.

20. Ibid.

21. Fallows, James. 1996. *Breaking the News: How the Media Undermine American Democracy.* New York: Pantheon. Pp. 47–73.

22. Ibid.

23. Turow, Joseph. 1997 *Breaking Up America: Advertisers and the New Media World.* Chicago: University of Chicago Press. Pp. 125–56.

24. Postman, Neil, and Steve Powers. 1992. *How to Watch TV News*. New York: Penguin.

25. Weiss, Michael J. 1998. *The Clustering of America*. New York: Harper Collins. Weiss, Michael J. 2000. *The Clustered World: How We Live, What We Buy, and What It All Means about Who We Are*. Boston: Little, Brown.

26. Turow, *Breaking Up America*, 90–156.

27. Dotson, Bob. 2000. *Make It Memorable: Writing and Packaging TV News with Style*. Chicago: Bonus. Arya, Bob. 2001. *Thirty Seconds to Air: A Field Reporter's Guide to Live Television Reporting*. Ames: Iowa State University Press. Freedman, Wayne. 2003. *It Takes More Than Good Looks to Succeed at TV News Reporting*. Chicago: Bonus. Kaiser, Robert. 2003. *The News about the News: American Journalism in Peril*. New York: Vintage.

28. Allen, Craig M. 2001. *News Is People: The Rise of Local TV News and the Fall of News from New York*. Ames: Iowa State University Press.

29. Fallows, *Breaking the News*, 47–73.

30. Ibid., 182–234.

31. Alterman, *What Liberal Media?* Fallows, *Breaking the News*, 74–128.

32. Alterman, *What Liberal Media?* 14–28. Sharlet, Jeff. 2003. "Big World: How Clear Channel Programs America." *Harper's* 307 (December): 37–45. Bagdikian, Ben Haig. 2000. *The Media Monopoly*. 6th ed. Boston: Beacon. McChesney, Robert W. 2000. *Rich Media, Poor Democracy: Communication Politics in Dubious Times*. New York: New Press. McChesney, Robert W. 1997. *Corporate Media and the Threat to Democracy*. New York: Seven Stories.

33. Alterman, *What Liberal Media?* 22.

34. Cook, Timothy E. 1998. *Governing with the News: The News Media as a Political Institution*. Chicago: University of Chicago Press. Chomsky, Noam, and Edward S. Herman. 1988. *Manufacturing Consent: The Political Economy of the Mass Media*. New York: Pantheon. Gans, Herbert J. 2003. *Democracy and the News*. New York: Oxford University Press.

35. Alterman, Eric. 2000. *Sound and Fury: The Making of the Punditocracy*. Ithaca: Cornell University Press.

36. Fallows, *Breaking the News*, 103.

37. Jamieson, Kathleen Hall, and Paul Waldman. 2002. *The Press Effect: Politicians, Journalists, and the Stories That Shape the Political World*. New York: Oxford University Press. Alterman, *What Liberal Media?* 148–74. Conason, Joe. 2003. *Big Lies: The Right-Wing Propaganda Machine and How It Distorts the Truth*. New York: St. Martin's. Pp. 29–51.

38. Palast, Greg. 2003. *The Best Democracy Money Can Buy: The Truth about Corporate Cons, Globalization, and High Finance Fraudsters*. New York: Plume.

39. Alterman, *What Liberal Media?* Conason, *Big Lies*. Corn, David. 2003. *The Lies of George W. Bush: Mastering the Politics of Deception*. New York: Crown. Franken, Al. 2003. *Lies, and the Lying Liars Who Tell Them*. New York: Dutton.

40. Jamieson and Waldman, *The Press Effect*. 2002.

41. Corrado, Anthony. 2000. *Campaign Finance Reform: Beyond the Basics.* New York: Century Foundation Press. Donnelly, David, Janice Fine, and Ellen S. Miller. 1999. *Money and Politics: Financing Our Elections Democratically.* Boston: Beacon.

42. McCarty, Nolan M., Howard Rosenthal, and Keith T. Poole. 1997. *Income Redistribution and the Realignment of American Politics.* Washington, D.C.: AEI. Bartels, Larry. 2002. "Economic Inequality and Political Representation." Paper presented at the Annual Meeting of the American Political Science Association, Boston, August. Gillens, Martin. 2004. "Public Opinion and Democratic Responsiveness: Who Gets What They Want from Government?" Paper presented at the Seminar on Inequality in an Age of Globalization, Woodrow Wilson School, Princeton University, January 7.

43. Phillips, Kevin. 2002. *Wealth and Democracy.* New York: Broadway. Palast, *The Best Democracy Money Can Buy,* 108–70.

44. Heftel, Cecil. 1998. *End Legalized Bribery: An Ex-Congressman's Proposal to Clean Up Congress.* Santa Anna, Calif.: Seven Locks. Hightower, Jim. 2003. *Thieves in High Places: They've Stolen Our Country–And It's Time to Take It Back.* New York: Viking. Phillips, *Wealth and Democracy,* 201–48.

45. Watkins, Sherron, and Mimi Swartz. 2003. *Power Failure: The Inside Story of the Collapse of Enron.* New York: Doubleday. McLean, Bethany, and Peter Elkind. 2003. *Smartest Guys in the Room: The Amazing Rise and Scandalous Fall of Enron.* New York: Portfolio.

Index

★ ★ ★ ☆ ★ ★ ★